D1193265

73

DATE DUE

INVIS

JUN 1 1 2009		
JUN 0 4 2009		
JUL 2 1 2009		
JUL 3 0 2009		

DEMCO 38-296

INVISIBLE SCARS

How to Stop, Change or End Psychological Abuse

by Catharine Dowda, M.Ed., LPC

New Horizon Press
Far Hills, NJ

Catharine Dowda
Invisible Scars: How to Stop, Change or End Psychological Abuse

Cover design: Wendy Bass
Interior design: Susan Sanderson

Library of Congress Control Number: 2008938369

ISBN 13: 978-0-88282-308-9
ISBN 10: 0-88282-308-6
New Horizon Press

Manufactured in the U.S.A.

2013 2012 2011 2010 2009 / 5 4 3 2 1

DEDICATION

For
Amanda and Rebecca
Ashley and Brian

In memory of:
My father, William,
and
In tribute to his namesake:
My exquisite grandson, Dixon

May you grow to live and love
with the kindness, thoughtfulness and enthusiasm
of your great-grandfather

AUTHOR'S NOTE

This book is based on research, a thorough study of the available literature and experience in counseling patients, as well as my clients' own real life experiences. Fictitious identities and names have been given to all characters in this book in order to protect individual privacy and some characters are composites. For the purposes of simplifying usage, the pronouns his/her and s/he are sometimes used interchangeably.

The information contained herein is not meant to be a substitute for professional evaluation and therapy.

TABLE OF CONTENTS

PREFACE

In 1976, I moved to Greensboro, North Carolina, with my one-year-old daughter in order for my husband to take a new job. I wanted to get involved in the community and make use of my Sociology degree. There, a group of people advertised a meeting for anyone interested in providing services for battered women. I attended on that evening and, as everybody introduced themselves, I said I was just a volunteer. The wise woman leading the meeting said, "There is no such thing as 'just a volunteer'." Little did I know that at that moment, I was headed down a life-long career path.

Grassroots services began in our community with many individuals and agencies becoming involved. A small group of us was trained to take calls from a crisis line that operated 24/7. Emergency housing was funded with donations. Eventually, we had our first shelter, and I began recruiting volunteers and organizing their training.

One of the groups that became involved in supporting the needed services was the Junior League of Greensboro. I became a member of the league and served as the project advocate and a member of the advisory committee for the group, which called itself Turning Point. I also served on the league's public affairs committee, where I was sent for excellent training in lobbying in my hometown of Washington, D.C. We did lobby for improved laws and funding for victims of domestic violence on state and national levels.

In 1983, I was employed by Family and Children's Service, where the Turning Point group had found a home. In 1985, Family and Children's Service was able to place me in the Criminal Investigation Division of the Greensboro Police Department to work as a Victim Advocate with victims of any serious personal crime. This included rape, robbery, child abuse, serious assaults and families of homicide victims. The detectives in the division were given no orders that they had to work with me. It was up to me to make my way and, needless to say, they were very skeptical of "do-gooders." It took one detective a year and a half to allow me to work with him. When he did, he walked up to me and said, "I'm seeing a rape victim tonight at 7:30. If you want to come, be at the seafood place on Battleground Avenue by 7:15. If you aren't there, I won't wait." Believe me, I was there plenty early and from that point on, he allowed me to work with him and we became friends.

I received extensive training from the National Organization of Victim Assistance. I spent six years in the police department and it was an amazing experience. I am forever grateful to the officers and victims who allowed me to assist them. I went to crime scenes, the hospital, victims' homes and through court proceedings. I did crisis counseling, victim assistance and provided support during hearings and trials. I even went to an autopsy in Chapel Hill, although that may have been the detectives testing me, to see if I could handle it. I saw firsthand the worst things imaginable that people could ever do to each other, which continues to be valuable, because there is very little that I now see or hear that surprises or throws me. I am truly thankful to the men and women of the Greensboro Police and Guilford County Sherriff's Department for giving me their confidence and support. In addition to learning to love country music, I learned that solving crimes and helping victims is rewarding, difficult work and, if you are going to survive, you'd better have a sense of humor. It was one of the hundreds of life lessons I've learned.

In 1992, I completed my master's degree and started a private practice. I knew I couldn't keep up the pace of crisis work that included going out to any place in the city, often in the middle of the night. I also knew I wanted to work with people in a calmer setting doing more in-depth counseling. I see adolescents and adults, individually or for couples counseling. I feel fortunate to work with the people who come in for therapy. I am continually impressed by their courage, compassion and desire to make changes in their lives. I believe that I learn as much from them as they may from me.

Introduction

Individuals, relationships, backgrounds, experiences, values, self-concepts, age and life situations factor into how we connect and disconnect from our partners.

QUESTIONS, RATIONALIZATIONS AND EXCUSES

Invisible Scars looks at the complexities of psychologically abusive relationships and the reasons people have for staying or leaving them:

- Why does she stay with him?
- She must enjoy the games.
- I'd never let anyone treat me like that. If she did that to me, I'd be gone.
- She's got quite a mouth on her. No wonder he's always leaving home. I'd need to shut her up if I was married to her. How does he stand it?
- Doesn't she know he's cheating on her? Everyone else in town knows it. Maybe she doesn't care.
- What a jerk. Did you hear the way he talked to her? How does she put up with that?

- He's jealous and controlling and she sneaks around behind his back and does whatever she wants. Maybe they deserve each other.
- She makes most of the money, but he counts every dime. She has to ask his permission to buy a pair of shoes. I don't get it.
- He's a scary dude. He gives me the creeps. Why doesn't she get out of there?
- She doesn't trust him at all. She goes through his phone, reads his e-mails and checks his bank accounts. I hear she even has him followed. How does he tolerate her?
- She's such a beautiful, sweet woman with no self-confidence. He puts her down all the time, so she feels lousy about herself. I can't understand why she's with him.

When people make these kinds of statements and ask me why people stay in psychologically abusive relationships, I find it hard to answer them, because there are so many reasons. Hopefully, you will find this book to be a compassionate look at human feelings of love and fear that will educate and enlighten.

My goals are to:
- Increase public understanding of the scope and causes of psychologically abusive relationships.
- Give support and guidance to people living with psychological abuse.
- Examine the multitude of reasons for remaining or leaving.
- Speak directly to the victims and abusers, offering insight and suggestions to bring about positive change.

I have learned from over thirty years of working with domestic abuse and criminal abuse that it is important to maintain an attitude of acceptance and a sense of humor. Each person has his or her own unique perspective and value system. It does not help to judge someone else. It does help to listen and really hear what is being said and offer new thoughts, support alternatives and present a fresh approach. We come to our decisions in our own time. No one else walks in your shoes.

If you yourself are experiencing psychological abuse, someone you care about is being hurt or if you just want to have a better understanding of this kind of complex relationship dynamic, this book is written for you. My hope is that reading it will give you a better understanding of your own and your partner's behavior and the nature of your interactions. As you will see, you are not alone. The final section of the book offers many suggestions for moving forward and making healthy choices.

Let's get started.

Part I

What's Psychological Abuse All About?

Chapter 1

Why Psychological Abuse is Heartbreaking

We are the walking wounded, but you can't see that by looking at us. The damage is not physical. You will not see bruises, cuts, breaks or marks. We hurt from the psychological impairment of abusive words, actions, thoughts and deeds. We seek to heal our wounds and form strong, healthy invisible scars.

Angie and Andy's dysfunctional relationship is telling:

> Angie arrives home from work exhausted. All she can see is clutter everywhere—toys, dishes, newspapers and clothes. Her husband, Andy, is asleep in his recliner in front of the television set. She begins washing the dishes, slamming drawers and cabinets, intentionally waking him.
>
> "Thanks for cleaning up," she says sarcastically.
>
> "I picked up the kids from day care, fed and bathed them and put them to bed. What more do you want?" he responds.
>
> "They are your kids, too. Do you expect a medal? I'm the one who was up three times with the baby last night. I can't work these hours and keep the house clean. *You never do anything around here.*"

"Here you go again. You are never satisfied! All you do is bitch at me. Bitch, bitch, bitch," he yells.

"Are you calling me a bitch? I am sick of the way you treat me. And stop yelling or you will wake the kids. All you think about is yourself. You are so selfish. Don't you think I'd like to be able to sit and watch TV at night? I never have time for myself, because I have all the work your lazy ass won't do. I bet you didn't even sell anything at your job today."

Throwing the television remote control device at Angie, Andy turns to leave and says, "Watch TV, bitch. I'm not listening to any more of this."

"Don't you walk away from me," Angie screams as she grabs his arm and turns him around.

Andy jerks his arm out of her grasp, "The next time you touch me, you, the kids or one of your pets is going to get it and one of you will end up in the hospital or worse."

Days later, Angie is at her parents' house with the kids. Her mom asks, "Why don't you two separate? You fight like cats and dogs."

Angie thinks about Andy, their marriage and the family they have created. She shakes her head and sadly responds, "I don't know exactly why we stay together, Mom. It is really complicated and it would break my heart to leave him."

PHYSICAL ABUSE

Physical abuse is any intentionally menacing or damaging physical action toward another person, one which may cause bodily harm. Amazingly, many people tolerate a certain level of physical contact and do not define themselves as abused if they are grabbed or pushed. Physical abuse may never be present in an abusive relationship or it may occur daily. Once is too much. It is never okay, no matter who is doing it or the supposed justification. Defending one's self may require a physical action, but trying to control, punish or express our anger through physical violence is unacceptable.

For many years, a cycle of violence has been observed where a violent incident is followed by a honeymoon period with apologies and good behavior. Over time, the tension begins to build over a variety of small daily stresses. Triggers can cause anger to explode into physical abuse. While this cycle is present in many cases, it is also common to have no clear pattern. There may be no honeymoon period. The buildup of tension may not be noticeable and rage can come in an instant. This unpredictability makes it difficult to relax and trust that the relationship is ever safe.

When reported, physical violence is the most commonly responded to and punished form of abuse. In America and some other countries around the world, laws against domestic violence have been improved but are not perfect. Women and sometimes men try and hide what is happening in their homes to avoid judgments, criticism or more abuse. They do not call the police. They may be afraid or not yet prepared to take a stand and seek help.

VERBAL ABUSE
Verbal abuse consists of the nastiest things imaginable that people say to each other.
- You are...fat, ugly, disgusting, cheap, filthy, old, worthless, sloppy, stupid, incompetent...
- Who else would want you?
- You never do anything right.
- What kind of mother are you?
- You are such a bitch, bastard, asshole, whore, cunt, dick...

Verbal abuse may be the most damaging, pervasive, contaminating form of violence. It lowers our self-esteem, steals our confidence and immobilizes us. With verbal violence, we can deal the most devastating blows any time of the day or night in any environment. Angry screaming or a malicious whisper can be equally effective. Verbal abuse can happen in the privacy of your home, at a party, in church, while driving, shopping, traveling, dancing or watching a movie. It can be delivered in person, over the phone, by e-mail or in a card or letter. It can happen in the middle of a fight or slip in during lovemaking. It's quick and effective.

Human beings sift for negatives. We remember the negative things that are said to us or about us. A lover, boss, co-worker, friend, spouse, acquaintance, teacher, child, doctor or store clerk may make one negative comment that we will take to heart and remember. The critical remarks by our parents and partners will be stored in the back of our brains and become our frames of reference about who we are. It is often the basis on which we form our self-concepts. Without a lot of insight, therapy and hard work, we take the negative messages of childhood and often find someone who will add to those messages in a way that reinforces what we were raised to believe. Hence, many verbally abused children unknowingly seek out verbally abusing partners to continue what is familiar and believable. The abuse received as an adult rings true because the negative beliefs have been implanted early.

♦ Oh yes, I know I'm stupid, because I've always heard that.

♦ I'm not surprised to be called a failure, because my father said I would never amount to anything.

♦ Of course, I'm ugly. My mother said I'd be lucky to have anyone want me.

In a fit of anger, or in an effort to be more powerful and in control, we often go for the jugular vein during an argument. We say the one thing we know that will push our partner's buttons and attack the main vein, which will quickly drain the blood out of the body and become lethal. We choose the areas of vulnerability that are most painful. If she is sensitive about her weight, he'll call her fat. If he is sensitive about his sexual competence, she will criticize the size of his penis or his ability to perform. If she hates her mother, he'll say, "You are just like your mother." If he is insecure about his job, she will say, "You just can't cut it at work." And so it goes. The possibilities are endless.

In this book, we will focus on psychological abuse, which the story of Angie and Andy illustrates. Be aware that psychological abuse can lead to two other kinds of abuse: physical and verbal.

PSYCHOLOGICAL ABUSE

Psychological abuse consists of mind games played out in a devious fashion, mostly to establish or maintain control. It is the Chinese water torture of abuse; usually a continuous pattern of behavior that can leave the recipients feeling like they are going crazy.

Profanity

Every ugly word that exists has been used in anger to degrade, humiliate and inflict pain. Calling someone a "fucking fat whore" or a "sick, stupid son-of-a-bitch" may be more potent due to the vulgarity. Words can wound. There is no way around that. Sticks and stones will break your bones but words really do hurt you.

Stonewalling

Psychological abuse can be totally ignoring your partner or refusing to communicate. The total shut down, known as stonewalling, is passive-aggressive behavior, the goal being to punish. "I don't like what you've done or what you are saying, so I refuse to look at you, talk to you or touch you. You do not exist. I am fine without you. You have no significance to me. I do not care what you want or need. It doesn't matter to me if you cry. I feel in control, because you can't make me talk to you." The icy emotional distancing is powerful at the time and very destructive in the long run.

If your partner continuously shuts down, you may try fruitlessly to communicate. No matter how kind or reasonable you are, he or she may refuse to look at you or speak. Frustrated, you may escalate your own anger to try and get a response. You may find yourself raising your voice, calling names, pushing buttons or attacking physically. At that point, you have lost control and exhibited your own abusive behavior. Your partner remains in the power position in this dysfunctional interaction.

Understand that stonewalling is a no-win situation; you may shut down, stop any attempts to communicate and gradually distance yourself in self-defense. The disconnecting process begins and, over time, hopelessness sets in and feelings for each other fade. As you love your partner less, his or her power over you diminishes, but the relationship can become irreparable.

Threats

Threats and intimidation are another form of psychological abuse, designed to control behavior and create fear. Examples are angry stares, slamming doors, throwing things, punching walls, standing over her, yelling, clenching fists, getting in his face, tearing up her favorite things and hurting pets.

- I'll knock your head off.
- You'll be sorry.
- I'm coming home and you'd better be ready.
- I'll mess you up so bad that no man will ever want to look at you again.
- You'll come home and find everything gone.
- I'll kill that dog of yours.
- I'll take the kids and you'll never see them again.
- You'll never get a penny of child support.
- I'll kill you and they'll never find me.
- I'll drive this car over a bridge and kill both of us.
- You'll never get away from me. I'll hunt you down wherever you are.

Sometimes the threats are carried out. She comes home to find her beloved cat poisoned on the porch. He takes the dog out back and shoots it. She smashes his favorite belongings. He takes scissors in the night and cuts off some of her hair. He takes the children on a "trip" without her, just to show he can. She cleans out the checking account and hides all the money. He smashes his fist into the wall next to her face or shoots off his gun in the house.

Threatening to harm one's self is a powerful threat: "If you leave me, I'll kill myself. I can't live without you." While this may appear to be a perfect solution, most people cannot tolerate thinking they caused someone they have loved to commit suicide.

Threats are scary, because they often become real. We read daily about the brutal tragic endings where people are killed or left permanently injured. The repercussions are numerous. Perhaps part of the psychological damage we all experience is becoming accustomed to the constant barrage of sad news stories and increasingly violent and deviant movies and television programs. Violence has become such a pervasive part of our culture that we cease to be shocked or motivated to take a stand against it. Our inaction is a kind of sanction, which contributes to the acceptance of violence in every part of our society.

Criticism

Criticism is a powerful psychological tool. As a way of acting superior, one partner comments on what the other partner says and does, how he or she looks, dresses or cleans the house or on his or her family, job, religion, intelligence, lovemaking, choices, friends, cooking, decorating, parenting, income or abilities. Anything is fair game. The idea is to undermine confidence and cause uncertainty and insecurity, thus allowing the commentator to feel more powerful.

Self-improvement suggestions may be presented as helpful but easily turn destructive and are experienced as critical.

- I'm just trying to help. You are taking it the wrong way. You are just too sensitive.
- I didn't say you were fat. I just said that outfit would look better if you lost a few pounds.
- Boy, your friend is such a great wife. Her house is spotless and her children are so well-behaved.
- My brother-in-law is such a great provider. He just bought my sister a new car and they are planning a great vacation. We never go anywhere.
- I'm just sharing this diet plan with you to help you lose those twenty pounds. Let's weigh in together every week.
- I'm putting this bathing suit model's bikini picture on the refrigerator. You'd look as great as she does if you'd get in shape.

Criticism paired with contempt is often deadly to relationships. Statements are delivered as absolute judgments and often contain the words "never", "always", "should" or "ought".

♦   You never help me around the house.
♦   You always interrupt me.
♦   You should be more assertive at work.
♦   You ought to spend more time with your kids.

Remarks are often accompanied with contemptuous body language. Rolling eyes, hands on hips, pointing fingers, shaking heads and looks of disgust cause the listener to take offense no matter how accurate the statement may be.

Isolation

Isolation is forbidding or strongly discouraging any contact with the outside world, including family members. Jealousy and insecurity fuel this punishing controlling behavior. If verbal edicts are not sufficient, some people have resorted to taking away transportation, removing phones and computers and even discouraging eye contact with anyone outside the home. Jobs, friends, volunteering and shopping are curtailed.

Much like solitary confinement is the ultimate punishment in prison, isolation is used to make sure a woman "knows her place." In other cases, she fears that if he has a glimpse of life outside their relationship, he just might leave. Keeping the other person in seclusion will reduce the chances of anyone knowing about the abuse and maintains the partner's position of authority.

Control

Controlling behavior definitely has a psychological component. Invasion of another person's boundaries is the common element. You feel you have the right to tell someone else how to dress, walk, look, feel, think, talk or behave. Control may be rearranging things in the house, always setting the thermostat to where you are comfortable, questioning or changing your partner's decisions, insisting you know more about any given subject or refusing to help at home unless it is done your way.

♦ I will grocery shop, but only if you make me a grocery list in the order that the items appear in the store.

♦ You may only use this bedspread.

♦ You may only have new furniture if I pick it out.

♦ I'll do the laundry—oops, was I not supposed to wash that new red shirt with the white stuff? (Maybe that one can be innocent—once.)

♦ Aren't you grateful for this new car I selected for you?

♦ You need to keep the schedule I made for you.

♦ Don't you question how I spend money after I bought you all those fucking gifts at Christmas.

Psychological Torture

Psychological torture is intentionally planned and orchestrated systematic mental abuse. The intent is to create fear and to cause someone to feel they are crazy. It often involves surveillance, setting traps and terrorizing behavior. Extreme measures involve mind control and programming techniques. Generally, the abuser is a very disturbed individual who is capable of creating a living hell for his or her partner. The victim becomes hypervigilant and can never relax, not knowing when the next scary event will occur.

The torture may begin gradually and become relentless. The abuser may begin by moving things around in the house or hiding objects, then putting them back. Light bulbs become unscrewed; computer or car parts go missing; the electricity is turned off; the mail is interfered with. The behavior progresses to monitoring all calls, e-mails and correspondence, hurting pets, cleaning out bank accounts or changing legal papers. The victim becomes off balance and is not always believed by people she is hoping will help her.

Denial

Perhaps the most common form of psychological abuse is causing your partner to believe that the abuse is either his or her own fault or is not really abuse at all. You deny having done anything wrong, minimize the events or accuse the partner of initiating or instigating the abuse.

Reality becomes distorted. Confusion is common. "I know what she did to me, but she makes it seem as if it was my fault." Often victims start believing the offender's perspective and question their own sanity or sense of reality. Some women have said to me, "I know it was my fault. If I had only made mashed potatoes instead of French fries, he wouldn't have become so angry and threatened me." Believing you deserved to be abused because of what you cooked for dinner, what you wore, who you spoke to or your tone of voice places your partner in a very powerful position. Victims may believe they are at fault, because they are scrambling to find a cause for their partners' bad behavior. "If I just do all of the right things, he or she will stop hurting me." It doesn't work, but it is an understandable way to attempt to alleviate the reality of the situation.

Financial

One type of psychological abuse can be financial abuse. It involves controlling the money, checkbook, credit cards, budget, assets, spending habits and purchases in the relationship. This does not include relationships where one person has requested that their partner be responsible for all the financial decisions. Abuse involves not allowing your partner to have any discretion or decisions as it pertains to money. Often this is accomplished with intimidation and guilt.

- Look at all I've done for you.
- You are never grateful.
- You know you are no good with money.
- This costs way too much. You need to buy a cheaper brand.
- You spent how much? I can't trust you.

Some women do not have access to any cash, checks or credit cards, even though they may work full-time jobs. In other cases, she controls the checkbook and he must go through her to get anything. Or she may not have any idea of how much money he makes or where it is kept. He may keep secret accounts or investments.

His or her motivation may be to control all the financial decisions or it may be to control the other partner and the children through cutting off any means to independent choices or actions. He may think she can't go anywhere if she doesn't have any money. She may feel she's being the benevolent benefactor as she hands out the cash as she sees fit. He may believe he's doing what is best for the family if he knows where every penny goes. Psychological abuse occurs when the real motivation is to eliminate a person's freedom.

Sexual

Sexual psychological abuse ranges from withholding all expressions of affection to systematic sexual torture. Frequency of sexual intercourse is a preference, which is mutually satisfying to both partners or can be a source of great dispute. If both partners want sex once a month or once a day, it works because both are happy. The problem occurs when one person wants sex once a day and one wants sex one time a month. In non-abusive relationships, compromises are negotiated. In abusive relationships, people have intentionally withheld affection for years or insisted on sex twice a day and became critical and abusive if it did not occur. Demanding sex is a form of abuse; forcing sex is rape. In the United States, however, many states have been slow to recognize that rape can exist within a marriage and only make charges of an assault where physical violence is evident.

Refusing to recognize and understand a partner's adverse reactions to sexual intimacy can become abusive. Many women (and men) have been victims of child sexual abuse or rape and this frequently impacts their ability to desire or enjoy sex. While this is certainly an issue to be dealt with in counseling, a person should be sensitive to difficulties his or her partner is experiencing. Forcing someone to participate in a sexual act they find distasteful or degrading leaves emotional scars. And if they have been abused in the past, the damage is compounded.

Jealousy and insecurity have spawned some forms of sexual abuse. Men who have been cheated on or have known one of their parents was unfaithful are particularly susceptible. They frequently make accusations and continually question behavior. Some force their partners to submit to physical checks of their vaginas to see if they can detect the presence of semen; accompany women to their gynecological exams; or even object to their partners' wearing tampons, because it might feel stimulating while inserting or removing it. Some cultures routinely remove women's clitorises to prevent them from seeking sexual pleasure. Can you imagine the fear and insecurity leading to that decision? *We want to control our women, so let's cut out a body part that provides them with pleasure.*

Incredible sexual violence has been perpetrated against women's sexual organs, which have been forcefully penetrated, kicked, punched, cut, burned and beaten. Rape victims have had their pubic hair dry-shaved and have had fists, bottles and various objects shoved up their vaginas. Inserting a gun and pulling the trigger is a sadistic game of Russian roulette. Men also experience sexual violence in relationships, suffering battered or severed sexual organs and forced anal penetration.

Having affairs can also be a form of sexual abuse. You expose your partner to a multitude of diseases. Innocence is destroyed, followed by a violation of commitment, trust and love. Nothing is ever the same. The damage is done. Repetitive sexual affairs can be a form of addictive behavior; the partner experiences the infidelity as abuse.

Women and Psychological Abuse

Most women are not as physically strong as their partners, but some are particularly adept at psychological abuse. Many women have little insight into their own destructive and provocative behaviors, but clearly identify themselves as victims when their partners become physical. No physical abuse is justified; however, we need to examine and understand the entire relationship before we can effectively make changes.

In this book, we'll look closely at how psychological abuse can be vicious. It is equally unacceptable. The sex of the partner does not make it less abusive. Some men are profoundly abused. One man described the verbal and emotional abuse he received as feeling as if he was publicly stripped naked and beaten with a stick. Humiliation and degradation by someone you love is devastating, no matter who is doing it.

Addictions

I believe addictions are a prevalent source of contamination in relationships. When people become involved in an addiction, their primary relationships are with the substances or activities with which they are involved. They become powerless and eventually their lives can become unmanageable. It has devastating consequences, physically, emotionally, mentally, financially, sexually and spiritually.

Addictions can be to alcohol, prescription or illegal drugs, gambling, food, shopping, sex, relationships, pornography, the Internet or video and computer games. Addictions alter the behavior of a person, lowering his or her tolerance, patience or inhibitions. They can cause loss of jobs, money, health, trust and security.

Use of alcohol and drugs is frequently mentioned as a part of the scenario in which abuse occurs. Individuals who are drunk or high have impaired judgment and control and may be quick to lose their tempers or just get mean. In some situations, abuse never occurs during sober periods but the family learns to be wary when consumption begins.

In all addictions, absorption with the behavior steals the person away from their loved ones.

- ◆ He's spent all our money on gambling. Now we are broke.
- ◆ She's eaten so much, I don't recognize her anymore. I miss the way she used to look.
- ◆ I never see him anymore. He spends all his free time playing games on the computer.
- ◆ She's run our credit cards up so high we'll never get out of debt.

The good news is that there is help. Twelve-step programs, counseling, rehabilitation, understanding, spiritual growth and hard work are answers to this problem for the entire family. Understanding how to live with an addiction is as important for the partner as it is for the addict. This involves learning how to set boundaries, to understand what you can and can't change or to live "one day at a time", to "listen and learn" and to "let go and let God." Working a twelve-step program involves a daily spiritual commitment. The rewards are numerous and productive for individuals and relationships.

All forms of abuse cause fundamental spiritual damage. What happens to us externally affects every cell in our body and impacts our spirit. Bruises from being beaten are merely the visible signs of spiritual trauma. If you choke me, hold me down, sit on my face and force me to perform oral sex, my soul is injured. I detach by going someplace else in my mind to be able to endure the trauma and to minimize you reaching who I really am. If I am to retain my real self, I must protect my spirit.

The worst damage from all types of abuse is changing or extinguishing the natural pure spirit that is our gift at birth. Faith, hope and love are replaced with confusion, despair and fear. Systematic abuse can take away our will to live. Prisoners of war and concentration camp survivors are often able to live, because they find a way to nurture their souls when everything else is taken away. Sadly, many homes in our country house prisoners of abuse.

I believe spiritual work helps you rise from the devastation to become transformed into your own special self. The essential part of who you are can heal, grow, understand and make healthier choices. Touching who you are as a spiritual being in the complex enormity of the universe is a humbling and empowering experience. Healing work is in the love, first of yourself and what you were given, then in the freedom from incapacitating fear.

According to the National Resource Center on Domestic Violence, in 2004, 1,159 females and 385 males were murdered by their intimate partners. That same year, there were 627,400 nonfatal intimate partner victimizations and those are only the reported cases[1]. Some left their partners; many stayed. Why did they stay? Take this journey with me to look at all of the intricate complexities in psychologically abusive relationships and why many of us—women and men—stay.

Does any of this apply to you? Before you say "no", consider that abuse occurs on a continuum that most of us will be able to place ourselves on, traveling from critical controlling behavior to calculated first degree murder. Abuse can be insidious and pervasive. It can creep in and permeate your relationship or it can erupt into one dramatic fatal act of violence. Along the continuum, we can see the behaviors of our partners, parents, friends, co-workers and ourselves. Abuse occurs in all social, economic and educational levels; in opposite and same-sex relationships; in all ages, religions, races and professions. It is in your neighborhood and may be found in the relationships of the couples you least suspect. Men and women are capable of abusive behaviors, but it must be noted that, statistically, abuse against women is more prevalent.

A relationship involves two people, and the contributions of each person to the dynamics of abuse must be examined to fully understand the problem. No one acts in a vacuum. For each action, there is a reaction. No action, however, justifies inflicting abuse and every person is ultimately responsible for his or her own behavior.

Chapter 2

Power and Control Issues

Relationships have power and control dynamics operating on a regular basis. Lovers, spouses, friends, parents and children, siblings, employees and employers, co-workers, clergy and parishioners, elected officials and citizens, law enforcement and suspects, countries, institutions, even the forces of good and evil, all struggle for power and control. Understanding relationships is complex and elusive.

In psychologically abusive relationships, the person who appears to be in power is often the person most out of control. If he makes out a daily schedule for her and calls at 10:30 A.M. to see if she's dusting the furniture, is he really powerful? If she criticizes him until he's miserable, is he or she getting what the person wants? Violence erupts out of anger, fear and insecurity. After exploding, you may look or feel powerful, but your actions caused you to lose control. Picture children on a seesaw: the repetitive up and down motion depicts how often the power in a relationship changes.

Tom and Tina had serious issues:

> Tom and Tina shopped for a new home for the first two years they were married. This was a complicated process, because they each had assets from past marriages and had

somewhat differing opinions on house hunting. It became apparent to Tina that Tom was not going to value her opinions even though he asked for them. Tom felt it was only satisfying to buy a house if he could get a real deal. Tina wanted to define a price range, find a home, make a reasonable offer, sell her house and move into the new one, combining their collective belongings. Tom let her know that he had no interest in using any of her belongings in their new home.

Tom planned numerous outings to look at homes, many out of their price range. He then made lowball offers which were ignored by the sellers. Tina became frustrated and began to shut down as she realized she had no control over what was happening, except to refuse to participate. Time went by and Tom convinced her to continue looking again. Finally, exactly two years later, they found a house that was a perfect fit and the price they had agreed they could afford. However, Tom insisted on making an offer forty thousand dollars less than the asking price with fifteen contingencies. Tina was shocked. The offer was countered, but Tom was in a competition to get the price down.

On Saturday morning of that week, Tom asked Tina's opinion on what she thought was a reasonable offer. When Tina responded, he gave her multiple reasons why she was wrong. He accused her of operating out of emotion instead of logic. Realizing she'd been had again and that he would give no merit to her opinions or desires, Tina snapped. She yelled and called him a "jerk" and an "asshole." She told him how fed up she was with the whole process and that she was done with the house hunting. She said she felt manipulated by his game playing and no longer found any joy in the idea of owning a home together.

Tom, as was his pattern, pulled the ultimate power play. He became the wounded victim of her verbal abuse and refused to talk to Tina for an entire week. It did not matter to him that Tina sincerely apologized for the name calling on several occasions. All he would say to her was that he wanted to be left alone. It did not matter to him that both of their birthdays were during that week. Tina was being punished and he refused to talk to her. Tina eventually collected herself, went to counseling, called a close girlfriend to go to dinner with her on her birthday and refused to allow herself to continue to be punished.

Tom finally came around and by the next weekend they talked for hours about their outlooks, feelings and goals for their relationship and for a new home. Monday morning, Tom went to make a reasonable offer on the house that would have been accepted had the home not sold to another couple that past weekend.

Notice the power and control dynamics in this couple's behavior. See how the power changed hands. These power plays are present in our ordinary daily life experiences, as well as during our angry chaotic events.

Many of us saw one "How to Be a Good Wife", which was passed along over the Internet. It is reported to be an excerpt from a 1950 high school Home Economics textbook and was also reprinted in *Housekeeping Monthly* on May 13, 1955. The article elaborates on instructions on how to be a good wife, including:

Have dinner ready: Plan ahead, even the night before, to have a delicious meal on time. This is a good way of letting him know that you have been thinking about him and are concerned about his needs. Most men are hungry when they come home and the prospect of a good meal is part of the warm welcome needed.

Some don'ts: Don't greet him with problems and complaints. Don't complain if he is late for dinner. Count this a minor, compared to what he might have gone through that day.

The goal: To make your home a place of peace and order where your husband can relax in body and spirit.

Let's look at why this often works. Dr. Carl Jung helped identify that masculine and feminine energies operate in all of us to varying degrees. Masculine energy is dominant, action-oriented, assertive, pursuing and leading. Feminine energy is accepting, feeling-oriented, submissive, nurturing and following. Each man and each woman has some kind of balance within them of masculine and feminine energies and their upbringing often determines which energies have been more fully developed[2]. Perhaps in a perfect world children would grow up in a non-abusive, two-parent household, where they would be taught to develop both energies. Each child could develop their abilities to be assertive, successful and dominant, as well as tender, nurturing, helpful and kind. Dreaming aside, what often happens is that men's and women's masculine and feminine energies crash against each other in a mismatch, which keeps both people from getting their needs met. We can't figure out how to compromise.

- Who is going to do the housework when both people work full-time?
- Who will stay home with the sick baby?
- Will you move when she finds a great job in another city?
- He wants a new car, she wants to go on a vacation and they can't afford both. How will they decide?
- Who meets the children's needs?
- Who makes the sexual overtures when both are exhausted but needing attention?

The list of dilemmas is endless.

In the old hit TV sitcom *Leave It to Beaver*, it looked easier in the Cleaver home. June knew "how to be a good wife". She had all the household matters under control and she looked great when Ward came in the door. No sweatpants and tennis shoes for her. Ward came home well-dressed, charming, kind and ready to help solve any major problem. Of course, the only real problems involved the kids, Beaver and Wally, and the issues were neatly wrapped up in half an hour. Many households during that time had roles that were well-defined. Women developed their feminine energy and men could be "real men". Many busy people of both sexes jokingly say, "I need a wife!", because that represents having someone to take care of everything and give a hug, a smile and a warm meal when he or she gets home. We don't just want a housekeeper; we want the hug, smile and maybe a backrub, too.

But what happens if Ward runs off with his attractive young secretary? After all, we never had any idea how June was in the bedroom. What is June to do now? Her résumé has no work experience listed and no specialized training or computer skills. Perhaps she could work for minimum wage in a store or even open a catering business with her half of the marital assets. Realistically, most of us now encourage our daughters to prepare themselves to be self-sufficient. Consequently, some of the caretaking, nurturing and homemaking skills may be underdeveloped. Over time, our society has changed. Roles and their expectations have become more confusing and frustrating. Everyone is expected to learn to do it all. Is that reasonable? It certainly is causing adjustment problems.

GAME PLAYING

It's amazing how many games we play with the people we are supposed to love the most. The majority of the time, we have no idea what is happening when we are involved in a non-productive dance with our partner and, hence, can't see how to remove ourselves from the destructive dynamics.

Here are a dozen commonly played games:
1. Punishment Game
2. Provocation/Victimization
3. No Win Interrogations
4. Competition
5. The Blame Game
6. Bait and Switch
7. You Are Perfect…Now Change
8. Citizen's Arrest
9. Just Try Harder
10. The Benevolent Dictator
11. The Drama Game
12. Tear Down/Build Up

1. Punishment Game

Have you ever felt like your partner is punishing you, but you're not sure exactly why? When you ask about it, he denies that anything is wrong or that he is doing anything unusual. The tension, body language, failure to communicate or his actions clearly indicate that something is bothering him. You can make guesses about the problem, but he won't admit to having an issue with you or admit to any behavior that is punishing. Whether it is subtle or obvious, you know when it is happening. He may even pretend to be cheerful, but you know what is brewing under the surface. The idea is to keep you engaged in and attentive to an unsolvable dynamic. Not discussing the issue is part of the game because the more you attempt to discuss or solve it, the more secure he feels that you are paying attention and are concerned.

2. Provocation/Victimization

This game involves provoking your partner until he or she snaps, then acting like the innocent victim. For example, breaking someone's boundaries is often perceived as threatening. Talk to abusive men and you will often find that their partners will break into their space when they are angry and upset. When the man reacts abusively, the woman becomes the victim and vice versa. The other partner is the bad one. Examples of provocation are:

- Getting in his face to talk.
- Pointing your finger into his chest.
- Sitting in front of the door or on the hood of the car when she is trying to leave.
- Making threats.
- Verbal taunting.
- Constant brutal criticism or putdowns.
- Grabbing anything and pushing it in her face.

It is essential to remember that while provocation may be a cause of physical violence, it is not a justification. Physical abuse is against the law and it is never acceptable behavior.

3. No Win Interrogations

Endless questions that are meant to confuse, dominate and intimidate are part of a game of offense. Often there is no "right" answer and any response could mean friction in the relationship.

- Where were you last night?
- What were you doing?
- Who did you talk to?
- What did you talk about?
- What were you wearing?
- When did you leave?
- Who left with you?
- Did anybody flirt with you?
- Did you give your phone number to anyone?
- Why didn't you call me?

This game can be about any topic, but the outcome will always be unpleasant.

4. Competition

Some might think the purpose of the relationship is to provide a field for competition.

- I am smarter, stronger, better looking, more knowledgeable, nicer, sexier or more desirable than you are.
- I am neat, you are messy.
- I am on time, you are always late.
- You ought to work out and get in shape like I am.
- I have a college degree and you never finished school.
- I make more money.
- I am good with a budget, you overspend.
- No one can talk to you. Look how hysterical you are.
- I could have any man/woman I want.
- I'm much better with the kids than you are.

Do you feel more powerful if you are putting your partner down?

5. The Blame Game

The purpose is to clearly define the other person as the problem.

♦ If it wasn't for you, I'd be more successful.

♦ I'm okay, but you are crazy.

♦ I wouldn't have stonewalled if you hadn't...

♦ It's your fault that I get so mad, because you always seem to provoke me.

♦ You wore those clothes on purpose to attract other men.

♦ I'd be nicer if you...were happier, cooked and cleaned more, complimented me, gave me more sex, appreciated the things I do...

♦ If you helped me more, I wouldn't complain so much.

♦ You ignore me, so you can't blame me for having an affair.

♦ How can you be unhappy with what we are doing? Don't you remember it was your idea in the first place?

Are you quick to say what is wrong with your spouse and very slow to acknowledge your own mistakes? It is easier to point the finger away from your body rather than toward yourself.

Another form of the blame game involves discounting, criticizing or shaming. The purpose is to make your partner feel that his or her thoughts, behaviors and emotions are off base.

♦ You are too sensitive. You can't take a joke.

♦ Toughen up. You wear your heart on your sleeve.

♦ You are making too much of this. I was just kidding.

♦ What a baby. You cry about everything. I'm sick of it.

6. Bait and Switch

We all are on our best behavior in the beginning of relationships. We want other partners to see our best selves. As we become intimate and comfortable in our relationships, we reveal our flaws and often our partners feel betrayed.

♦ I thought I was getting a winner; instead I got a loser.

♦ I wanted to date her, because she seemed so sweet.

♦ I didn't know we could be like this until it was too late.

♦ He seemed so nice and attentive but he became obsessed with me.

♦ He never lost his temper when we were first together.

Most people experiencing psychological abuse say, "I just want it to be like it was in the beginning."

You can bait and switch by saying one thing and doing another. For example:

♦ Asking for the other person's advice or opinions, allowing him or her to think he or she has some influence and then doing whatever you want with no regard for the other person.

♦ I love you, now go away. If you please me, I will reward you with attention, affection, gifts or praise. If you misbehave, I must punish you.

♦ Being a hot sex partner while dating and cold after marriage. This is a prevalent problem, because of game-playing.

♦ Calm and chaos—the person appears to have his or her life together but you find that underneath is turmoil. No matter how often you attempt stabilization, chaos ensues because it is the person's essence.

♦ Planning a holiday, vacation or any special event, then spoiling it so that an important time becomes disastrous.

7. You Are Perfect...Now Change

Did you ever fall in love with someone, then try and change the person? Women particularly do this, but men do as well. Instead of focusing on what we like about the person with whom we fell in love, we put a lot of energy into changing what we don't like. Out of ten characteristics of our mates, we may like seven qualities, but we focus on the three we don't like and begin trying to fix them. It's our mission. We think we are being helpful, but we are actually attempting to satisfy our own needs. A partner in this position is left confused by how he or she went from being the good person to the bad person. When you are a fixer, the game becomes to attract someone to you with approval and admiration, then make the person into a reconstruction project. Rather than being grateful for what we have, we convince ourselves that life would be so perfect if we could just change the qualities we don't like. Like the prince discovers in this short tale, trying to change a person to fit a certain ideal does not result in what we expect:

> A prince was looking for a bride. He was not interested in the multitude of "acceptable" women that his family paraded in front of him. Instead, he was enchanted by the gypsy girl he saw in the village dancing barefoot with an abandoned nature that he found bewitching. He brought her to the castle, introduced her to his horrified parents and eventually married her. But in order to make her a proper princess, she had to learn the rules of propriety and decorum. As her mentors were teaching her etiquette, how to speak, table manners and how to curtsy, she lost her wild, free, joyful nature. She became someone who blended in. She lost her individuality and her spirit. The prince became disenchanted. How had his gypsy bride become so mundane and ordinary?

Can we change? Certainly, if we choose. Can we change someone else? No—not unless the other person chooses to change. Do we want the result of the changes we request? Not always. We often fall in love and then go about destroying someone's spirit by requesting alterations. What you see is what you get. Don't expect your partner to change simply because he or she loves you. Each person wants you to accept that person for who he or she is. If you see a major trait or behavior that you can't accept, walk away.

8. Citizen's Arrest

Some feel compelled to tell others what they think the other people are doing wrong even when they may do exactly the same thing. Did you ever see your partner correcting other drivers in traffic when he drives the same way? Some common examples of this mind game:

♦ Accusing him of lying when she lies on a regular basis.

♦ Accusing her of having an affair when he is the one with a mistress.

♦ Accusing her of hiding money when he has secret assets.

♦ Accusing him of looking at other women when she flirts all the time.

Correcting other people's behavior is a way of feeling powerful.

9. Just Try Harder

If you can keep your partner trying to please you, you are in a dominant position. This may be accomplished by alternating approval and disapproval so that the other person doesn't feel that it is futile to try. Human beings strive to achieve or attain what we know is possible. The right balance of praise, affection or positive behavior can cause some people to keep trying to please, even when the good is interspersed with negative, nasty behavior. Often we are attracted to a challenge that does not seem totally out of reach.

Another way of hooking a person into trying harder is changing the facts of a situation to suit your own purpose. For instance, when he discusses an incident or argument he alters important details, engaging her in a dispute over what really happened. She may try to convince him that his memory is incorrect, become enraged at the devious deception or start to question the accuracy of her own memory. He may act superior, condescending and certain of his position. These games divert any blame away from him or her and leave the other person struggling.

10. Benevolent Dictator

Sometimes, the abusive partner plays the role of tolerant tyrant.

♦ You can have anything you want, as long as I approve it.

♦ Be sure and bring me all your merchandise receipts.

♦ I am so generous; you have no right to complain.

♦ How can you be unhappy? I give you everything you need.

♦ I know you had your heart set on that car, but this one that I

bought you is much better.
- I bought you these expensive shoes. I don't want to hear that you are uncomfortable.
- I spent a fortune on these clothes, now I want to see you in them.
- I want you to redecorate the house but you need help, because I don't trust your taste.
- Look at all I do for you. How can you say I'm controlling?

11. The Drama Game

In some relationships, it seems there is always drama. Everything is a major issue with no simple solution. A calm, relaxed environment is rare. The game is to create chaos and the person in control gets to decide when the chaos ends and the problem of the minute is resolved. The drama queen generally enjoys this process and often can act totally innocent. Both parties may contribute to the uproar. If you let your partner continuously create and resolve chaos, they are in control. If you do not buy into or create drama, you maintain your own personal power.

"I'm leaving" is a type of drama game. This is not to be confused with people who express needing "time out" to cool down and are then willing to come back and discuss the issue in a calmer manner. The "I'm leaving" drama game can be played two ways:
- I'm leaving and I refuse to talk to you.
  Walking out of the room, house or relationship and rejecting any attempt to discuss the problem means taking control and avoiding any unpleasant confrontation. It generally enrages the person being shot down and abandoned and does not solve any issue.
- I'm leaving and you'd better chase after me.
  I'm walking out, because I'm angry with you. However, I want you to chase after me and prevent me from leaving. It is unlikely that I will allow you to fix the problem, but I will feel important. You could look foolish and controlling for interfering with my departure, but the drama will be very satisfying.

12. Tear Down/Build Up

"I can give and I can take away." In this game, your partner reduces you to your lowest point emotionally, psychologically and perhaps physically and then becomes kind, loving and giving. You are so relieved and grateful the negative behavior has stopped that you welcome all the positive attention you can receive. This reinforces the power the abuser feels and implies permission to continue the game in the future.

This same dynamic is seen when a person is abducted and abused, then appears to be choosing to stay. Subjected to the worst behavior that one human being can inflict on another, the fear and terror becomes relief and gratitude when the abuse stops. Complete submission is an attempt to avoid the horrendous behavior from returning.

WHY CAN'T SHE OR HE BE MORE LIKE ME?

There is often a basic power struggle between men and women. In this game, men are "reasonable thinkers"; women are "emotional messes". However, women are often more emotionally evolved and that scares many men. Women want to talk about their feelings. Men want to understand what the problem is, then think up a solution. Women then feel misunderstood, undervalued and frustrated. Men are confused, because they intended to be helpful. Many men want women to feel happy and be less complicated. Many women want men to share complexities. Some men can see women as irrational. Some women can see men as too controlled and logical. In many cases, a woman's life force is connected to her emotions. For many men, a man's power and self-worth are connected to his perceptions that he is in control and feelings are way too messy.

In the chapter called "When Men Don't Feel" in the book *Making Your Second Marriage a First Class Success*, Doug and Naomi Moseley say it beautifully:

> In an intimate relationship, a man who cannot express his anger in a clear and clean way is really just a covered-over boy. The same is true of a man who can't receive a woman's anger. A man who looks to his partner to set the emotional tone in his

relationship, because he has not explored his own emotional capabilities sufficiently, is weak. He doesn't have his full resources available to him and will ultimately be perceived by his partner as crippled in some way. A man who dies early, because he has frozen over his feelings is a sacrifice, not a hero. The demand for feelings is not some kind of anti-male conspiracy; it is a prayer for men to discover and bring forth the best that they can be.[3]

Even though Rhett Butler in Margaret Mitchell's epic novel *Gone with the Wind* was an exciting rogue, he felt weakened by becoming smitten with Scarlett O'Hara. She was conniving and detached, perpetually in love with Ashley Wilkes. At the end of the saga, she finally realizes that it's Rhett she loves. But her neglect has finally caused his indifference and he leaves her, uttering the famous line: "Frankly my dear, I don't give a damn."[4]

The ultimate power is indifference. Abuse and neglect of someone you love pushes them away and their feelings for you die by millimeters. It can take years. Eventually, no loving feelings remain. Some men will beg at this point to go to counseling, something she may have been requesting for years. She may feel betrayed and angry that he was unwilling to work on the relationship until it is too late. A counselor cannot give you back your feelings for another person. If a person has gotten to the point where he or she calmly says, "That's it, I'm done. I can't do this anymore," it often means there is simply not enough love left to do the hard work required to build a healthier marriage.

Chapter 3

Why Psychological Abuse Occurs

"I don't understand why he or she does this to me. How can my partner treat me this way when I love my spouse so much?" A huge number of factors contribute to how a person becomes psychologically abusive. In this chapter, we will focus on many of the reasons. Understanding that most of the circumstances which create these conditions cannot be changed helps individuals and couples evaluate their situations and devote energy toward making possible improvements. There are some situations that cannot be successfully treated, but the majority can be helped with therapy and medications.

Let's look at four major categories:
1. Trauma and Shame
2. Physical Illness and Conditions
3. Psychological Disorders
4. Fears

1. Trauma and Shame

Our earliest traumas can occur during childhood. Children who are abused are profoundly changed. Abuse molds personality and character and the message to the child is that they are bad, wrong, defective, unwelcome, despised or exist to be used. Physical abuse involves every horrible imaginable and unimaginable thing that someone can do to his or her child. Recently, our local paper reported the arrest of a couple for killing their child by tying him to a tree for two days in the scorching heat as a discipline for misbehavior. In the six years that I spent working in the Criminal Investigation Division of our police department, I saw and heard the most excruciating stories of child abuse that happened at the hands of people who supposedly loved their kids. They haunted me. Children are often prisoners, because they have few options for escaping their situations.

Sexual abuse can occur at any age and is commonly unreported. There are a huge number of adults who were sexually abused in some way as children. The abuse ranges from indecent exposure, fondling, oral and anal sex to intercourse. The abuser can be a family member, teacher, scout leader, church member, neighbor or stranger. One incident is enough to cause serious damage, particularly if it is held inside and kept secret or is reported and not believed or handled very inappropriately. Children are often additionally traumatized by a parent who knows or discovers what is happening and does nothing to protect them from the abuse, report the offender or provide the needed help.

Verbal and emotional abuse involves using nasty, derogatory, demeaning words to criticize and control. A child who grows up with taunting over who they are, how they look or how they act gets the message that they are not good enough and should be embarrassed. Some parents abuse, because it is all they know to do. It was done to them, they believe it is sanctioned by their religion or they actually think it is appropriate parenting. They may be trying to break the child's spirit or be trying to toughen them up. Verbal and emotional abuse is the epidemic of our time, as is the flipside of overt abuse. Covert abuse is lack of any appropriate parenting, discipline or guidance. Afraid to do anything, they do nothing and the children develop the insecurity of feeling too powerful at an inappropriate age. They don't know how to self-discipline, so they become undisciplined. They have no appropriate boundaries and often feel unrealistically entitled to behave in any way and have or take anything they want. Some parents who do not know appropriate discipline procedures were themselves poorly parented or abused and are bending over backwards to not repeat their parents' mistakes. They have the best intentions to not cause harm, but they err in the direction of permissiveness and leniency. The children from these parents often have difficulty when their partners do not like or approve of their conduct. They may seek relationships with people who either give them a lot of freedom or who attempt to monitor or control them. They may seek what they are used to or choose a mate who attempts to give them what they never got. Conflict ensues as they struggle over control. You may seek what you never had and then push against it, much like a child who is angry when punished. The undisciplined partner is saying, "I want you to love me enough to care about what I do, but I'm not going to like you trying to change me and I may throw a temper tantrum."

Childhood abuse invariably leads to shame. If the people children depend on and love treat them badly, they are never capable, during their youth, of seeing the offenders as the people at fault. They blame themselves. They must have caused or deserved this bad behavior. They feel deficient and flawed, ugly and stupid, bad and wrong, evil and empty. They are deeply ashamed and embarrassed.

As children, we can be victims of our parents' criminal behavior. However, all through our lives, the potential exists for us to become traumatized by crime. We can be assaulted physically or sexually. We can be robbed, burglarized or kidnapped. We can have our money, assets, house or business stolen through individual deception or corporate crime. We can be discriminated against, harassed or stalked or unjustly accused of something we did not do. We can be victimized at work, during any of our daily activities or while we are sound asleep in our own home. September 11, 2001, left hundreds of innocent people murdered by terrorists and left our entire nation traumatized. We are also impacted by having someone we love become the victim of crime. The murder or rape of a child, parent, sibling or spouse is a crime no one fully recovers from. Every crime victim, at some point, searches his or her mind for what he or she could have done to have prevented or stopped it. It is normal to have thoughts and feelings of wanting to retaliate. The helpless feelings and anger are sometimes vented on the person you are closest to. You can't punish the criminal, so you end up punishing your partner.

You can also be victimized by a serious accident or an act of nature. If you caused the accident by carelessness, neglect or a situation such as driving under the influence of alcohol or drugs, you are angry at yourself. If the accident was random and blameless, you may feel angry at the world or at God. You may also feel angry at your higher power for a fire, storm, flood, tornado, wind, lightning, etc. that changed your world. Human accidents and acts of nature can kill, maim, disable and financially, physically and emotionally devastate you and your family. If another person caused the accident, even unintentionally, you may be able to sue them and recover some financial losses, but the anger and trauma remain.

Wars are fought to protect and defend. Our country may benefit, but individuals and families often pay enormous prices. Having a loved one deployed during conflict creates enormous tension, worry and fear. Losing that loved one in combat or by an accident is heartbreaking, even when you are enormously proud of his or her sacrifice. No one fully mends the hole in his or her heart from that loss. For the soldiers, what they hear, see and feel while doing their duty can create lifelong traumatic memories. Life as they knew it is forever altered as they have horrific insights into human behavior. Fully relaxing without using alcohol or a drug is impossible for some. Nightmares haunt their sleep and constant vigilance haunts their waking hours.

A very different trauma is caused by the loss of a job, income and a way of life. We live in a time where many people are impacted by unemployment and inflation. Some industries are dying out or are being outsourced to other countries with cheaper labor. Companies are laying people off or eliminating benefits to save money. Prices are rising, with gasoline leading the way and impacting everyone. Home mortgages are at a record rate of foreclosure and people and pets look for places to live. Rising food costs mean that more people are going hungry and people must adjust their lifestyles while more of their budgets go to cover necessities. The stress is enormous.

Mike's sad story illustrates the results of such stress on his life and marriage as he turns into a psychological abuser:

Mike was laid off from yet another job, as his only training was in a dying American industry. He dreaded going home and telling his wife, Mona. He didn't know if her patience would hold out and he hated to see the look of disappointment he knew would be on her face. More than that, he hated what lay ahead for him. He'd have to update his resume and spend all day sitting at the computer applying for jobs. If he was lucky enough to get an interview, he'd try to be positive and present himself in the best light, but he knew his age, former high salary and the growing number of jobs on his resume worked against him. He despised all the coming rejection and the possible months of being unemployed. If he got a job offer, he'd probably have to take another pay cut. He had no idea how he and Mona would pay all their bills if that happened. He knew Mona would be upset if they had to sell the house and move, but they might have no other choice.

When Mona heard the news she *was* frustrated and disappointed. She hated to see Mike depressed and deflated. She understood how he could be losing his confidence, but it was hard to watch the dynamic, successful man she had married become so discouraged and scared. She hated to admit it, but she was angry at his weakness and ineffectiveness. It was hard to work all day and come home late to find him sitting and staring at the television news full of depressing stories and statistics about unemployment.

It was difficult for both Mike and Mona to not know how long Mike's current unemployment would last and when and where his next job would come from. The clock was ticking on their savings. When would the money run out and how would they ever retire? Their situation seemed impossible.

Mona tried to find a silver lining in Mike's latest job loss. She did not think it was fair for her to work all week and spend nights and weekends on all the household chores. She began making "Honey Do" lists. Eventually, she directly told him that she felt he should do all the household cleaning, shopping and cooking, since he was unemployed. Maybe she was trying to punish him, but mostly she felt it was only fair, considering his new leisure time. She was trying to ward off the resentment she felt over his free time, no matter how miserable he was, and all the increased pressures on her to carry them through the crisis.

Mike understood her logic, but he *did* feel punished for a situation that felt out of his control. He hated being without a job again; he hated the job search process; he hated the idea of disappointing Mona; he hated cleaning the bathrooms; and, most of all, he hated feeling powerless.

All of these circumstances converged into escalating incidents of anger and frustration as Mike erupted, making nasty psychologically abusive attacks on Mona that relieved his immediate pressure, but left him feeling like a totally incompetent jerk. Part of him thought, *How dare she pile more on me at this difficult, vulnerable time in my life.*

Mona felt victimized by his joblessness, his depression, the change in life circumstances, the loss of security, the fear of more losses to come, the uncertainty of the future and now, the abusive attacks he was directing at her. She felt it was fair that he take more responsibilities, since he had more time. She knew she did not deserve to be his figurative punching bag, just because there was no one else around to take his frustrations out on. She asked herself how much longer she could take this.

Abandonment causes deep psychological and emotional trauma. There are multiple ways that a person can feel abandoned at all stages of his or her life and often we experience them simultaneously. The common result of being abandoned is we do not get our needs fulfilled and we subsequently experience the shame of feeling unworthy of being properly cared for, respected and appreciated. Here are some of the many ways we end up experiencing abandonment:

♦ Inadequate nurturing through neglect. Some children fail to develop physically and emotionally from being neglected. They fail to thrive.

♦ Abuse of every description robs children and adults of the ability to feel good about themselves and master healthy coping skills and interpersonal relationships.

♦ Any addiction causes the other people in your life to be deprived of your sober self.

♦ Death of a parent, child or partner causes abandonment feelings. If the death was a suicide, these feelings are particularly acute, but any loss of a loved one can be traumatic.

♦ Complete absorption of self by a parent or partner is referred to as narcissistic deprivation. You are deprived of a loved one's appropriate care and attention.

♦ Over-absorption or enmeshment causes you to feel inappropriately bonded to a parent or spouse. You end up feeling you exist to meet their needs. You must please them in order to matter. You lose yourself.

♦ Separation, divorce, lying and infidelity. If you are abandoned by a parent or partner or if you are lied to or cheated on, you feel alone, angry and ashamed.

♦ Demand for perfection. If you are expected to achieve and be perfect to meet a parent or partner's needs, you experience having your normal flawed self abandoned. You are not acceptable the way you are. You must continually prove yourself.

♦ Shaming and guilt. Many people are disciplined and controlled through shame and guilt. Their true selves are disrespected.

Trauma and shame play a tremendous role in shaping who we are and who we become. It is not unusual for a person who has experienced trauma to become psychologically abusive in his or her relationship. Sometimes the behavior is overt and clearly definable, but sometimes the other person retreats inside his or her self, leaving his or her partner emotionally abandoned.

2. Physical Illness and Conditions

Our human bodies are complex and miraculous. Designed to operate perfectly, there are many things that can go wrong. Our body chemistry has a negative impact on our feelings, thoughts and behavior and often our emotions, thoughts and actions have an extremely negative impact on our bodies.

The brain is fascinating and it runs the show. To learn more I've read many articles about the brain and attended a workshop called *Understanding Hostility: The Physiology and Psychology of the Hostile Client* by Jeffery Baker, Ph. D. At an autopsy at the medical examiner's office, I was surprised to view the brain's size and complexity. Put simply, the thalamus is the central processing system that breaks down what it hears and sees and sends signals to the cortex, which gives it all cognitive meaning. The small almond-shaped amygdala adds the emotional meaning and can trigger the fear response and sends out electrical signals. Genetics, trauma, depression, anxiety, diseases and brain damage can cause the brain to function poorly enough to cause some people to have a quick temper and possibly become violent. At times, the brain can flood due to extreme fear or rage and the person may lose control of their actions and may not be able to remember what they have said or done. Low or erratic levels of the neurotransmitter serotonin can increase aggressive behavior. Hence, the use of medications that increase and steady the serotonin levels is helpful to many in dealing with their abusive actions.

The director of Behavioral Research at Duke University Medical Center, Dr. Redford Williams, and his wife, Virginia, were interviewed by Donald Patterson of the *News and Record* in Greensboro, North Carolina, about their book entitled *Anger Kills*. In the article, Williams explains that when we are angry, our brain sends an alarm down nerves to signal our adrenal glands to send large amounts of adrenalin and cortisol into our bloodstream. The nerves also constrict our arteries that carry blood to our kidneys and intestines. The adrenalin causes blood platelets to become stickier and fat cells to be dumped into the blood for energy. The liver changes the fat cells to cholesterol. The heart pumps more blood and our blood pressure goes up. The coronary artery can become damaged over time, and sticky platelets and cholesterol clump and build up at the damaged site, clogging an artery. Each time you are angry, the plaque can build, which sets a person up for a heart attack.[5]

Another factor involving the brain is the ability to distinguish right and wrong and to control our negative impulses. Brain damage can result from injury, illness, stress, trauma, concussions or seizures. If the impulse control is damaged, the person may develop an Intermittent Explosive Disorder or at the extreme level, become a predatory psychopath who feels no guilt or fear. In relationships with a person whose brain has been damaged in this way, he can behave with charm, an elevated ego, have no remorse or ability to empathize and be very manipulative and deceiving.

There are many diseases and conditions that can trigger negative behavior. High blood pressure, diabetes when the blood sugar is elevated and many degenerative diseases can cause grumpy, nasty moods. The aftermath of serious surgery often involves becoming severely depressed. Having chronic pain anywhere in the body is draining and tempers can easily flare. The aging process and particularly Alzheimer's disease cause extreme mental and behavioral changes. Alzheimer's patients have physical and psychological symptoms and can become very verbally and physically violent and aggressive as parts of their brains are damaged; but as the disease progresses further, they become helpless and docile.

Research on violent men has shown that a small percentage have the capacity to be calm and calculating when angry or when they experience any perceived aggression. Neil Jacobson and John Gottman, in their book *When Men Batter Women*, sampled sixty batterers. They found that 20 percent became "Cobras" when angered. They did not have higher blood pressure, heart rate or perspire more. They used violence and verbal aggression unemotionally to control. The "Pit Bulls" were the other 80 percent and they did have the elevated physical symptoms as they resorted to abusive behavior. The cold, calm Cobras were scarier and generally unfit to participate in couples counseling.[6]

Is the ability to be very calm under pressure or in a crisis, genetic, biological and inherited or created through our environment and experiences? Is the development of any disorder because of our body chemistry or more situational? For a fascinating look at the connection of your body, mind and spirit, read *Anatomy of the Spirit: The Seven Stages of Power and Healing* by Caroline Myss, Ph. D. She connects how everything we experience, think and feel impacts and changes the cells in our body. She states, "I believe that our cell tissue holds the vibrational patterns of our attitudes, our belief systems, and the presence or absence of an exquisite energy frequency or 'grace' that we can activate by calling our spirits back from negative attachments."[7] The book examines how seven sacred truths, or chakras, impact our organs, mental and emotional issues and physical dysfunctions. Dr. Myss maintains that experiencing problems in specific areas of our lives will directly impact specific areas of our bodies, minds and emotions.

3. Psychological Disorders

People experiencing psychological disorders who seek treatment from a physician or therapist are given a diagnosis found in the *Diagnostic and Statistical Manual of Mental Disorders* or DSM-IV, published by the American Psychiatric Association. This process of diagnosing is for the purpose of accurately understanding and treating a person's difficulty. It is also required before any insurance company will reimburse the provided services. I hate the focus on labeling, because many people have stigmas towards psychological issues and will not seek help for their problems. You know what your symptoms are and hopefully you now understand that our mind, body and spirit are interrelated. Some of the most helpful healing treatment comes in counseling your mind and comforting your spirit. Here is a brief overview of the many disorders that can result in triggering psychologically abusive behavior. More complete technical information can be found in the DSM-IV or online.

- ◆ Depression – sad, tired, little pleasure in life, no energy, losing or gaining weight, trouble concentrating, difficulty sleeping or staying awake and feeling worthless or guilty; may contemplate suicide.

◆ Anxiety – excessive worrying, restless, irritable, tired, can't think clearly, tense and problems with sleeping.

◆ Panic Attacks – can feel similar to a heart attack, heart accelerates or pounds, chills, sweating, shaking, trouble breathing, chest pain, dizzy, nausea, feel like you are choking, losing control or dying.

◆ Bipolar Disorder (formerly Manic-Depressive Disorder) – a combination of experiencing depression with manic episodes in varying frequencies. Manic episodes can include inflated self-esteem, not sleeping much, rapid talking with racing thoughts, incredible energy used to accomplish tasks and relentless pursuit of pleasurable activities which may have negative consequences.

◆ Schizophrenia – break with reality, delusions, hallucinations, disorganized behavior and speech.

◆ Dissociative Disorders – parts of the self split off. Dissociative Identity Disorder includes forming other distinct personalities.

◆ Obsessive-Compulsive Disorder (OCD) – obsessive thoughts which cause worry, stress and compulsive, repetitive behaviors.

◆ Posttraumatic Stress Disorder (PTSD) – caused by a traumatic event that gets relived and re-experienced, nightmares, distress, flashbacks, may try to avoid talking or thinking about event, can't experience many normal feelings, outbursts of anger, can't think clearly, hypervigilant and easily startled.

◆ Addictions – dependent on a substance or activity, feel powerless to stop, relationship to substance or activity takes priority over any other relationships, characterized by lying and compulsive behavior .

◆ Personality Disorders – there are ten types:
  ▸ Paranoid – distrust and suspicious, holds grudges.
  ▸ Schizoid – detach from relationships and don't show any normal emotions.

‣ Schizotypal – very uncomfortable in relationships, distorted thinking and eccentric behavior.

‣ Antisocial – uninterested in other people's rights or feelings.

‣ Borderline – unstable in relationships and with themselves, very impulsive, will make *you* feel crazy.

‣ Histrionic – drama queen or king, overly emotional and craves attention.

‣ Narcissistic – "It's all about me." Feels important, needs admiration and lacks empathy.

‣ Avoidance – socially inhibited, feels inadequate and sensitive to criticism.

‣ Dependent – submissive and clingy, needs to be taken care of.

‣ Obsessive Compulsive – must be orderly, perfect and in control.

‣ Not Otherwise Specified (NOS) – catch-all for other kooky behavior.

People who come in for counseling are experiencing adjustment disorders with disturbances in their behaviors or moods. They are attempting to deal with situations in their lives that have caused them to feel out of sorts and unsettled. Any one of these disorders can cause problems in relationships. A depressed person may have absolutely no interest in connecting with his or her partner and an anxious person may worry his or her mate to death. A person with PTSD may pound his spouse unknowingly during a nightmare or immediately be in attack mode when startled. Someone in the manic phase of a bipolar disorder may have sex with multiple partners and at least one of the personalities of a person with dissociative identity disorder will be erratic and potentially combative. A person with schizophrenia or a person under the influence of certain drugs may hallucinate or become so paranoid that they act aggressively due to imagined threats or dangers. Men and women with obsessive compulsive disorder can demand rigid compliance with their ideas of cleanliness and order. If *you* have been diagnosed with one of these conditions and are married to an abusive mate, the very symptoms of your disorder may infuriate your partner and trigger more abuse. All of these considerations factor into the treatment of individuals and couples in distress.

4. Fears

The traumas discussed earlier are the foundation for our fears. We each experience fear in varying degrees. If we understand our fears and deal with them in healthy manners, we do not allow them to cause us to act out against our partners. If we do not have insight into the depths of our fear and if we do not know how to resolve or manage them, they become the underlying motivation for many of our negative actions. We can harm loved ones and we also damage ourselves in the process. The more we struggle to force our spouse to act in a way that we believe will try to reduce or calm our fears, the more the relationship becomes conflicted and uncomfortable.

♦ Fear of Failure – We all hate being judged, criticized and feeling that we do not measure up. We are afraid of failing at anything, because this can reinforce the shame we already feel. We despise being teased, tormented or discriminated against. Enough failure leaves us feeling worthless.

♦ Fear of Abandonment – The person feels and often expresses: Please don't leave me. I can't bear it if you reject me and I am left alone. I've become way too dependent on you, which causes me to be jealous of anything and anybody else to whom you pay attention. I am very insecure.

On July 18, 2002, the *Greensboro News and Record* reported on a plea bargain in the case of a man who murdered his wife. According to the article, the marriage was in trouble and he "felt embarrassment that his wife spent more time with her female friends than him. She was planning a trip with them when the slaying occurred."[8]

♦ Fear of Commitment and Intimacy – Although it is a basic need to be loved and accepted for who we truly are, the risk of becoming vulnerable is too scary for some people. We'd like a guarantee that our feelings are totally reciprocated and we never get one in life. Men, in particular, can have difficulty with deep emotions. They are often uncomfortable with their feelings and unwilling to express them. They may avoid hearing about or responding appropriately to difficult or painful problems or situations. Women often end up holding their pain on many issues. At times, people are so desperate to connect with another person that they will rush in with their own fantasy of a perfect relationship. As the newness wears off and real life difficulties present themselves, they can't handle it and make a hasty retreat.

Let's look at a letter written (but not sent) by Jennifer, a young woman trying to deal with her extreme frustration and anger after being abruptly abandoned by a man in his thirties who had never been able to stay in a relationship longer than six to eight months, which is often the time "in love" feelings begin to lessen. When the normal problems and issues developed, he left, even though he had acted as if he was *fully* invested and committed to the relationship. He used her issues to criticize her, even though she sought professional help on an ongoing basis, took mild medication and had been sober for six years. He was unwilling to acknowledge or deal with any of his own issues, preferring to remain alone.

Wow, well I certainly never thought that I would be in this place with you. You were the one that I trusted to never hurt me like you did. I feel as if I have been on a roller coaster with you and like I was hit by a tornado. You come in and sweep me off my feet; telling me how much you love me, telling me how happy you are with me, asking me to move in with you, telling me that there is nothing that I could say about myself that would surprise you, talking about having kids with me, sending me roses, telling me how perfect I am, telling me that I am the first girl that you have ever bought jewelry for, telling me that you would never leave me or hurt me…all of this within the first three or four months!!! I didn't know how to take it. I had never had someone treat me so good. But I see the irony in all of this now. I told you several times that I felt overwhelmed and like things were going too fast and that it was too much. But you never seemed to understand or respect that. And you wonder why it felt as if I was pushing you away or why I wasn't as excited as you thought I should be. I didn't even know how to breathe for a while. Of course, every relationship is happy and exciting and seems perfect in the beginning; but it doesn't stay that way. That is just reality. Once we started running into problems, it didn't seem as if you knew how to handle them or get through them and it proved true that you wouldn't. I tried to be honest and open and communicate throughout the whole relationship and I told you everything about me at the very beginning at your request, never thinking that it would come back to slap me in the face. Boy was I fooled! You made me out to be such an unhappy person, when really I was feeling overwhelmed, stifled and frustrated. Yes, I know that I had my times where I was unhappy and/or complaining and I was always willing to admit that. But I don't think that you ever fully understood why and I don't know that you ever will be able to understand. Yes, I know that we took a break for a reason. Both of us needed it and wanted it. And I did ask you questions for a reason. But I think that those were things that you should have thought about all along. And they were definitely things that you should have known the answer to before you were planning a future and communicating to me about it. Life and relationships are not fairy tales or fantasies. They are real; they have real issues and problems and feelings. And these things should never be taken lightly when you are committed to someone. I feel like you thought I was your "Cinderella" and that you were going to sweep me off my feet and we were going to run off and get married and live happily ever after. Don't we all wish things could be that easy? But instead you swept me off my feet and dropped me on my ass, before I even had time to try to get on my feet. And the second I felt like I was ready to open up and be happy with you, it was "I just don't want to be with you

anymore and I don't see you in my future." What the hell???
Love is not a switch that can be flipped and if you felt that way
for a long time, then you sure as hell were a good actor. I don't
think you know how to have any kind of relationship, except
maybe with your computer—because at least that's safe and it
could never hurt you. You are such a surface person and you
think that life is and/or should be so simple and cheery. You said
there was "too much to deal with, with me." But you knew all of
these things from the very beginning and appeared to be supportive. But instead, I got slapped in the face with my "issues"—
"How many medications are you on?" "That sounds like your
counselor talking." "When are you going to another meeting?"
"How can you forget to take your medicine?" Well at least I am
in reality; I am looking at my issues and I am taking steps to deal
with them on a daily basis. What are you doing? Do you think
that you don't have any REAL issues? Because if you do, you are
a fool. Everyone has issues, all different, but they are there. I
never had anyone make me feel so good and then turn around
to make me feel so bad. Like I was beautiful on the inside and
out and perfect; and then BAM I have so many issues and seem
so unhappy, and why should I have to work to be happy?? No
one is happy ALL OF THE TIME!! You made me feel like I
am weak because I have things like depression, alcoholism, anxiety and physical issues. When in fact all of these things have
made me strong, deep and unique. These things have made me
become the person that I am today and they give me true color.
When we finally broke up, you knew that I had said that I
couldn't just be your friend right away. But yet, you contacted
me on a regular basis; "Are you okay?" "Do you hate me?" "Buy
Dave Matthews tickets, I will go with you." "How are you?" And
then when I finally give in and tell you that I think that we can
be friends, you suddenly stop texting, questioning and seeming
to care. Is this what you think a friend is? Because I certainly
don't. I do not treat my friends this way and my "true friends"

would certainly not do that to me. I guess I sort of jumped the gun, thinking that we could just be friends. I am hurt. I am mad. And I need some space to breathe, let go, accept and move on. You know, I thought that I had finally kissed enough frogs. I thought that I had finally found "my prince". But again, I was proved wrong. And isn't it all so ironic??

It can be therapeutic to write a letter that you do not send to someone who has hurt you. Do not worry about what you say or how you say it, simply let your thoughts and feelings flow. You may be surprised at the depths of your hurt and anger, plus the letter serves as a record of what you are experiencing, allowing your mind to not continue obsessing over your thoughts.

♦ Fear of powerlessness – This goes hand-in-hand with the fear of failure, but this fear is closely connected with most abusive relationships. When people feel inadequate, ineffective or disrespected, they may use their relationship with their partners to try and get their needs met. If the effort to establish power and control in the relationship causes them to become abusive, then they have actually lost control, which reinforces the feeling of powerlessness. Some men are afraid of the power that women hold, if the woman possesses the ability to be confident, kind, nurturing, articulate, sexual and compassionate. It scares some women, because of the strength they see in him and maybe don't possess.

A final reason people psychologically abuse each other is because they can. They rarely have true negative consequences or only minor ones. Their partners have quietly sanctioned abuse by tolerating it. The partners make excuses for it, analyze, diagnose or attempt to correct it.

♦ If you knew you would lose your job if you brutally cussed and criticized your boss, would you do it?

♦ Would you mock, provoke or shove a police officer if it meant going to jail?

♦ Would you refuse to look at or speak to someone who was trying to help, serve or provide for you if it meant you got passed over for things you wanted and needed?

Some people would risk the above behavior. Most would not. But, we live behind closed doors with each other. Fear, shame, anger, sadness and embarrassment get in our way. We live with the people we love and have chosen to make a life with. We try to understand and be tolerant and patient. We try to forgive and move on. We find excuses for their behavior and our own. We know no one is perfect.

This is NOT to say that as individuals we allow or want abuse. No one enjoys being hurt or ignored. However, people have the ability to exercise much more self-control than they often do in the privacy of their homes. Sometimes we show our partners our worst behavior. We believe they will tolerate it because of love, traditions, values, understanding and compassion.

Are there people who will treat the psychologically abused better? The answer is yes. Then why do we stay with someone who psychologically abuses us? Read on.

Part II

Why We Stay

Chapter 4

Needy Relationships

For me, the Broadway musical *Oliver*, based on the book *Oliver Twist* by Charles Dickens, is mesmerizing. The central romantic relationship is between Nancy and Bill Sikes. Bill is a particularly cruel character who takes pride in the fear he evokes. Nancy loves him and sings about Bill needing her, explaining that she will be loyal, loving and will cling to him steadfastly. In the end, he kills her. Many women and men see being "needed" by their partners as a powerful reason for staying in a relationship.

I need you…

♦ to feel loved and complete;
♦ to feel safe and secure;
♦ to feel wanted and desirable;
♦ to feel accepted and included;
♦ to feel powerful and important;
♦ to feel turned-on and sexy.

Healthy relationships have a balanced interactive quality where we are able to need and count on our partners, while not being hurt or sacrificing our personal power. Some abusive relationships have a skewed enmeshment, or codependency, where people feel they are only meaningful and significant when connected to their partners. The vulnerability this creates is frightening. You realize how much the other person can hurt you. So you pull away, then come back, yo-yoing between tension and unhappiness. If my significance is associated with being in this relationship, then your disapproval or anger causes me to feel desperate. I must reconnect in order to regain my balance. If I feel you really need me, I can forgive and come back to you, no matter what you have said or done. This will meet my need to feel whole. If I only matter in a relationship to you, then I must be in a relationship with you.

- I can heal him through my love for him.
- She says I make her life complete.
- I feel sorry for him.
- I can help her.
- He cries afterwards and begs for my forgiveness, so there must be hope.
- I know he needs me, so if I can say or do just the right thing, I can make it better.

It is normal for us to want to save what is important to us, whether it is our love, relationship, family or lifestyle. Our need to be connected causes us to search for solutions.

We rationalize and attempt to understand why our partners might be abusive. They can't help what they're doing, because...

- alcohol makes her mean;
- he saw his father hit his mother;
- she was abused as a child;
- he has a bad temper;
- I make her angry;
- she gets jealous because she loves me so much;
- if I show my anger, it upsets him;
- his mother constantly criticized him;
- he's stressed out over his job;
- our kids cause problems;

◆ money is really tight right now;

◆ I don't want sex as much as he does and that frustrates him.

These rationalizations cause many to think they have the power to eliminate the psychological abuse by changing or improving the external situations. They don't clearly identify the abuse as unacceptable. Failure to do so ensures that the mind games will continue.

Human beings are relational creatures. Unless we are severely damaged, we enjoy being connected to other people. We search for our soul mates. Somehow, the world looks, feels, smells, tastes and sounds better when we are in love. We become intoxicated by the intensity of experiences which occur when we are in sync with a partner. The initial sweetness is so wonderful. As the relationship continues and problems occur, many people say, "I just want things to be like they were in the beginning." The fact that we have experienced such joy with someone else is powerfully seductive. We often attempt to regain or recreate the initial state of happiness. We want the special connection that brought us joy, without the ugliness.

What happens when reality confronts us and illusions fade? We feel betrayed and misled. Daniella shares her thoughts about her psychologically abusive husband:

> Surely this is a mistake. This person, who is so dear to me, is now shouting obscenities one inch from my face and has shoved me to the ground. It seems that I don't matter quite as much and my world feels like it is crumbling. I'm feeling desperate to fix it. When the nightmare passes, he seems contrite. He's apologizing. He's begging me to stay and promising it will never happen again. He needs me after all. That was stormy, but what relationship isn't?

Often women in these situations are caregivers who attempt to soothe and correct problems. This role can be developed in childhood. We might have been the person family and friends turned to for understanding, attention and solutions. We learned that taking care of others is how we mattered. Experiencing problems in our adult interactions, we continue striving to be the peacemaker. We feel compelled to help.

Rationalizations allow us to stabilize our relationships in order to find a personal value that we feel we cannot find on our own. Remember, our importance is connected to our partnership with our mates. Alone we are existing, together we are living. In *Oliver Twist*, Nancy has a hard life on the street and Bill gives her some attention and significance. Loving him is how she feels alive, how she matters. We can understand the emotion. We can identify with her feelings. We get it. We yearn to experience the intensity of the relationship, and we accept the bad to keep the good.

The same dynamic applies to men who are attracted to needy women. He can feel more powerful and necessary in her life if she needs him. Her dependency creates his sense of security. He feels assured that she will not leave him if he continues to meet her needs. Dale talks about the psychological abuse he endures:

> I know my wife needs me. I've always wanted to take care of her and keep her safe. It makes me feel good to do that for her. Growing up, she was abused, physically, psychologically and, even though she has only sketchy memories of it, we believe she was also abused sexually. She no longer wants any sexual contact with me. It has been years since we made love. She likes for us to be close and hold each other, but the thought of sexual intimacy terrifies her. I feel sorry for her, but I feel sorry for me, too.
>
> She has a need to control everything. Her therapist says that, because in her childhood, she had no control over the terrible things that were happening to her. She is stubborn, at times demanding and will dig in her heels and not budge. It's so much easier to let her have her way. It is sad and very draining but it is important to me to always be there for her.

Neediness can be very frustrating if the needy person is like a bottomless pit. No matter how much you give, it is never enough. They are like buckets with holes in the bottom. A continual stream of whatever they ask for will not fill them up. Cravings for attention, love, sex, money, communication or reassurance can never be satisfied.

Roger explains his bad behavior:

> I never felt as good or as bad about myself as I did with her—I had the highest of highs and the lowest of lows. She brought out my best and my worst. I found that, at times, I wanted to put her on a pedestal and sometimes I wanted to drag her through the mud. She was all things to me, but I couldn't let her know that. So, sometimes, I made her feel like she was nothing to me. I needed her so much that it scared me to death. My feelings were unbelievably intense. I couldn't make love to her enough. I wanted to bring her inside of me the way I pushed myself inside of her. I couldn't get enough. She had me completely, but I could never let her know that. It was way too frightening—her energy and my fear, her sexuality and my desire, her heat and my intensity. I could never get enough of her, but I kept trying.

Staying in a psychologically abusive relationship, because you are needed by the abuser, can certainly crush your spirit. Regardless of how much you give, you keep getting knocked down. You are like the children's toy—a Weeble—you bounce back with a smile on your face, ready to serve.

What does it mean to be really needed by another person? It means that, to at least one person, we are very important. We share an intensity of our essence that we fear we would never feel without our partners. We are convinced that he or she would be lost without us. We define our purpose in life based on meeting the other person's needs. He or she can do anything and I will stay, as long as that person needs me. The relationship isn't ordinary. It is intense. It involves a value that many, especially women, may never have felt before. To this one person, no matter how imperfect, the partner is vital. She grasps and accepts his frailties, flaws and failures. He knows her secrets. She sees his passions, fears and insecurities. He feeds off her and she feels influential and expansive. She sees the side of him that no one else sees, because he needs her. His or her vulnerability is the other partner's power, even though that person may get punished for it. It is a double-edged sword. He craves her passionately, but he hates feeling weak due to his neediness. She erupts in anger to assert her power. His and her eventual acceptance of the psychological abuse is based on intensely feeling that the one partner knows the other one's strengths and weaknesses.

Ask yourself:

♦ What do I feel about him or her needing me?

♦ Do I feel grateful, relieved, powerful and important when he or she apologizes or acts nice again?

♦ Am I a caregiver? If so, is that how I feel I matter? Is that a role I want to continue?

♦ Have you ever thought you would die if your partner left you, only to wonder six months after the relationship ended, *What was I thinking?*

Chapter 5

Fear

Fear can be the motivation for staying in a relationship or for leaving (which is covered in chapter 20). Living with fear is difficult. Unfortunately for some, it is a way of life.

1. My partner says he or she will kill me if I try to leave. I'd always be looking over my shoulder.
2. Where would I go? I don't think I can support myself.
3. My partner will try and get custody of the kids. He or she will do anything to make sure I am miserable.
4. He or she will never leave me alone.
5. What would people say? I'd be embarrassed and humiliated.
6. I'm afraid to be alone. What if I never find anyone else?

1. My partner says he or she will kill me if I try to leave. I'd always be looking over my shoulder.

Living with the known fear can be easier than a life where you never know what could be around the next corner. The news media highlights stories of women and some men who are murdered, because they separated from their partners. You may know, from living with your spouse, what that person is capable of doing, so your apprehension is well founded. A woman or man who is threatening, mentally unstable or who has a sense of entitlement over his or her partner is dangerous.

- She is *my* woman.
- He has *my* kids.
- She's living in *my* house.
- She won't get *my* money.
- No other woman will have *my* husband.
- He *belongs* to me.

Threats can be extremely frightening. A man or woman who says, "I'll kill you, the kids and then myself" is scary. If your partner actually feels life is meaningless and that he or she has nothing without you, it is hard to trust that the partner won't snap. Always having to look over your shoulder is an alarming way to live. Never knowing when he or she might be following or waiting to ambush you means you never relax. Thoughts of losing the person he or she loves or feels ownership of may push some over the edge. Choosing to stay seems safer for the victim.

2. Where would I go? I don't think I can support myself.

If a woman needs to leave her home and has no place to go, most communities have some sort of shelter or short-term housing. While these temporary lodgings provide important assistance, not everyone can deal with leaving familiar surroundings to go to a new situation, which involves living with other women and children in crisis.

Most states in America have civil orders available for domestic abuse cases, which give the victim time-limited rights to stay in his or her home and order the abuser to get his or her possessions, leave the premises and not see or contact the victim. He or she may also be granted emergency financial relief, but this process may require the services of an attorney.

The reality is that issuing a court-ordered forbiddance to come near his or her spouse does not mean that the person will honor these mandates. Some men will abide by the rules, but others will flagrantly ignore them. When a woman or man obtains a restraining order, what does that person actually have? He or she possesses a piece of paper, which feels like little protection if the spouse is breaking into the home. It does pretty much guarantee an arrest, *if* one has the order in hand *and* can get the police on the scene fast enough.

A low-paying job or being unemployed makes leaving scary. Along the way, your partner may have convinced you that you have no value in the workplace and can't survive without him or her. The effort it will take to make yourself marketable seems overwhelming and exhausting. Believing you can't make it on your own, you sabotage attempts at success by sending out negative energy, which is unimpressive to potential employers. You become unable to recognize opportunities and available resources. Fear of failure often brings failure. If you have been made to feel worthless, you won't be able to project your positive qualities.

3. My partner will try and get custody of the kids. He or she will do anything to make sure I am miserable.

Psychologically abusive behavior often continues long after a divorce. Some men and women have made a project out of torturing their ex-spouses, even after they have remarried. The range of behavior is varied, but some people have an endless capacity for devious, destructive behavior. The ex-spouse justifies punishing the person, because he or she left the other. That person's misery is his or her pleasure.

Examples of this destructive behavior:

♦ Filing for sole custody of the children.
♦ Not paying child support.
♦ Quitting a job in order to have support reduced.
♦ Allowing the house to go into foreclosure.
♦ Saying derogatory things about the ex-spouse to the kids.
♦ Neglecting or abusing the children.
♦ Hurting pets.
♦ Continuously harassing the other person.
♦ Stalking.

♦ Breaking into the ex's home.
♦ Threatening anyone the other person dates.
♦ Making hang-up calls.
♦ Nasty voice or e-mails.
♦ Turning friends or family against the ex.
♦ Causing the person to lose his or her job.
♦ Flattening car tires.
♦ Cutting phone lines.
♦ Taking or opening the other person's mail.
♦ Hacking into the ex's computer.

The list of possibilities is endless.

4. He or she will never leave me alone.

If you truly feel that your partner will never leave you alone, you may choose to stay. Feeling defeated before you even begin is paralyzing: If I can never be free of him, why would I spend my life running? Living in fear offers no peace, but at least if I am facing him, I'll see it coming.

Kathy reveals her own insights into her current psychologically abusive relationship:

> I dance his dance always. If he says go, I go; stay, I stay. Like a well-trained dog, I'm there to serve my master. Unlike the dog, I hate him most of the time. He has an endless capacity to hurt and a creative calculating mind to control everyone around him. I am afraid. I loved him once. Our union was supposedly blessed by God, but I fear I sold my soul to the Devil instead. He swears I'll never get away and I believe him. He never gives up on anything. I've learned to be a robot. I do what he wants and I hide my feelings, so that some real part of me is mine and not his. No one can rescue me now. It's hopeless.

Helpers often feel helpless. Whether you are family, friend, law enforcement, counselor or volunteer, there is only so much you can do. Great strides have been made in laws and services for victims of abuse.

The fact remains that help is often inadequate. Leaving can be very risky and dangerous; it is no wonder that fear causes many, especially women, to stay.

5. What would people say? I'd be embarrassed and humiliated.
It's a rare person who has no concern with what other people will think or say. We worry about the impact of leaving on ourselves, our children and our families.

♦ No one in my family gets divorced.
♦ My kids will be devastated.
♦ None of my children's friends have divorced parents.
♦ My church frowns on separations.
♦ What will my friends say?
♦ Everyone thinks we are such a great couple.
♦ My parents wouldn't speak to me if I left my husband.
♦ My father said he'd write me out of his will.
♦ I could no longer be in my couples Sunday school class.
♦ People will wonder why this is happening.

It is tough to have people you know and people you don't know gossiping about your life. After a story is repeated several times, it often bears no resemblance to the truth. It seems common for others to need to identify a bad person and a good person, so that they can malign one and feel sympathy for the other. In the attempt to define who's "at fault" in the separation, people may guess or even manufacture information. They piece together bits of hearsay and create a scenario that can take on a life of its own. Some of the folks are curious about hearing the story, while others want to know who is now single and available. It can be humiliating to hear what is being said about your life. Generally, you are powerless to correct it, because anything you say gets transformed as it is repeated. Often there are several variations of your situation being circulated. Gossip from family, friends, neighbors, co-workers, church or any other organization's members can each have a different spin.

All of these rumors are happening at such a difficult time. You also can't control what your partner is saying. If you live with a psychologically abusive person, it is unlikely that your partner will say, "I treated my spouse terribly and my partner had every right to leave me. I deserve what I got, because I was a total jerk. It is all my fault." It is more likely for the abuser to turn him or her self into the wronged party, to solicit sympathy and preserve self-respect. Fear of what will be said about your life may keep you at home.

6. I'm afraid to be alone. What if I never find anyone else?

- The empty side of the bed.
- Noises you hear in the night.
- Being sick or hurt with no one to care for you.
- Nobody to talk, laugh or share a meal with.
- Feeling like a fifth wheel with your coupled friends.
- Difficulty finding single friends.
- Holidays alone.
- Awkwardness.
- Being without the kids when he or she has them.
- Never being intimate with another man or woman.
- Fearing no one will ever want you.

Edward reveals his fears that keep him trapped inside of his dysfunctional relationship:

I can't imagine a life without seeing her and the kids every day. I would be lost without them. It terrifies me to think of us separating. I can't imagine being alone. I'm not very good at the cooking, cleaning, homemaking, nurturing part. I don't know how I'd handle having the kids by myself and I'd be afraid that they would not really want to be at my house without their mom. She makes everything work. She's the feeling, caring, loving part of our family. I count on her to know what to do in situations that frustrate or confuse me. I depend on her always staying with me. I would hate having to date again. Sometimes women frighten me. I often can't tell what they want or need, and nobody likes rejection. I would hate the sad emptiness I would feel from losing all that we have together.

Perhaps you have never lived alone and have no concept that you could survive a solitary environment. Maybe you have spent a portion of your life by yourself, were miserable and at all costs want to avoid being alone again. The fear of loneliness keeps many people in abusive relationships, particularly if the good still outweighs the bad.

- ◆ We have a lot of good times. I'll take his crap just so I'm not alone.
- ◆ I wouldn't know how to handle everything by myself.
- ◆ At least there is someone around to help in an emergency.
- ◆ I'm less afraid with him in the house.

Lack of confidence in your ability to function is particularly normal if your husband or wife has attempted to completely control every aspect of your life. Examples of the control:

- ◆ Making out your daily schedule and then calling during the day to see if you are doing the task assigned for that hour.
- ◆ Completely controlling the money by giving you a small allowance and requiring receipts to show how it is spent.
- ◆ Forbidding any contact with the outside world unless he is present to witness it. Surveillance equipment can be used to ensure this rule is followed.
- ◆ Demanding daily sexual activity, believing he is preventing any infidelity.
- ◆ Requiring you to check with him on every decision, even down to what programs can be watched on television and what food will be prepared for dinner.

Never finding another significant love relationship is a very real fear. There are no guarantees that we will get a shot at a better partnership. Women and men may feel the only people left out there are someone else's rejects who are bound to have loads of problems, so why not keep their familiar situations. At least they know what they are dealing with. "The devil you know is better than the devil you don't know."

Women and men in psychologically abusive relationships often feel like damaged goods. Low self-esteem is common. Egos have been badly bruised. Negative self concepts have been reinforced.

- You are lucky to have me.
- Who else would want you?
- You'd never make it without me.
- Look how fat you have gotten.
- How are you going to properly inform some other woman about having herpes?

Even though it may not seem possible, there is always another person. Whether you want those you come in contact with may be questionable. Before you consider a new relationship, do some homework. Learn to love yourself and understand what you want and deserve. Make peace with your core being. Practice forgiveness for your own mistakes and frailties. Nurture your damaged spirit. Believe in your future and make the most of the present. Begin each day as a fresh start and work at being your best self. Emotionally and spiritually healthy people believe they deserve healthy partners. You *can* have what you want.

You may have many other fears that are not mentioned here. Each of the things of which you are afraid is very real to you. Try making a list that answers "If I left my partner, I'd be afraid of..." Sometimes identifying our fears helps our ability to discuss them and do some problem solving. Living in a state of fear brings so much anxiety and turmoil that we can't make good decisions or sort through what we want to do. We feel confused and disoriented; never peaceful. Remember, as you work through your list of fears, look for options. You only have control of yourself, your decisions and your part in the relationship. An outside, objective, trained person can help clarify your thoughts, understand your issues and search for solutions. You deserve better than a life lived in fear.

Chapter 6

Who Am I?

"In the beginning of the relationship, I felt like a flower blooming. Then, one by one, my petals fell off and, bit by bit, little chunks of me were gone."

Her story reveals how Carole gradually lost herself. She forgot who she was. She couldn't remember what she enjoyed; how to laugh or play or how to nurture herself when she was sad. She did each next thing that was expected of her and those duties filled all of her time.

Not knowing who you really are is not uncommon. Many go through the tasks of the day with little awareness of their true selves. Women may nurture others and spend no time caring for themselves. Days are packed with responsibilities and they don't even put themselves on the list. They may squeeze exercise into the schedule, because they know it is good. Beyond that, some can be clueless as to what is liked or enjoyed.

How does self-esteem develop? From birth, we receive messages from the people around us. Were your parents joyful about having you in their lives? Were you loved and appreciated? Were you disciplined appropriately? The messages about what others think of you continue through your life. Family, teachers, classmates, friends, neighbors, church members, boyfriends/girlfriends, co-workers and spouses all react to us and we internalize all the negative responses, discounting the positive.

Often we are labeled by our gender, race, nationality, religion, memberships, socio-economic status and even our political choices. Within those labels we have roles. As a woman or man, you can be a girlfriend, boyfriend, wife, husband, mother, father, daughter, son, sister, brother, friend, co-worker, employee, volunteer, church member, professional and homemaker. Each role has responsibilities with cultural or self-imposed expectations of how you will perform. Ask yourself what traits, habits, values and characteristics you possess that determine how you will behave?

In psychologically abusive relationships, we are continually fed negative messages. Write down all of the things those you love have said that hurt your feelings. Even if the comments were intended as "constructive criticism," include them on your list if you felt badly when you heard the remarks. Now, put a check mark beside the comments that you believed or still carry around in the back of your mind. Those comments helped form your negative thoughts and feelings. Over time, we grow to feel unworthy and unremarkable. We can't feel special or valuable unless we are continually proving ourselves or being useful.

Let's look at four outcomes of all that negativity. Regardless of which position you take in the psychologically abusive relationship, both people have damaged self-esteem. People who are centered and at peace with themselves do not abuse another person.

1. Dominance and submission
2. What can I get from you?
3. What can I give to you?
4. No deep feelings allowed

1. Dominance and submission

I may not feel good about myself, but I plan to be in control. If I have to feel empty and lousy, I don't intend for the world to know it. I'll be master of my universe. No one will get too close. I'll not let myself fall head over heels in love so I won't be vulnerable. I'll use my words and actions to intimidate. I'll keep what is mine and not share more than I have to. I'll do enough to have people accept me and I'll hide my weaknesses.

-OR-

I've always been told that I won't amount to much, that I'm not very attractive or bright. I feel lucky to be married. I need to do everything I can to make this work, because I feel more included and worthwhile being in the relationship. I may not be treated well, but it is better than being alone. I'm sure if I work hard at this and do what is expected of me, I can stay. I don't deserve more.

2. What can I get from you?

If you are primarily the "taker" in a psychologically abusive relationship, you are expecting to have your needs met. What are some of these marital expectations?

    a.   Services
    b.   Physical/Sexual
    c.   Financial
    d.   Children

a. Services

Ask any caregiver (usually the woman) to list all of the jobs she or he does and you will be amazed. Most "takers" take these tasks for granted or aren't even aware of them. Perhaps your family divides the tasks equally, but a taker often expects the household perfectly maintained, children's needs met and everything operating smoothly.

b. Physical/Sexual

Whether the taker is sick, craves attention or wants to have sex, the giver better cheerfully respond. He may want a backrub, a blow job or to be waited on hand and foot. Whatever the demand, there is pressure to provide.

c. Financial

Historically, women depended on men to provide for them financially. While in some families this is still the case, gradually women have taken an equal or primary provider role. The taker may say:

◆ What did you buy for me?
◆ How much was your raise or bonus, because I have plans for it?
◆ I want new furniture. I'm tired of this old stuff.
◆ Let's sell your car. You take my old one and I'll buy myself a new one.
◆ Can't you get a second job to cover these bills?
◆ You are spending too much. You don't need those things.
◆ I'm getting a new flat screen, high definition TV. You will love it.
◆ We can use the tax return for the new fishing equipment I want.
◆ You should ask for a raise.

d. Children

Wanting you to agree on having and raising children is a "taker's" expectation. Do you have any, one, two, three or more? If you do have children, the taker expects that most of the needs, nurturing and discipline will be done by the giver. The partner may be around for the fun, but not the necessary work.

Burt's story of being a giver is telling:

> He thought of her as a "pusher." Whatever he did, it was never enough. He could never fill her wants and needs for very long. They always needed to buy something else or go somewhere else. She wanted to do every social thing that her friends did. Shopping, entertaining, traveling, it was always "What's next?" He felt he worked hard, made a decent income and did more than half of the housework, all the yard work and paid the bills. He loved being a dad, so taking charge of the kids was a

pleasure; one he didn't think she shared. He was an introvert and he needed some alone time to recharge his batteries. His extroverted wife was constantly pushing him to go out or have people in. In reality, he didn't really enjoy her friends, finding them superficial and a bit pompous. If he didn't want to participate, she got angry and berated and belittled him. Changing his mind became her personal challenge. She would repeatedly ask the same questions until she got the answer she wanted. It was easier to let her have her way. He didn't like confrontation, so he'd let her take whatever she wanted.

3. What can I give to you?

The "giver" is alert for all the family needs. It is how he or she is worthwhile. Whether they are working three jobs or staying in the home, they are busy every minute of the day. They must be busy to justify their worth. Sheila's story of her psychologically abusive relationship is eye-opening:

In retrospect, she realized she had been a doormat; not a fancy intricately woven one, but a plain ordinary doormat. The house and the kids were her job. Her husband said she also needed to have an income. She could do it all. She wouldn't let anyone see the tears of frustration and exhaustion that ran down her face as she scrubbed her bathroom late on Sunday nights. She had to keep up or she'd get behind.

Sex was a thing of the past, which was probably good, because she didn't have much leftover energy. However, she did miss it. She suspected, from the hang-up calls and time he happily spent on the computer, that there was another woman. Instead of confronting him, she added dieting, exercise and a makeover to her regime. If she was more attractive, then maybe he wouldn't need anyone else. He didn't seem to notice. As she was cleaning up his muddy shoes one evening, a realization came: This is what doormats are good for, cleaning other people's shoes.

4. No deep feelings allowed

If you have been verbally and psychologically abused by parents and/or partners, you probably internalized the negativity and feel unworthy and fearful of being fully engaged with your feelings or with another person. Jarred tells his sad story:

> I felt so ashamed growing up. I thought people could look at me and see how bad and shameful I was. I still do punish myself. I am always on guard and somewhat detached. It's as if I watch myself doing things. I don't allow feelings. As I go through something pleasant, I comfort myself with the thought that when I am alone I can think back and the memories will be joyful. When I am hurt or angry, I think it would be reckless or irresponsible to show intense feelings. I am in awe of people who show their emotions.

Have you ever noticed that fearful people with a poor self-concept seem to be spinning? We are a culture bombarded with auditory, visual and emotional stimulation. How can we learn to be still when there is such a deluge of electronic provocation? Computers, phones, televisions and a multitude of handheld devices give us constant sounds, images and information. We stay spinning in our heads. We dwell on the surface, moving through life unaware of our depth. Running faster and faster on a treadmill does not lead to any destination.

Some people have another handicap. Many parents have become overindulgent and have failed to discipline appropriately. Rewarding every ordinary accomplishment does not help children see themselves accurately. Parents should assist with good decision-making, healthy interactions and being accurately conscious with an appropriate perspective. Otherwise, kids may feel the world owes them something, and they shouldn't have to work too hard to get it. Anyone who is critical or suggests improvements is being unfair or discriminatory. We often have been unhelpful in equipping our children with the skills to master adult tasks and share in adult relationships.

WHO ARE YOU?

The great survivors of this world are those people who experience adversity and discover how to stop their spinning minds and be peacefully present. In books, they have eloquently shared their experiences with the world in a way that resonates. Among the stories that have especially moved me personally are *When Things Fall Apart* by Pema Chödrön, *The Power of Now* by Eckhart Tolle, *The Seat Of The Soul* by Gary Zukav and *Night* by Elie Wiesel. The amazing history of Oprah Winfrey as she rose from poverty and abuse to being one of the most influential women in the world, all done with hard work, graciousness, gratitude, spirituality and a whole lot of joy, is very inspiring as well.

Some everyday people are also great survivors. They are successful not by simply living through painful and tortuous experiences, but by transcending them. They have risen above and beyond their fears into the peacefulness of loving awareness.

The good news is that peace is there for all to find. The journey may be difficult, but incredibly rewarding. We never have to be stuck in the prisons of our pasts. We can't know if things are better in the future, because we cannot live in the future. Inner peace is only available to you in the present. But this knowledge can be wondrous and transforming. It is not a constant thing you achieve and at which you never have to work. It requires the constant uncluttering of our lives and our thoughts. Finding your strength and knowing who you are may disturb anyone who wants to control you, but it may be the most important work you ever do. It requires less action, more stillness and greater sensual awareness. Recognize and accept your entire self. Take that self into every present moment and be fully conscious of living within your world just as it is. You will begin avoiding negativity as a matter of choice. You may stay in your relationship or go, but your enlightened self-awareness will free you to make decisions that harmonize with maintaining your inner peace.

In Nora's story, which follows, we see how dawning self-awareness can affect a dysfunctional relationship.

NORA'S STORY

I met him when I was twenty, married him at twenty-one. We were married twenty years and have two children.

When we were dating, I had second thoughts and he got very psychologically abusive. We got engaged and he said he would kill me if I did not marry him. I was in a panic state. I felt it wasn't a good relationship, but I couldn't break up with him. I went home for a wedding shower that friends of my mother were giving me. He telephoned when they all were around, screaming and yelling at me over the phone that I would be a lousy wife, that I was a pig and he could find someone better. I began crying as I tried to answer his criticisms. He never acknowledged that he'd done anything.

I was so young and I didn't know about alcoholism. He was drinking. After we separated, I read some books on problem drinking and went to Alcoholics Anonymous. Then I realized he had been having blackouts and didn't remember what he did. To this day he denies doing anything wrong. He played mind games with me all the time, refusing to talk or getting in my face. He didn't tell me where he was going or when he'd return. I never knew him not to be drinking. His excuse was everybody was doing it. I grew up in a household where you didn't talk about things that weren't pleasant. I never knew what alcoholism was, so I didn't recognize it.

His parents never drank. He was one of five boys. He told me his mother ran a strict household and was verbally and physically abusive. His parents were very nice to me.

In the beginning of our marriage I thought our misunderstandings and friction were all my fault, that I was doing something wrong. If I was a better person or cleaned better, it would be okay. Each day he came home and found something else wrong. He ran his finger over the door ledge all the time and said it was dusty. If there was one crease in his shirt, he threw it back into the laundry and told me to iron the shirt again. He was a perfectionist.

When I got out of school I was pregnant and I had my first child at twenty-two. I started teaching school. He didn't want me to work. When I was at work a neighbor babysat my child. My husband expected the same degree of perfection in the house as before our baby was born. I had to fix him a big breakfast every morning as well as have the house clean before I could leave. Work was my haven. I could be my own person there. I had friends, but I thought no one knew what my life was like at home.

I felt like I was a bad person. In my family, if you didn't have anything nice to say, you didn't say anything at all. My husband and I didn't talk a lot. Sometimes he was totally silent. At others, threatening. He worked all the time. He worked late and drank at bars before he came home. I never knew when he was going to arrive, but he expected a meal when he got there. Sometimes he came home for lunch, too. He expected three hot meals a day, even if I had to get out of bed in the middle of the night to fix one. Lunchtime could be more pleasant, because he hadn't been drinking. Dinner had to be a real meal, not hot dogs. I had to walk on eggshells all the time. I didn't want to make a mistake, because if I did he clenched his fist and made threats.

Our second child was born two and a half years after the first. He wasn't around much for them, because he was always working. I was always running, trying to be perfect. I actually thought he drank, because I wasn't good enough.

The worst part was the unknown—not knowing at what he'd be angry. He never took the children to do things. He never offered to watch them. He played favorites with the two of them and told me constantly I was a lousy mother.

I told our good friends that everything was fine, but later I found out they knew more than I thought they did. One night, I couldn't go to play bridge, because I didn't iron his shirt right. If I cried, he told me to stop being a baby. He fussed at me all the time, but I never acted upset around my kids.

My father was my idol. He was the perfect gentleman and I was his princess. I didn't want my children to see their father in a bad light.

Once when I talked about leaving my husband, he said he would make sure that the children and I would starve. He said no one would like us. He said he'd tell my family what a terrible wife and mother I was, and they wouldn't want to have anything to do with us.

Many times, I got through the days by packing our suitcases. I spent hours packing things, thinking I would leave while he was at work. When he was nice, I unpacked and put everything back. He didn't know I was doing that. It was the way I coped. Also I did menial tasks, folding and unfolding things to make them perfect. One time at work, my boss told me my desk was a mess and I said, "Please don't make me clean it up. This is the only place I have where I can be messy."

My husband was very controlling with money. He gambled. Sometimes he came home drunk with wads of money. I often took some and stashed it away, because I knew he wouldn't remember how much he had won. I was on a strict budget. He told me what, when and how much I could spend. I had to ask his permission to do even minor things. I was expected to stick to the budget he set, which was very meager even though he made good money. One time, my mother sent me a check for my birthday. He came home and I was dressed to go to dinner. He said he was tired and wasn't going anywhere. I said I'd go by myself, and he asked how I expected to pay for it. When I told him I'd use the money my mother sent me for my birthday, he stood over me with clenched teeth yelling, "Give it to me right now. You overspent this week."

When we separated, money was a huge issue. Other things were important to him only if they mattered to me. He knew I'd always dreamed of owning a certain kind of car. After we separated, he ordered my dream car for himself, just to spite me. He wanted us to have things that impressed people. He picked the house in which we lived and the neighborhood. I never argued with him about money. Even if I left a light on in a room, he would be enraged.

Sexually he was very abusive. He wanted to have intercourse all the time. He never got enough. He threatened to get it somewhere else if I didn't give it to him. When we had sex, I'd just lie there. It was miserable. I don't think I ever had an orgasm with him the whole time we were together. He didn't care, because it was all for him. I faked things to make him happy. I thought if he left me, I'd be nothing. I had no self-esteem. He threatened to leave me if I gained weight. I was so intimidated. He conditioned me not to think and to do whatever he wanted.

I never knew if he was unfaithful. He stayed out late in bars. Sometimes women telephoned the house. I'd hang up. I didn't want to know the truth. I never confronted him about it.

I liked my friends, my work, my children and my civic volunteering. I could be myself in all those situations.

He switched jobs and traveled. It was wonderful when he was gone. When he was home, we all had to do whatever work he ordered us to do in the house and yard.

I was afraid to leave. I was afraid of what he would do. No one in my family had ever left a spouse, so I never thought it was an option. One time, early in our marriage, I decided to leave, but I had no car. I called the bus station and purchased a ticket to my parents' town. One of my friends took me and my baby to the bus station. After a couple of weeks at my parents', he came to get me and my parents encouraged my husband and I to talk and work our problems out. I went back.

Another time, much later, we were with a group of couples out of town at a concert. He left to go to the bathroom and never showed back up again until the end of the show. Then he came walking back through the parking lot with a blonde woman. We were going home and I told his brother that I was leaving him and he said he didn't blame me. The next day, I was packing to leave and my husband said, "Don't go. I'm the one with the problem. I'll get help." He started going to see our minister and called a friend in Alcoholics Anonymous. He decided to stop drinking liquor and just drank beer and wine. I said I'd support him if he would get help. After a couple of AA meetings, he said he wasn't "that kind of person." He thought he'd handle his problem by sticking to the beer and wine. Verbal abuse continued even when he wasn't drunk. He was volatile and critical. He called me terrible names and put me down in front of people. Each time I just walked away.

Once, we were on an airplane going on a company trip. He had left our seats and was drinking heavily in another part of the plane. He was always the life of the party, always charming to women. We got to our destination, but he didn't get off the plane with me. I couldn't find him. Friends took me to the hotel. Three days later, he showed up. He said he didn't know where he'd been. I had forty dollars and my return ticket. I was planning to fly home when he walked into the hotel room.

After twenty years, the final encounter was when we were working together in a family business. We disagreed over how to handle something. He stuck his finger in my face and yelled at me that I was dumb, to stay out of it and just do my job. His business manager was watching. It was the final blow. I looked at him and said, "You will never talk to me that way again." I drove home, packed my things, walked out and never went back.

We went through therapy. He got mad when the therapist asked him to stop badgering me. He said that "all you women stick together" and he got up and left. That day I had my own car. I had already learned that he would leave me stranded. Once, he left me forty miles from home. I started walking. I had no money. I flagged down a car and begged them to help me. They took me to a restaurant. I knew someone there who gave me a ride home. He never asked me how I got back.

I worried about how I would live if we separated. I've kept my divorce papers, because they were incredible. He put in there that spousal support would stop if I inherited anything. He tried to control my future. My attorney advised me not to sign, but I just wanted out. I wasn't going to go to court. I knew I would survive. By the time I left, my children were grown and I could take care of myself.

I was always looking behind me wondering what would happen. He had threatened to kill me. I still feel fear when I know I have to be around him at family events.

I always wished he would have apologized and taken responsibility for the things he had done. I repressed so much anger that I didn't even know how to talk about it. I was like a volcano and when I started remembering and later talking about my life during therapy, I got physically sick. Driving home, I had to pull over to throw up. I had pushed things down into my subconscious for so long that I didn't even know how to speak about the past. Once I dreamed that I was stabbing him. When I finally expressed how angry I was, my therapist said, "There is hope for you now."

I can't believe I took his psychological abuse for twenty years. Nevertheless, sometimes I still feel like a failure. I hate that I broke up my family. I hate that my children suffered.

When we separated, the best part about being in my own place was that I could relax. I didn't have to be perfectly neat. No one was going to yell at me or take the car away or tell me I couldn't do something. My space was mine. To this day, I find my peace by being alone.

Chapter 7

Hope Springs

If "hope springs eternal in the human breast," then it is natural for both men and women to have hope for our love relationships. We don't want to give up. We believe in the ability of human beings to change, no matter what the problems are. We take someone we find attractive and think he or she can be molded into a shape that would be perfect for us. Ever so helpful, we have requests, suggestions and demands.

Hope keeps our spirits alive, striving for change, growth, improvement and fulfillment. The optimism of hope is positive. Miracles can happen. Believing in and expecting positive results creates a powerful living energy. Trouble arises when we think we can use that positive energy to change someone else, instead of understanding that we can only make the miracles happen in our own lives.

Lynn talks about her psychologically abusive husband: "He apologizes. He cries and promises not to do and say things that hurt me again. He says this time will be different, because he'll really try. He asks me to help. He's a good man in so many other ways. How can I turn my back on him now? I'm the only one who cares enough to really make a difference. I just know we can fix this if we stick together and work harder."

Do we stay because we hope he or she will change? Of course we do. What keeps us hanging in there?

1. Love and sympathy for the little boy or girl
2. Seeing the multidimensional man or woman
3. Fear of failure
4. Believing you can change him or her

Four Reasons for Staying in the Relationship

1. Love and sympathy for the little boy or girl

Inside all of us are the children we once were. We carry that child into adulthood. If we pay attention, we notice our partner's inner child, particularly when the other person is afraid, angry or just playful. Often, we can connect with that little boy or girl and desire to love and nurture the person. If our partners were neglected or abused in any way while they were growing up, we can feel such sympathy and compassion. Seeing how their upbringing impacted them, we may understand and forgive their adult behavior. We have hope that our tolerance, nurturing and guidance will help him or her be a better man or woman.

When a man connects with his partner's little girl, he often becomes more understanding and forgiving of her bad behavior if he knows about her difficult childhood. He may feel protective and tolerant as he seeks to give her a better life as an adult than she experienced as a child.

In either case, when we empathize with our loved one's inner child, we hope for change as they learn and mature. If our mate is crying, scared, unsuccessful, misunderstood, hurt or begging for attention, we may see the child. If there is anger, name-calling, throwing things or tantrums, we certainly can see the child. We hope and expect that the misbehaving adult child will grow up and leave childish ways behind.

2. Seeing the multidimensional man or woman

We see and experience the complete person. There are so many components that make up the other person's personality. He's not just a psychologically abusive man. She is many different things. He has various roles in his life. Potentially, the person is a son, daughter, husband, wife, father, mother, brother, sister, worker, church member, volunteer and friend. Within these roles, he or she can possess a combination of desirable qualities. What positive characteristics does your partner have?

+ Good with children
+ Patient
+ Tolerant
+ Good provider
+ Handy around the house
+ Sexually exciting
+ Generous with his or her time
+ Loving
+ Helpful
+ Funny
+ Talented
+ Skillful
+ Generous with money
+ Leader
+ Intelligent
+ Thoughtful
+ Hard worker

You can certainly add to the list. These positive roles and good qualities determine the ways in which you value your partner. As you notice the many good things, you are hopeful that the person's better parts will win out. It seems logical that he or she should treat you as well as your partner treats others. You are determined not to give up on a person who possesses so many positives.

3. Fear of failure

No one wants to fail. We don't want to admit defeat. Hopelessness is depressing. We are taught to compete, try harder and not give up. We can feel ashamed and discouraged if we fail. Society may judge us.

+ What is wrong with him or her?
+ He or she failed at two marriages.
+ What is the real problem?

We strive not to become "damaged goods," a person with "baggage," a person with a bad reputation, a "statistic" or a "loser." We expect that hard work will pay off. If we persevere to achieve what we desire, then it should work out. Our efforts should be rewarded. We hope that endurance will make our dreams come true.

4. Believing you can change him or her

In this letter to her partner, Alycia reveals her lost hope for the relationship she once valued:

I hoped that you loved me enough to change. You wouldn't want to hurt me. You wouldn't want our relationship to end. You would want us to be kind and keep each other safe.

I thought if I was patient it would pay off. You would learn how to love me. You'd want all the good, without all the bad. We could grow and learn new ways to treat each other that didn't hurt.

I believed there was more; more ways to be nice, more ways to feel good, more ways to experience loving each other. I didn't want to think that what I was seeing was all I would ever have. I saw the promise of a more kind, loving you. I thought I could make it work.

When you did listen, I told you what I wanted. I explained specifically what you could say and do that would make a difference to me. Were you just not interested or was it some kind of power play: if it mattered to me it was not going to happen. I tried to do what you wanted. You didn't return the favor or, if you did, it never lasted very long. What I asked for was simple: stop cussing at me and calling me names; stop trying to control me; stop accusing me of things I haven't done. I have never betrayed you in any way. Will you try again? I want us to stay together. Will you stop hurting us? I hope so.

Alycia's is a common plea: Please listen to me and make changes. We try everything. We ask, plead, cry, yell and pout. We attempt to demonstrate good behavior or we try doing the same bad things to him that he does to us, to "show him how it feels." We tell him "we need to talk" and then proceed to explain, in every rational way imaginable, why change is necessary and how to go about accomplishing it. We assume he will appreciate all of our efforts. The struggle becomes familiar: "If I say and do just the right things, a light bulb will come on in his head and everything will improve. However, I'm not quite sure what will work, so I'll keep trying multiple strategies. It is hard work but I hope it will pay off."

Peter tells about his psychologically abusive marriage:

We had such a good life—plenty of money, great kids, lots of family around, a beautiful home, expensive cars and fabulous vacations. I was gone a lot for my job, traveling during the week, but home most weekends. My wife always wanted to be the center of attention, particularly with other men. Over time, I became suspicious that there was more going on than flirting. I hired a private investigator, which provided proof of her having an affair in my own home. I was devastated, but I loved her and wanted to keep our marriage and family together. We went to couples counseling, worked on our relationship and continued to enjoy raising our kids. I hoped she would not ever again be unfaithful. I was not a perfect husband. I've always had a problem verbalizing my feelings, and when I am frustrated, it is hard for me to resolve issues through talking them out. But, I was loyal, faithful, hard-working and I loved my family.

Now she has done it again. She left me for another man, taking over half of what we have accumulated and a big chunk of my pride. The irony to me is that she has never admitted to or acted like she has done anything wrong. Somehow, she has managed to spin things around to where I am the bad guy and she is the victim. She is a strong, capable woman, who has always done exactly what she wanted and yet she acts like she is afraid of me and needs to be protected. It is truly amazing. She has the sympathy and support of family and friends, while openly having an affair with the guy she maintains had just been a "good friend" prior to her separation. It was a knock-out punch: leave me for another guy, take most of what you want and act innocent and justified.

Hope is natural and understandable. Nevertheless, we live with uncertainties. We do not have a crystal ball to see the future, so we visualize what we would like to see happening. If we give up, we can experience depression and despair, feelings we want to avoid. So we live with the unanswered questions about how and whether the relationship will progress. We put forth our best efforts to create the changes we desire. The more time and energy we invest, the more committed and determined we are to make it successful. We project our dreams, wishes and desires onto the person we love and we hope he or she will meet our expectations.

Chapter 8

He's Their Daddy/She's Their Mommy

Concerns over the well-being of the children can be a major reason why people stay or leave a psychologically abusive relationship. Among these concerns are:

- ♦ The children love their other parent.
- ♦ How would I take care of the children by myself?
- ♦ They would be so unhappy if we didn't all live together.
- ♦ We would have to move into a different neighborhood.
- ♦ They would be angry and blame me.
- ♦ I was a child of divorce and I don't want them to be.
- ♦ I don't trust my spouse not to hurt the children if he or she gets partial custody.
- ♦ My family says I must stay for my kids' sake.

There are three major factors to consider:
1. Practical Matters
2. Emotional Consequences
3. Well-being

1. Practical Matters

There are many practical difficulties involved in the separation of any family.

♦ Will I have to move out of my house? I may not be able to afford the house payment. I can't pay him for his half of the equity we have built up. He may insist on living here himself.

♦ How can I afford to live on my own? There are so many expenses. We were just making ends meet with both of our salaries.

♦ Will the children have to change schools? If I have to move, what if I can't find a house in the same school district? I can't drive all over town to get them to school and make it to my job on time.

♦ Will I have to get another job? My job doesn't pay enough to support us. Will I be able to find a better one or will I have to work two jobs? If so, then who would care for the kids while I'm working all those hours?

♦ What custody arrangement can I be comfortable with? Is she going to ask for total or joint custody? I'm not sure I trust her to take good care of them. I'm afraid she'll fight for them just to punish me.

♦ Will the kids lose contact with their friends? If we move, they may not be in the neighborhood or same school with their friends. I would hate for them to go through that loss, too.

♦ Will they have to drop out of their activities? The kids have so many activities that cost money and involve driving them places. How can I make all of that work?

♦ How can I handle parenting responsibilities all on my own? I fear the kids acting out as a result of this separation. I also don't think she will have the same ways of disciplining them, and it could become so confusing and chaotic.

♦ Will he actually pay me child support? He may be court ordered to pay child support, but I fear that I won't see any money. He's always said if I left, I'd never see a dime.

♦ Will I be able to find the time and money to take them on vacation or do anything that is fun? He'd be the good-time dad, and I'd be too poor to afford any extras. It would be so difficult to always struggle.

♦ Will she ever let me see my stepchildren? I love them and fear that I will lose them forever. I know I have a right to my own children, but she wouldn't be forced to let me see them. Her kids and I have become so close that it would be devastating to be kept from them.

2. Emotional Consequences

It is natural for children to love both their parents. Knowing that, it is difficult for some people to decide to deprive their kids of seeing one parent for a part of their lives. You may hesitate to disrupt your child's world, fearing that he or she will grieve and change.

Do you feel that your partner only abuses you and never the children? The truth is that even very small children are the silent observers, hearing and noticing everything. Even if they are in another room, they sense the tension and are often tuned for danger. They learn by what they see, hear and feel. Beliefs about relationships, trust and security are being formed. They are learning about power and control, dominance and submission and how to communicate their feelings, wants and needs. Observing abuse makes them victims of abuse.

Even conceding that your marriage does not provide an ideal environment for child rearing, you may believe it is preferable to the alternative. Children who go through divorce suffer and grieve. They experience a loss of security and stability. They may feel abandoned by one or both parents as they struggle to understand custody arrangements. They can be fearful of change and new, unfamiliar situations. They may feel guilty and think that they are partially responsible for the breakup as they struggle to make sense out of what is happening. Children who experience sadness and despair may regress to younger behavior or lose their ability to concentrate at school or enjoy normal activities.

Anger toward the parent they perceive caused the divorce and anger over their life changes is often vented toward the parent they feel is safest to express it to. Therefore, the parent they see as least to blame may receive the brunt of their anger. Possibly they do not feel safe expressing their anger at all, so it is suppressed and turns into various acting-out behaviors. Often an abusive parent fuels a child's anger and confusion. If your husband or wife is angry at you for wanting to separate, the person may do what he or she can to punish. Knowing that you love your children, the other partner may use them as the ultimate weapons by manipulating their opinions about you:

- ♦ Your mother or father doesn't care about you.
- ♦ He left you with me, because he doesn't love us anymore.
- ♦ She cheated on me with that guy she is seeing.
- ♦ If you love me, you will come live at my house.
- ♦ You don't have to listen to what your mom or dad tells you to do.

As he plays his destructive mind games with the children, he may also be the good-time dad who buys things, takes them places and never sets up appropriate rules or healthy boundaries. The kids become pawns in a chess game with disastrous results. They enjoy his attention and the goodies, but are enormously conflicted. If they feel they have to choose sides, it is a huge emotional burden. When parents attempt to garner support and justify their own positions, children become more confused and disoriented.

Older children may feel responsible for their parent's well-being. Their capacity for insight and the demands made by Mom or Dad can turn them into caregivers and protectors. These are inappropriate roles that often determine their actions in future relationships. The divorce sets up anxiety about the instability of intimate partnerships and their ability to trust, love and allow vulnerability is damaged.

Parents in a psychologically abusive relationship who stay together will often see their children carrying their misery. The kids may feel they are to blame, especially if they are the topic of arguments, threats and criticism. They blame themselves, instead of the parents they love and on whom they depend. They may misbehave to be the focus of anger and discipline, thinking they deserve punishment. They could try to control the situation without understanding why. When they grow up and interact with friends and romantic partners, they often express themselves inappropriately, because the lessons learned at home about relationships are all they know.

Whether you stay or go, psychologically abusive relationships have definite emotional consequences for your children.

3. Well-being

The well-being of children weighs heavily on the mind of someone considering separation from a psychologically abusive partner.

♦ Will he be responsible? What kinds of rules will he have? Will he supervise them or let them run wild? Will he be too harsh and psychologically abuse them?

♦ Will she take care of them? Will she talk to them, notice when they need help and be sure they are well? I'm afraid of what will happen if I'm not there.

♦ Who else will be around? I don't trust his or her family or his or her friends. I'd never leave my children in their care, but he or she would.

♦ What kinds of men or women will he or she subject them to? I think my spouse will bring all kinds of people around who will stay at the house and try and tell my kids what to do or be a terrible influence.

♦ Will she abduct them? I'm afraid she'll take them, disappear and I'll never see them again. She's always said I'd never see the kids again if I left. I'm petrified that she would really do it.

♦ I can't keep them safe from his psychological abuse if I'm not there. He has zero patience. I can usually distract him and get the kids out of his way. They will eventually misbehave, and I'm afraid of what he will do to them.

♦ She says terribly damaging things to them. I try to be a balance and soften her criticisms, threats and contemptuous body language. If she's angry, she is relentless. I can't imagine leaving them in her damaging care.

It is important to know that although statistics indicate more abusers are men, women abuse as well. And this is especially true of psychological abuse.

DAVE'S STORY

One of the people with whom I met is Dave, who revealed his experience with a psychologically abusive wife in our interview.

C. *How old were you when you met her?*

D. Twenty-seven.

C. *How long did you date before you got married?*

D. Two years.

C. *During those two years, did you ever feel there was any indication that she could be an abusive person?*

D. No. I knew she was an independent-type personality. It never crossed my mind that she could be a mean or abusive person.

C. *How long was it before you had your first child?*

D. Two years after we were married.

C. *What is the first time you remember something happening where you thought, "Wow, this is not good. There is something going on here"?*

D. My dad died and we were living in a small town. My dad owned his own business and I worked for him for almost ten years. After he died, economics in this small town were getting stressful and I discussed it with my mother and we sold the business. I went to work with my brother and my wife and I moved to a bigger city. I noticed that after we moved we seemed to quarrel a lot more. I remember standing in the backyard and she was mad, but it didn't have anything to do with me. She looked me in the face and said, "You are the one who destroyed my life and made me move here." I looked at her and I was stunned. My interpretation was that everything that had been decided we had thoroughly discussed. It hadn't happened instantly. It was over six or eight months. But for her, whatever was wrong with her life I was to blame. I had gone through the death of my father and the grueling process of selling the business while dealing with the questions and doubts of my brothers and sisters who had no involvement in the business. When she said that to me, I thought, *Why do I get blamed for it all?*

C. *As she accused you of things or got angry with you, how did you learn to deal with her?*

D. Be careful. Watch what you say. Any stress would bring on verbal abuse. One Sunday, we were going boating. We got to the lake and the boat wouldn't crank. She started in on me about how stupid I was. Why didn't I test the boat before I put it in the water? She said she was so embarrassed. She raised so much hell. She sat on the back of the boat like she was Cleopatra. Hundreds of people were around, including our kids. She stood up on the back of the boat and yelled, "By noon tomorrow, I will have me a new boat and he can take this boat and do whatever he wants to do with it." She badgered me all the way home. I didn't say anything. The next day it was like nothing ever happened.

C. *When is one of the most telling times you remember?*

D. We were married eight or nine years. We had been to the lake again. Coming home, she was mad that I had missed a turn. She kept telling me how stupid I was. At home, I unhooked the boat, put a block under it so it wouldn't roll and chained it to the basketball goal. She came outside and said I had to move the boat, because she couldn't get the car out in the morning. I unhooked it and started to move it. It jumped the block of wood, rolled down the backyard and hit a pine tree. You've never heard such a string of curse words coming out of a Sunday school teacher in your life. She was letting me have it. I was watching in stunned horror. It totaled the boat. She called the sheriff's office to tell them I had destroyed the boat. I said that it wasn't a crime and they told her that as well. She was quite furious.

C. As the marriage progressed, did things get much nastier and more frequent?

D. Yes, more frequent. It was extremely volatile or nothing. It was amazing what would trigger it. You never knew. It got to be common behavior that when I got home from work, my son met me at the car and said, "This is not a good day. You need to be careful when you go in the house. Mama is in one of those moods."

C. How did you keep yourself from losing your temper?

D. One time, I danced with someone else. She was angry. It wasn't even a slow dance. When we got in the car, she started hitting me. I stopped at a convenience store to get gum. While I was inside, she saw a police car, jumped out of our car and told them I had been hitting her. I came out of the store and they put me against the car and frisked me. She was looking at me like, *I've got you now.* The officer said he would put me in jail if she wanted him to. It was a Friday on a holiday weekend and he told me he would put me in jail and I wouldn't have a chance to see a judge until Wednesday. She was grinning, but finally said no, she thought she could handle it. They told her she had to drive, even though she had had a lot more to drink than I had. She drove a block and stopped the car and told me to get out. It was eighteen miles to the house and it was 2:00 A.M. I told her no. She said she'd go back and talk to the police. I got out and she shut the car door and drove off. I walked to a Laundromat and called a friend to pick me up. My wife went home. The next day, she acted like nothing ever happened. I swallowed my pride and kept on going.

C. What was the straw that broke the camel's back or the most traumatic thing for you?

D. She humiliated me in front of our friends. The things she said were stunning. It would have felt better if she had beaten me with a club. One night, we were at a restaurant. She stood up and announced to twenty people that she had found a $2,500 ring that she wanted and if she didn't have it the next day, she was filing for divorce. I was so embarrassed. The next day I went and bought the ring.

C. *Why did you stay?*

D. The children were the primary reason. The kids and I were close and I knew she would emotionally abuse them. It would be so unjust and I knew I deflected a lot of her anger. Another reason I stayed was we had friends, family and a lifestyle that were hard to separate from. There were some good times between us. We talked, enjoyed each other and had a good sexual connection. But she was like a drama queen with an ax. Her fury would override the problem. I didn't want to admit failure. I didn't want to tell my family I had screwed up. I hoped I could work harder not to trigger her anger. I wanted to keep trying to make things better and minimize her rage. I told myself don't argue, don't fight back, don't defend yourself; just say, "Yes ma'am."

C. *Did she ever apologize?*

D. She would say, "I'm a pretty nice person, until I'm provoked." This was her way of saying that I made her do it.

C. *How did it end?*

D. The night she took the hammer and chopped the door down, I left. I stayed with a friend and then rented a house. A thousand times she asked me to come back. She told me I was selfish, that she and the kids needed me. I never went back. For the next two years, I was very alone, thought of returning. But each time I felt that way, I told myself to wait forty-eight hours. Then I would realize why I couldn't go back.

Chapter 9

Religion, Marital Peace and Discord

Religion has a strong influence on marital relations. Each denomination harbors its own tenets in the case of divorce:

♦ My church does not sanction divorce.

♦ I could not remarry unless I got an annulment.

♦ I said vows in church where I pledged to be married to him until I die.

♦ My church understands separating for physical abuse, but the verbal and psychological abuse would not carry the same weight.

♦ She has damaged my spirit, and yet the guidance my church gives me is to stay with her.

♦ The Bible says...

There are many interpretations of what passages in the Bible convey. It has been translated and deciphered through centuries by scholars, theologians, religious leaders and laymen. Different denominations use the same book as the foundation for varying beliefs, rules, customs and ceremonies. Passages are used to justify opposing positions. Phyllis Trible, a feminist Biblical scholar who taught at Union Theological seminary and Wake Forest University, discusses the Bible in the March/April 2006 issue of *Biblical Archaeology Review*:

> The Bible is a mixture of blessings and curses. It doesn't speak with a single voice. It has competing voices, contradictions in it. As it moves through history, it encounters new settings and new occasions, and we're ever called upon to do something with this text.[9]

Later in the article, as she examines many passages, she states: "The Bible sets before us blessing and curse, good and evil, and it tells us to choose. It doesn't make the choice for us. The text that in one setting can be a blessing, in another setting can be a curse."[10]

At times, when people express that they remain in their marriages because of their religions, it is not really about what the scripture dictates, but more about what they feel their church friends, family and congregation will say about their decisions. The church family is often a vital, pivotal part of a person's support system and being ostracized is never desirable. However, for some the fear of rejection from the church community is more important than what doctrine dictates.

BIBLICAL SCRIPTURE RELATING TO MARRIAGE

The Bible is the foundation and guidebook for Judaism and Christianity. This book has been much translated and interpreted over the course of history. Then each man or woman who has studied it and speaks before a congregation gives his or her unique interpretation and inflection. As individuals who hear them, we listen, often read for ourselves and then develop a personalized meaning to help guide us through our lives and our relationships.

Let's look at some parts of scripture that surround the concepts of marriage, husbands' dominance over their wives, loving relationships and forgiveness. Although I am not a Biblical scholar nor will I attempt to explain these passages, I have found that many of the clients I've met with through the years have told of being influenced in one way or another by them.

In Genesis chapter 1, after God has created Adam and Eve and placed them in the Garden of Eden, he specifically instructs them not to eat the fruit of the tree in the midst of the garden. The serpent tempts Eve to eat the fruit, and she gives some to Adam. God is angry, and Genesis 3:16 says: "To the woman he said, 'I will greatly multiply your pain in childbearing; in pain you shall bring forth children, yet your desire shall be for your husband, and he shall rule over you.'" Eve was disobeying God and this passage forever challenges women.

Genesis 3:23-25 discusses making the union of man and woman into one flesh, as does Mark 10:6-12:

> But from the beginning of creation, God made them male and female. "For this reason a man shall leave his father and mother and be joined to his wife, and the two shall become one. So they are no longer two but one. What therefore God has joined together, let not man put asunder." And in the house the disciples ask him again about this matter. And he said to them, "Whoever divorces his wife and marries another, commits adultery against her; and if she divorces her husband and marries another, she commits adultery."

Former U.S. President Jimmy Carter referred to Matthew 5:27-32:

> You have heard that it was said, "You shall not commit adultery." But I say to you that every one who looks at a woman lustfully has already committed adultery with her in his heart. If your right eye causes you to sin, pluck it out and throw it away; it is better that you lose one of your members than that your whole body be thrown into hell. And if your right hand causes you to sin, cut if off and throw it away; it is better that you lose one of your members than that your whole body go into hell.

> It was also said, "Whoever divorces his wife, let him give her a certificate of divorce." But I say to you that everyone who divorces his wife, except on the ground of unchastity, makes her an adulteress; and whoever marries a divorced woman commits adultery.

Romans 7:1-4 also talks about a woman being bound to her husband for as long as he lives. Only if he dies, may she remarry. Ephesians 5:21-24 says:

Be subject to one another out of reverence for Christ. Wives be subject to your husbands, as to the Lord. For the husband is the head of the wife as Christ is the head of the church, his body, and is himself its Savior. As the church is subject to Christ, so let wives also be subject in everything to their husbands.

Ephesians instructs men to love their wives, not be subject to them, but each should be kind and compassionate.

First Timothy 2:18-15 and 3:1-5 discuss the church, where men clearly dominate and women should be silent and submissive. In First Peter 3:7-12 women are referred to as the weaker sex and both are instructed to be nice to each other. Verse 10-11 says: "For he that would love life and see good days, let him keep his tongue from evil and his lips from speaking guile; let him turn away from evil and do right; let him seek peace and pursue it."

First Corinthians 11:3 also says that "the head of a woman is her husband", but in 13:4-13, the popular wedding reading about love instructs us:

Love is patient, love is kind. Love does not envy or boast; it is not arrogant or rude. It does not insist on its own way; it is not irritable or resentful; it does not rejoice at wrongdoing, but rejoices with the truth. Love bears all things, believes all things, hopes all things, endures all things.

Now this last sentence may present a problem. After saying all these wonderful things about what love is and isn't, we then are told that love bears and endures all things. Some have interpreted that statement to mean that if you really love someone you will endure all things or possibly that pure love transcends anything.

Bob discusses the constant criticism of his wife:

I married my wife when we were both young and right out of college. We have had a long and basically happy marriage. I love her deeply. The most trying and difficult part of our life together has been her need to constantly talk, dominate conversations, judge other people and always be right. We both grew up going to Christian churches, and I wonder if she somehow missed the part about if you are without sin, you can cast the first stone. She comments, usually unfavorably, on people's weight, appearance, personality, religion, political persuasion, race and life choices. She feels she is right and other people are wrong. She grew up with a stern critical mother and while I wouldn't call my wife stern, she is very critical. She will loudly interrupt or talk over whoever is speaking. She believes that everyone should want to hear her opinions.

She is very active in our church and generous with her time and money. I know she feels good about herself when she is caring for others. I am proud of her achievements and efforts to support what she believes in.

At home she disciplines the children by trying to guilt them into behaving. She lets them know when they aren't measuring up to her standards and she will be critical of how they look and act, even using words like stupid, dumb, fat, clumsy and retarded. If one of them becomes upset, she'll say they are way too sensitive and that she was just kidding. In private, I try to intervene and get her to soften her approach. She pressures them to be popular, successful and friends with the "right" people. She has an incredible memory and will repeatedly bring up things from the past she feels you have done wrong. She never lets things go.

She does not really listen to what you are trying to say, because she makes everything about her. If you try and talk about something that happened to you, she immediately turns it around to how it relates to her or how the same thing happened to her or someone else she knows. It never gets to be just about you. We even joke that if someone comes to the door collecting money for a disease, she will have the same disease by dinner that night. Her saving grace is her sense of humor and even she laughs about her hypochondriacal tendencies.

I have managed by spending time by myself, exploring my hobbies and interests. She knows when I want to retreat and for the most part she gives me my space. We all have things we have to endure and the good has always outweighed the bad, which is fortunate because my beliefs and values would make divorce unacceptable.

Proverbs describes women's conduct. In Proverbs 31:10-31 is a description of what a "good wife" should be, and 12:4 states, "A good wife is the crown of her husband, but she who brings shame is like rottenness in his bones."

Forgiveness is discussed many times in the Bible. In Ephesians 4:25-32, we are instructed not to lie, cheat or steal. Verse 31-32 tell us, "Let all bitterness and wrath and anger and clamor and slander be put away from you, with all malice, and be kind to one another, tender-hearted, forgiving one another, as God in Christ forgave you."

In Matthew 19:21-22: "Then Peter came up and said to him, 'Lord, how often shall my brother sin against me, and I forgive him? As many as seven times?' Jesus said to him, 'I do not say to you seven times, but seventy times seven.'"

Forgiveness is a complex issue in psychologically abusive relationships. Very often we are given the message that we "should" forgive, when perhaps it is way too soon in our process to realistically expect that to occur. Dr. Janis Abrahms Spring, who has long studied forgiveness, writes in her early work, *After the Affair*: "Those who forgive too quickly tend to interact with a false or patronizing sweetness, punctuated by sarcasm or overt hostility. The result is a relationship ruled by resentment, petty squabbles, numbness, surface calm, and self-denial—a relationship lacking in both vitality and authenticity."[11]

Jewish faiths have a concept called Teshuvah, where a person is expected to acknowledge his or her transgression, repent and make a plan to do better. Yom Kippur is a day of atonement where Jews gather to confess individual failings and pledge to let the realization of mistakes help them make improvements. In an article in the June 2003 issue of *O, the Oprah Magazine*, Rabbi Susan Schnur explains that each person is expected to admit wrongfulness and make amends directly to the individual he or she has harmed. "When you apologize, you're really purifying yourself. 'I'm sorry' becomes a redirecting of your life. This requires a commitment not to err again in the same situation."[12] This concept provides such a strong owning of our flaws and failures and certainly facilitates forgiveness.

Often, religious institutions embrace the repentant one at the possible expense of the victim. That was made so clear to me during a sentencing hearing of a music teacher in a Christian academy. He was pleading guilty to his "popsicle game" of blindfolding his students and having each child guess whether or not what was inserted into his or her mouth was actually a popsicle. He had apparently openly confessed his crime in his church and asked for forgiveness and support. His side of the courtroom was filled with deacons and church members, while the children, who were also church members, only had their supportive families behind them.

OUR DARK SIDES

We have been taught that our dark sides are negative things that we should avoid owning and from which we should make every attempt to distance ourselves. The Bible is filled with explorations of the dark side of nature and life. Opposites exist within the same whole: heaven and hell, good and evil, dark and light, humility and pride, greed and generosity, gluttony and moderation, anger and serenity, fornication and chastity, life and death.

In Robert A. Johnson's short book *Owning Your Own Shadow*, he gives fascinating insight into this complex subject. His theory is that we must embrace our own shadows and not project them on other people.

We project, because we are uncomfortable with owning our worst selves, so we accuse our loved ones of possessing the very qualities that we are attempting to disown. The projection causes turmoil and prevents self-discovery. He describes validating every virtue with its opposite and the tremendous compelling energy that a person's shadow contains: "To own one's own shadow is to reach a holy place—an inner center—not attainable in any other way. To fail this is to fail one's own sainthood and to miss the purpose of life."[13] He says that we can be more creative if we incorporate our own darkness: "This is pure genius. Its attributes are wholeness, health, and holiness. We are talking about sainthood in the original meaning of the word—a full blooded embracing of our own humanity, not a one-sided goodness that has no vitality or life."[14] In a discussion of the paradox of love and power Johnson writes:

> Most of the recrimination between quarreling lovers or spouses involves the collision of power and love. To give each its due and endure the paradoxical tension is the noblest of all tasks. It is only too easy to embrace one at the expense of the other; but this precludes the synthesis that is the only real answer. Failure invites a breaking apart—divorce, disunion, quarrel. A true paradox makes for a strong devotion and a mystical union powerful enough to endure the problems.[15]

There are some terrible consequences as a result of man's interpretations of religious texts, theologies and sermons from religious leaders. Wars are fought and people are killed over religious differences and principles. Children and adults are beaten and abused in the name of discipline believed to be helpful and corrective. People are tortured and brainwashed into following certain religious beliefs and practices. Some polygamist sects abuse women and children by physical punishment, psychological control and forcing young girls into marriage, sex and childbearing. Satanists practice ghastly rituals, using Bible verses to guide their ceremonies. Some religions, predominantly practiced in other cultures, force women into totally restricted, submissive and at times silent positions.

Religion is a powerful force in many people's lives. In Richard Rohr and Andreas Ebert's fascinating book called *The Enneagram: A Christian Perspective*, the authors explain that the Enneagram is an ancient map that describes character types, dynamics of personal change, energy derived from our "sins" and guilt and many other mysteries:

> The Enneagram can lead us to this inner experience of dignity and power. Indeed, it unsparingly shows us our mistakes. All too often we do the right thing for false motives.
>
> But if we "work our way through" our compulsion and emerge again on the other side, then we stand before the depths of our self. There we find a purified passion, a chastened power—our best and true self. Tradition has called this place the "soul", the point where human being and God meet, where unity is possible and where religion consists not only of words, norms, dogmas, rituals and visits to church but becomes a genuine experience of encounter.[16]

How can we deal with our questions about the way our religion views staying in or leaving a psychologically abusive relationship? Try and find leaders in your religious community who have knowledge and training in abusive relationship dynamics and who will listen compassionately, answer questions with deep insight and not judge you and your decisions. Do your own study of available resources and be open to finding your own answers.

While religious beliefs, customs and traditions often cause people to remain in marriages, religion can also be the reason people choose to leave a relationship. If we are strongly grounded in our faiths, compromise is possible if two people work together to create a family of open-mindedness, options and possibilities to learn, accept and grow. Cate, one young woman, tells how she tried unsuccessfully to develop those compromises and commonalities:

> It started with the simplest of insults, always framed as my own supposed moral indiscretions: How could I have dated that guy? How could I have told someone else I love them?

Why didn't I save myself for him?

He saw himself as pure, wholesome and "religious" and me as spiritually deficient. Throughout the years of our relationship, it felt as though our spiritual pasts were pitted against our potential future together. Every conflict ultimately boiled down to our respective belief systems, with mine clearly recognized as inferior: "You don't go to church every Sunday? The Bible says that's a sin."

And yet, week after week, we pushed the conflict below the surface and I told myself that we could resolve our religious differences. I started developing my own spiritual support system—separate from him—of a church community, family and friends. I became strengthened by this, with the belief that we could find a way to resolve our problem. Over and over again, this hope was justified. I was told, "I'm willing to try for you. Let's find a compromise that works for us both. After all, we're both Christians." And I was content with that thought.

Then the other shoe dropped. My faith and my church were insulted and ridiculed, described as "not a true church," even though it was a large Protestant church in the city where I grew up. My religious upbringing was questioned. My family's background was described as "pagan." I was told that "the man of the house decides what religion is practiced." Even the physical structure of the church was attacked—it was unadorned, simple, unworthy of praise. When I attempted to talk about faith and its purpose and role in my life, I was dismissed. He told me that his traditions and those of his family were of utmost importance. I asked him about *my* traditions. Would my family even be included in our spiritual life? Of course, he responded that family isn't important when it comes to religion; but his family's religion mattered more. I questioned his past willingness to compromise in the four years we had been together. I was told that he was trying to pacify me. This seemed wrong. It hurt. It damaged my faith in him, and his insults and questioning made me reconsider my own faith. Was *I* the one being small-minded? My attempts to relay this were brushed aside. Faith was pushed away in favor of religion and traditions. So I walked away. I couldn't stand for the criticizing of my beliefs, values, religion and family. I lost faith in our relationship and in him. How could I spend my life with someone who wanted to dictate my beliefs? In no time, he thought of the "solution." Since I no longer trusted that we would make future decisions as a couple, he found a way to ensure that all decisions would be a joint effort. They would ALL be arranged by an all-inclusive, in-depth pre-nuptial agreement. We'd make decisions "together"—with an attorney. In exchange, we'd split time between our two churches, though we would officially be members of his church. There was no room for love, faith or feelings. He said that I lost the ability to make decisions as a "normal" couple when I pushed for a compromise. He said that I "took the romance out of our relationship." But what about *my* feelings, thoughts, hopes, desires and traditions? They were to be lost, along with my religion, in an attorney's office. Finally I decided I deserve better than that.

Religious observations and rituals can be forces which strengthen marriage, binding relationships and families, but they can also be misused by a psychologically abusive person against the other partner.

Chapter 10

Money, Money, Money

The issue of money is huge, complex and the source of many arguments in relationships. Money should be the means to pay for our needs and some of our wants. Instead, in a psychologically abusive relationship it is often the cause of so much frustration, anger, pain and sorrow.

MONEY AND CONTROL

There are numerous ways that couples handle the financial side of their marriages. Conflicts arise from differences of opinion over money management. Power dynamics emerge over divergent philosophies.

- ◆ Who makes the money? What percentage of the total income does each person contribute?
- ◆ Is the money kept in joint or separate accounts?
- ◆ Who pays the bills? If you keep separate accounts, who decides what portion of each income goes toward expenses?
- ◆ If there is any money left over, what percentage do you spend and save? Who makes the decisions on how money is spent? Do you compromise?

♦ Does each person have full access to viewing your total financial picture? Is anything hidden or undisclosed?

In many abusive relationships, money is used as a means to control the other person. The abuser may dole out money as he or she sees fit and expect an accounting of how every penny is spent. He or she may put a partner on an extremely tight budget as a way of being aware of where that person is and what that person is doing. It is also a way to convince a partner that he or she can never afford to leave. A psychological abuser may tell his or her partner there is no money, only to miraculously find some for whatever he or she wants. He or she may hide money or investments and keep several accounts to facilitate deception.

Here are some ways both people in a relationship may hide or sneak money.

Small Ways

♦ Getting money back from a store by writing a check for more than the actual purchase total.

♦ Lying about what something costs.

♦ Sneaking purchases into the house.

♦ Saying things were a gift or that you have had them for a long time.

♦ Being deceptive about what money is spent on: food, alcohol, drugs, cigarettes, gambling, hobbies, gifts for another person or any form of recreation or entertainment.

♦ Not discussing your bonuses, tips or cash payments from work.

Larger Ways

♦ Secret accounts or investments.

♦ Stashing money in hiding places or with another person.

♦ Subsidizing an affair or an addiction.

♦ Lying about the total amount of income.

♦ Not paying taxes at all or paying on inaccurate figures.

So why does money cause people to stay in an abusive relationship? Let's look at three reasons:
1. Lifestyle
2. Fear
3. High cost of divorce

1. Lifestyle

Many people have come to enjoy higher standards of living in marriages. If there are two incomes, more can be afforded. While money can be used to control and punish, it can also be used for indulgence and pleasure. In some relationships, money is not an issue and both people agree on its usage and purpose. It can meet their needs as well as be used for fun. Combining assets can provide couples with objects and experiences they would not otherwise have: houses, cars, appliances, electronic devices, furniture, toys, hobbies and vacations. The list is endless. Many people also enjoy giving gifts and donations that they couldn't afford on their own.

Often a person understands his or her partner's approach to money, based on the person's issues. Perhaps he or she grew up poor or had huge losses in life due to the death of a parent, an expensive illness, the cost of divorce or the loss of a job. When you know a person's history, you often make allowances for the person's feelings about money.

Jeanette's attorney said it was the most restrictive, controlling prenuptial agreement he'd ever read—a work of art—and should be an example in law books. The lawyer gently suggested that this might be an indicator of things to come and she might want to reconsider her decision to marry him. But, she loved him. She knew he had been through a brutal divorce settlement and understood that he felt he had to protect himself. He needed to feel safe. He couldn't stand any more losses.

When she went to the law offices for the signing of the agreement, she felt ashamed and embarrassed. She was paying for someone else's greed. She had never in her life tried to take anything away from anyone. She signed her name to prove to him that she loved him, not his money.

It was a setup for sorrow and resentment. Her attorney's words echoed in her head as she had to negotiate the division of household expenses. How much could she give toward their monetary needs? He showed no mercy. She clearly saw that he would protect what was his and expect an equal contribution to their joint responsibilities, even though she had fewer assets. She never expected a break or a free ride, but she felt she was being punished for what he'd lost in his divorce. There was always the pressure of how much more could she give. All money was separate until he wanted more. Then it would be "*We* need to buy this" or "*We* need to drive your car on all trips, because it gets better gas mileage." She went from rarely focusing on money to feeling that a huge heavy dollar sign had to be constantly carried around and continuously fed or it would lash out and kill the relationship.

Jeanette didn't want the marriage to end. She'd been through her own divorce and lived some lean years when paying the basic bills was often a stretch. She'd done without a lot of things she enjoyed that this marriage now provided. Together they had a nice home to which she had grown attached. They had a pet that she adored. They could occasionally take a vacation. She could buy gifts and do things with her children. She preferred the way she lived now to returning to the struggle.

In some marriages, the income of one spouse is seen as sufficient, which allows the partner to stay home. The joys of parenting, homemaking, volunteering, social activities and exercise can be fully experienced. Many women want to stay home and raise their children. They may put up with a lot of bad behavior from their husbands for the privilege and responsibilities of being a full-time mother. Some women also enjoy their positions or status in their communities and the way they are able to spend their time, which is made possible by their husbands' careers and incomes. Money allows participation in activities that a forty-plus hour workweek does not. It can also offer the opportunity to return to school or learn a skill that could lead to a desired career or simply be for personal enrichment. Lifestyle changes are a very real consideration when contemplating leaving a marriage.

2. Fear

Financial threats made to keep women from leaving are frightening and effective.

♦ You will never have anything.
♦ I'll take everything you've got.
♦ You can't pay for much with your salary.
♦ Who would hire you?
♦ I'll quit my job before I pay you a dime of support.
♦ I'm staying in the house and the kids should stay here, too. You'd never be able to afford it.
♦ I had all these things before we got married, so you can't have any of them.
♦ All those gifts I gave you are marital assets, so you can kiss your precious jewelry goodbye.
♦ The kids will do all the fun things with me.
♦ We are close to retirement. I'll have fun spending my money on someone younger and more fun. You may have helped us become financially secure, but another woman will benefit from it if you leave.

These fears tap into the anxiety we already have in our hearts about how we will survive. For some, an inheritance, a huge raise or a new job provides the means to leave. Some women have left and then returned home, because just barely surviving was too difficult.

The current climate of the United States' economy can cause enormous pressure. Recession, foreclosures, home equity loans, failing industries, loss of jobs, credit card debts and bankruptcies tear at the fabric of our society. We are all impacted by the trickle down and domino effects of our overall chaotic financial picture. Because many cannot afford health insurance, their lack of good care and use of emergency services drives up the cost of insurance and expenses for everyone. As industries die out or transfer to foreign countries, there are more people competing for the remaining jobs. As home sales suffer, every industry associated with building and selling homes is impacted. The list is endless. Frightened people hold on to what they have, just hoping to pay their bills and survive.

3. High cost of divorce

Contested divorces are expensive. The adversarial nature of the proceedings causes people to hire the best attorneys they can afford. Unfortunately, it is often at this point that the level of anger, contempt, frustration and revenge spirals out of control, fueled by two attorneys adept at creating "billable hours." Attorneys love billable hours. It is how they matter in their law firms. It is how they get paid.

Divorce attorneys accrue more billable hours if they help orchestrate animosity. Initial instructions by some attorneys are for their clients not to talk to each other, thus creating four-way conversations, which can be manipulated by using inflammatory inflections and interpretations, thus escalating tension, fear and confusion. Every effort is made to have their clients feel that they have been unfairly wronged or mistreated and, therefore, each attorney will have to fight the "unreasonable" opposing attorney to have a victorious outcome. You will be charged for each minute spent on the phone, "researching" the law (as if they didn't already know it), listening to voicemails, reading e-mails, making copies, preparing documents, filing motions and, perhaps, going to court. The bill *can* mount up to six figures.

Imagine that you and your husband have a financial pie. Divide it down the middle. From each side of the pie cut a large slice for attorneys, mediators, court costs, moving expenses and shared debt. The larger the total of these items, the larger the slices need to be. What remains is what each person has to live on. It is not an appealing picture.

The stark realities of how separation and divorce impact the standard of living for a family can be daunting. If you do choose to separate and divorce, consider a better solution. The more you argue and battle each other, the more money you lose. It is all so unnecessary. It happens because you feel angry, hurt and betrayed. You want your spouse to feel the same pain or you are trying to protect yourself from the onslaught of his legal attack. Wake up. The attorneys get richer at your expense. There are state laws to educate you about your rights. There are guidelines that can be accessed online.

Be smarter. Seek out qualified divorce mediation or attorneys who facilitate cooperation and compromise. You can work out reasonable, fair arrangements yourselves and draw up your own documents to be reviewed by your legal advocate. Agreements should be signed and notarized. Move on with your life with a bigger slice of the pie.

Everyone wants financial security and independence. Since only a small percentage of the population has that luxury, money factors into a person's decision about whether to remain in or leave a marriage. Facing the loss of an income, a home and a lifestyle is daunting. Regardless of the health of a marriage, money is a fundamental reason that people stay.

Chapter 11

Secrets and Shame, Pride and Guilt

Psychologically abused individuals often have pasts that are filled with fear and anguish.

SECRETS AND SHAME

- ♦ Don't tell.
- ♦ People don't need to know your business.
- ♦ What would they think?
- ♦ What will the neighbors say?
- ♦ My family does not believe in airing our dirty laundry.
- ♦ I am so embarrassed.
- ♦ This is the worst thing that has ever happened to me.
- ♦ I don't know anyone else who is going through what I am.
- ♦ People will wonder what is wrong with me.
- ♦ No one in my family accepts divorce.
- ♦ My kids will be ashamed and self-conscious.
- ♦ What will he do to me if I mention what is really going on in our marriage?

Like physical abuse, there is a code of silence surrounding psychological abuse. We worry about how others will view us. We feel ashamed of our situations and perhaps do not realize that many other people are going through the same experiences: We think everyone we know will be curious and want to know the details. We fear the gossip that takes on a life of its own and adds fictitious details. We fear damaged reputations or having our families hurt by the distress and humiliation of exposing our abusive relationships. Another concern follows: What does it say about me if I tell people what is happening and then I choose to stay? They will think that I am crazy or that I caused, deserved or enjoyed the abuse; otherwise, I would leave. It's too complicated to explain all the reasons why we stay, so we might decide to keep quiet. If people don't know our business, we avoid disgrace.

When the abuse is psychological, it is even more difficult and complicated to explain. For each intricate mind game your spouse has played, you may have had a reaction that you don't want exposed. The games themselves are tough to identify, because they continue for years and are hard to pluck out of context and comprehend their damaging effects. As you unravel the fabric of your relationship, it is a struggle to communicate the destructive and complex control dynamics.

Secrecy creates isolation that allows the abuse to continue. What is not exposed flourishes. There is little consequence for the abuser, because only the supposedly powerless victim knows. Threats of additional abuse may have been implied or communicated: "If you tell anyone, I promise you will be sorry." She feels alone in her private hell. She fears what would happen if she exposes his behavior. He dreads the reactions of his partner and the responses of the people he values, so he remains silent. The spouse may also have convinced the person that if he or she speaks out, the other spouse will spread vicious rumors. The truth will be hard to determine, so the damage will be done. Threatening to ruin others' reputations with the truth or with lies is a powerful way to control their actions.

We may stay with our partner because of what John Bradshaw refers to as "toxic shame." In his book *Healing the Shame that Binds You*, he explains that "the excruciating loneliness fostered by toxic shame is dehumanizing."[17] The isolating shame can cause us to cling to whatever relationship we manage to keep while we hide our inner feelings. He describes how parents often shame children for their natural emotions. Boys, in particular, are criticized, ridiculed or punished for crying or being afraid. Toxic shame is what a person carries with them into adulthood, thwarting the ability to communicate feelings. We become detached from our natural emotions, because we are taught to be ashamed. We stuff our feelings down inside of us and refuse to acknowledge them. The result is that the emotions morph into something more dangerous. Our anger becomes rage; our sorrow becomes despair and depression; our fear becomes terror or paranoia. Why do parents shame and try to control their children's emotions? Because it was done to them. The "shame on you" or "I'll give you something to cry about" statements become a multigenerational mantra. It is no wonder that so many people, particularly men, have no idea what they really feel. The one emotion generally found acceptable for boys is anger. We encourage boys to be aggressive and powerful. From sports to business, dominance is rewarded. However, if the boy is raised in an abusive household, his anger may be suppressed by the controlling parent. If so, he will internalize his shame and be more likely to have a raging response to things and people that anger him.

PRIDE AND GUILT

Pride has two dimensions. One aspect involves appropriately valuing yourself as a human being, taking your commitments seriously and desiring to behave with honor and dignity. The other aspect entails taking pride to the extreme, escalating a haughty self-impressed air and acting superior, arrogant and overbearing. Both dimensions play a role in why people stay. If you feel too proud to ask for help, to report what is happening in your life or to risk living with less income or status, you may remain. You also may stay, because you feel a sense of duty and obligation. You have pride in yourself, standing by your values, morals, religious beliefs and responsibilities. Brian shares his feelings of pride while in a psychologically abusive relationship:

> She constantly complains, orders me around or makes unfair accusations. She ridicules me, to the point I don't feel like much of a man. I'm not perfect, but I try to do everything she asks of me and I've never betrayed her. Since we've been together, I've never had anything to do with another woman, although I sure have fantasized about it, wondering if I could find a better relationship. I stay out of a sense of duty. No one in my family gets divorced. I've always taken care of her, and she's not prepared in any way to live alone. She depends on me. It is my responsibility to take care of my family. I can't abandon them. I need to be around to help with the house, raise the kids and try to meet her needs. I took my marriage vows seriously and I am obligated to stay.

Guilt causes us to blame ourselves for the problems in our relationships.

♦ It's all my fault.
♦ What is wrong with me?
♦ I do things that trigger the abuse.
♦ He's told me I'm the reason that he loses control.
♦ I am so selfish.
♦ I'd never forgive myself if I hurt my children by leaving their father/mother.
♦ What would he do without me?
♦ If I was a better person this wouldn't be happening.

A critical negative partner reinforces the guilt we have assumed. You also may have had a parent who was an expert at creating guilt, so you are conditioned to believe that everything is your fault. To compensate for all your bad behavior, you may have taken on the job of caring for other people, no matter how they treat you.

Jordan tells of her psychologically abusive partner:

> I've taken care of him for so long. There are so many things he has no clue about. I run the household, pay the bills, plan all

our holidays and social occasions, take care of all the children's needs and cover all of our insurance and house maintenance. I even schedule his doctor, dentist and hair appointments. I am the wife, lover, mother, housekeeper and personal assistant, all rolled into one; plus I work a full-time job.

In return, he never seems to appreciate me or notice me. He takes for granted that everything magically gets done. He drinks, often calls in sick to work and is a slob around the house. He is disrespectful and sometimes downright mean, calling me names and putting me down. The kids are now grown and gone, and the thought of spending the rest of my life with him is unbearable.

My problem is, every time I think of leaving him, I feel so guilty. Who will take care of him? How will he cope? Making his life easier has always been my job. I don't hate him. I want him to be okay. I feel like it is selfish of me to want out. I know I'll be fine on my own, but I'm not sure he will be. I don't want him to fall apart. I'm not sure how to be at peace about leaving.

Whether it is worrying about what people will think, a sense of pride, being ashamed, a belief in a duty to endure or fear of the consequences of disclosure, a code of secrecy surrounds psychologically abusive relationships and can lead us to stay in the relationship.

Chapter 12

Bad Boys and Girls

Why do women and men love bad boy and girls? Edgy and exciting with danger lurking beneath the surface, bad boys and girls are unpredictable and bold. Many people are attracted to them like moths to a flame. The synonyms for the word "powerful" serve as an explanation for why these people are appealing and risky: influential, controlling, authoritative, dominant, strong, energetic, potent, strapping, vigorous, persuasive, forceful and impressive.

THE FAMOUS AND THE INFAMOUS
1. Sports Figures
2. Politicians
3. Movie Stars
4. Musicians
5. Criminals

1. Sports Figures

America is in love with sports, particularly the violent aggressive ones. Golf is fine, but give us a great football, basketball or hockey game, where enormous men are crashing into one another and we are smitten. Even NASCAR fans can't wait for the cars to smash, roll and burn. We idolize our top athletes and pay them incredible salaries for playing a game. Is it surprising if these heroes are aggressive and violent at home? When angered, it certainly must be second nature to use the same skills for which they are so admired. If "might makes right," why not use physical power to get your way? What if someone actually dies? Does society punish them? Rarely are they punished to any noticeable, costly extent.

2. Politicians

From the state capitols to the White House, the power of creating and enforcing laws, running a government and making huge international decisions is fascinating and alluring. The December 2, 2002, issue of *People Magazine* listed Secretary of Defense Donald Rumsfeld as one of the fifty sexiest men alive. Even though he is an attractive older man, it is the power he held that caused him to make the list. The article quotes Henry Kissinger as saying "Power is the ultimate aphrodisiac."[18] We are sometimes shocked by the sexual conduct of our presidents, but the temptations must be numerous. What makes these public figures appealing is that they have the ability to make things happen that the ordinary individual can only comment on or wonder about.

3. Movie Stars

Bad boy and girl movie stars sell tickets. Women and men flock to see the criminal, the lover, the manipulator, the fighter, the bitch or the scoundrel. We are fascinated with their passion, strength and appearance. The essence of the cinematic bad character is that he or she creates fantasies that make us squirm a little, as we imagine spending one night with them to experience their intensity.

4. Musicians

Whether your favorite bad boy or girl musician is a rocker, a rapper or a blues singer, the image may be as important as the talent. Some musicians make it to the bad list through their performances both on and off the stage. Their music glorifies sex, drugs, rock and roll and violence. They are defiant in their dress, movements, body art, piercings and lyrics. They may have chaotic personal lives that their fans find intriguing. It seems popularity and wealth follow outrageously pushing the limits. Female groupies are women who follow bands in order to feel a part of the aura. They may be willing to have sex with band members only to be casually discarded or passed on to another.

5. Criminals

Criminals are society's ultimate bad characters. We are riveted by their violence. Nowhere is this more evident than in our fascination with the mafia. Many of these men would appear ordinary or downright unattractive if we simply saw them on the street. From the real life criminals that we follow in the news to the fictitious ones we watch on television or in movies, we make these bad boys into sex symbols. The connection seems to be if they are that graphic, powerful and intense in the outside world, what must they be like inside the bedroom?

Sexual chemistry is there or it's not. You can't manufacture desire and you definitely know when you experience it. Some women feel passion toward raw male dominance. Think about all of the movies, novels, plays and even television soap operas where we are fascinated by the hesitant female who is swept away by the persistent aggressive male. In fiction, her submission to his insistence is followed by great romance and sexual pleasure. This can be the case in the real world, but unfortunately these assumptions have also led to confusion over whether "no" really means "no." Josh, one young man interviewed about his approach to women, said, "If 'no' meant 'no', every guy would die a virgin. I just work on the neck and boobs and try back in five minutes."

I once attended a conference featuring sociologist Murray Straus and English activist and author Erin Pizzey. Our community was beginning to provide services for victims of domestic violence and Ms. Pizzey had been instrumental in the development of shelters for battered women in

England in the 1970s. In explaining why many women go back to their partners after they have escaped the violence, she addressed a key factor. Paraphrasing, Pizzey said: It's not that women enjoy or want to get hurt, but you must understand that just prior to the violence, the intensity may be the most powerful connection that they have ever felt. Even though it is negative, the focus of his attention and energy creates a rush that can bond a woman to her partner and keep her returning home.

A dangerous man or woman can evoke fear, which floods some systems with adrenaline. Senses are heightened. We feel alive. Perhaps this is not unlike our attraction to other things that scare us, be it a roller coaster, haunted house, horror film, sky diving, rock climbing, cliff jumping or any other dangerous sport. We come back to the bad for many of the same reasons—fun with some fear mixed in. It is not the abuse that we are seeking. The extreme, concentrated focus prior to the outburst may draw us back. After an abusive incident, many men will lavish positive attention on their partners in an expression of remorse over their actions. He or she may be more loving and kind during this period than at any other point in the relationship.

BAD BOYS IN YOUR TOWN

What about the bad boys we encounter in our daily lives? Let's put them into eight categories.

1. Scruffy with an Attitude
2. Hot Bodies
3. Dangerous Dudes
4. Innocent Looking Devils
5. Little Men/Tough Guys
6. Clean-Cut Warriors
7. Successful Tycoons
8. Players

1. Scruffy with an Attitude

Some women are attracted to a little grunge. If he gets dirty at work, doesn't always shave or shower, doesn't keep his hair trimmed or wears his clothes in a defiant way while copping an attitude, we pay attention. Perhaps we imagine that not minding a little messiness or dirt will mean that he will really delve into exploring sexual connections.

2. Hot Bodies

The profusion of gyms and fitness centers means there are a fair number of hot bodies walking around. We notice the sculpted shapes. The serious bodybuilder or sports figure often takes steroids to enhance his muscles, performance or endurance. "'Roid rage" has been responsible for violent behavior that may not happen without the use of steroids.

3. Dangerous Dudes

They seem to have an intensity bubbling under the surface. They may drive too fast, use drugs or alcohol to excess, get angry easily, take lots of risks, commit crimes or be mentally unstable. A broad range of people can be dangerous. The unknown, frightening quality is curious and interesting. How close can we get without getting burned?

4. Innocent Looking Devils

Watch out for the quiet ones.

- ◆ He looked so sweet, but underneath his exterior there was trouble.
- ◆ I trusted him because he looked so honest and sincere.
- ◆ He was so nice to my family and friends, but when we were alone I saw his other side.
- ◆ I kind of liked the fact that no one could tell what we did in private just by seeing us together in public.

Unfortunately, some of the most heinous mass murderers looked innocent and trustworthy and that is how they lured their victims.

5. Little Men/Tough Guys

Some men of smaller stature attract more women by being tough guys. Aggressive behavior often translates to having power, and we are attracted to his raw energy and ability to have positive or negative influence over others. The physically unattractive man can also be appealing if he is in some kind of powerful position. Some women admire toughness regardless of how it is packaged.

6. Clean-Cut Warriors

A warrior can fight on a football field, a school, a neighborhood, a battlefield or in the streets. The clean-cut warrior is meticulously groomed and may wear a uniform during part of his day. Men in uniform have always been appealing, especially if they exude strength, pride and power. The aggressive force and dominance required to get the job done can be turned against us.

Generally, servicemen and police officers are the "good guys" willing to give their life for our country. Military men represent power, aggression and protection. Fighting with weapons or their bare hands, they are skilled at surveillance and lethal destruction. However, they are trained to kill. What happens when soldiers bring their violent experiences home to their personal relationships? In July 2002, the Army began examining its family counseling programs, following the murders of four wives in six weeks at Fort Bragg, North Carolina. Three men had just returned from Special Operations in Afghanistan. Two women were shot, one strangled and one stabbed at least fifty times.[19]

Some police officers use intimidation and physical strength in the line of duty. He may expect to use the same skills to feel he has control and respect at home. Exhaustion from long hours and dealing with ugly criminal behavior leaves little tolerance for relationship conflicts. Being constantly on guard and suspicious can spill over into a lack of trust for his intimate partner. To complicate the issue, many officers will "protect their own." In 2007, newspapers and magazines reported that a Bolingbrook, Illinois, investigation into the disappearance of a young wife of a police officer found that, in a two year period during his former marriage, police were called to his home eighteen times about domestic disputes. He was never arrested.[20]

7. Successful Tycoons

Men who have risen to the upper levels of their professions are noticed for their achievements, particularly if they are innovative, risky or profitable. In the July 29, 2002, issue of *Forbes Magazine*, one article concerned "Bad Boys." Beneath the title it said, "From rape allegations to fraud convictions – some companies will ignore anything to protect their top performers."

Money, power and success are the goals. There is very little room at the top, so we are in awe of the few who make it. The ultimate American dream is to have that kind of status. Some women have made their own journeys to the top, but statistically the most money and powerful positions are men's. How many women who marry tycoons excuse, endure and cover up abusive behavior to keep their connection to the upper echelons? We celebrate the winners and seek to be associated with their power and strength. We want to share in the exhilaration of success.

8. Players

Any of the bad boys in the other seven categories can surely be players, but a womanizer is in a class by himself. Attentive to women and their needs, he understands what it takes to get what he wants. He may really enjoy and appreciate females or simply be notching his belt and getting a rush from the conquests. Why are we so vulnerable to his manipulations? Because he is good at it. He has learned to listen and respond to our feelings and concerns, he has become our friend and helped us in some way or he simply exhibits a raw sexuality that sends an electric current through us that we find hard to resist. Saying and doing the most outrageous sexual things, he doesn't worry about rejection, because he knows he can move on to the next woman. The player studies his next interest, assesses what it will take to be successful and then enjoys the manipulation, attraction and consummation.

Cindy, one young woman contemplating getting involved with a bad boy, said:

I'm attracted to his spontaneous wild side, because I have the same wildness in me that I have to keep hidden. I feel turned on by his attitude of, "Look at me the wrong way and I'll beat the shit out of you."

Gayle, who kept returning to her husband, explained:
Growing up at home, I was always held to such a high standard. I felt I was never quite good enough. My bad boy husband loved me with all my flaws and imperfections. I didn't have to worry about measuring up, because he accepted me as I am. His behavior was so bad he couldn't expect perfection from me. When things were good between us, I could relax and enjoy myself. It was the most *alive* I've ever felt.

We reinforce bad boy behavior by rewarding it with our attention and attraction. If we find the nice guy boring and the bad boy exciting, this sends a negative message to our teenage boys. Young people pick role models who are popular or famous, so many young men will aspire to be bad boys.

What happens when women try and stay with bad boys?
- We think we can change them. If they just loved us enough, they would not treat us badly.
- We continue to be attracted to what is difficult to trust and count on. If we need to work to keep him, he seems more valuable.
- We grow to expect that we will be treated badly. We may feel it is worth it.
- We find ourselves doing things we never thought we would do. It is the reason he is "bad news."

WOMEN AND PSYCHOLOGICAL ABUSE
Who are some of these women who are capable of psychologically abusing a man?
1. Sweet Manipulator
2. Dominating Caregiver
3. Insatiable Carnivore

4. High Maintenance
5. Superwoman
6. Ms. Perfection
7. Negative Nell
8. Psycho Bitch

1. Sweet Manipulator

What you see is not what you get here. She's the wolf in sheep's clothing who will befriend you with kindness and concern to gain an advantage. The more she knows about you, the more dangerous she becomes as she uses her knowledge to manipulate and control. She may use sex as a weapon or a reward or she may let you believe that sex has never been as wonderful as it is with you, to make you feel important. Underneath, there is another agenda. Perhaps she has expectations of you that you don't want to fulfill. But all along she appears syrupy sweet and passive. She may play dumb or cry to get her way, hoping that you will want to help or please her.

2. Dominating Caregiver

She'll provide all the comforts of a loving wife, mother and home-maker. She's generous, kind, hardworking and efficient. What's the catch? She expects to be in control of you, the money, the kids and the household. She wants things done her way and if it's not, there are unpleasant consequences.

3. Insatiable Carnivore

She's the black widow spider who lures men into her web, has her way and then destroys them. This man-eater will chew you up, spit you out and move on to the next guy. Her past usually reveals a reason why she is angry with men, and she can spend a lifetime retaliating. She'll draw you in and get you hooked, without letting herself get too emotionally involved. What you do for her will never quite be enough to satisfy her. She will never be totally happy or content, but you will find yourself trying to meet her needs in order to keep her.

4. High Maintenance

She may have been born with the silver spoon in her mouth or she may always wish she had been. Her expectations of you are as a provider: you will pay for everything, treat her like a queen, buy her anything she wants, put up with her moods and not expect anything in return. She's the spoiled brat who will complain if things don't go her way or she is desperate for attention from men. Life is all about her.

5. Superwoman

There are amazing superwomen with wonderful relationships. However, the psychologically abusive superwoman is too busy to possibly pay attention to you. She has way too much on her agenda, and she'll let you know about it in a passive/aggressive way of explaining why you should feel ashamed or guilty if you expect her time, attention or maybe sex. She's avoiding you and you find it difficult to criticize, because all the things she is doing are valuable or important.

6. Ms. Perfection

Some women feel they're perfect and expect you to remember that:

♦ I will notice everything you do and while you can't possibly be perfect like me, I will always remind you of your feelings and flaws.

♦ You should be ashamed if you do not meet my expectations.

♦ I want you to tell me what you do, think or feel and everything about your past.

♦ You have no right to ask me to do the same, because I am perfect and therefore you will not dare criticize me.

7. Negative Nell

Some women complain constantly:

♦ The kids have been impossible.

♦ I hate my boss.

♦ You never do anything to help me.

♦ I'm exhausted and don't feel well.

♦ I think I'm getting the flu.

- We never have any money to do anything.
- It's too hot/cold out.
- I hate rainy days.
- My cramps are killing me.
- I don't feel like going to work today.
- I am so depressed.
- We are probably going to have to sell our house.
- I might lose my job.
- I feel fat and ugly.
- Why are you gone all the time? You seem to be avoiding me!

8. Psycho Bitch

All I really have to say is illustrated by Glenn Close in *Fatal Attraction*. It's every man's nightmare: the gorgeous woman who seems so normal, willing and appealing, but who ends up stalking you and boiling your pet. Women who are mentally and emotionally unstable can become very psychologically abusive in close personal relationships.

WHAT ABOUT BAD GIRLS?

It used to be said that bad girls were only good for one thing. Times have changed. From their clothes and their trash talking to their outrageous behavior, bad girls are glorified. Let's consider the exact same categories for bad girls as we did for the boys.

1. Scruffy with an Attitude
2. Hot Bodies
3. Dangerous Dolls
4. Innocent Looking Devils
5. Tough Girls
6. Clean-Cut Warriors
7. Successful Tycoons
8. Players

1. Scruffy with an Attitude

Mean girls have become popular and powerful. From superstars to the girl next door, women are wearing clothing that is skimpy, tight and seductive. Leather and lace, spandex tops, tattoos and piercings, heavy makeup and sexy hair are common. They'll gang up to exclude or gossip about other girls, steal each other's boyfriends and tell someone off in a heartbeat.

2. Hot Bodies

She may have luscious curves or tightly sculpted muscles, but many women are celebrating their hot bodies. Since many men are visual, there is power in understanding the impact of women's appearances. If women's bodies make them desirable, then bad girls can choose to use them to manipulate.

3. Dangerous Dolls

Bad girls can have a crazy, wild streak that makes them both exciting and dangerous. Risky behavior, drug and alcohol use, thrill seeking and a fearless pursuit of whatever interests her, she's the attractive flame that will burn you.

4. Innocent-Looking Devils

She's the girl in your Sunday school class or working for your favorite charity. She's the soccer mom, school teacher or even the local librarian. She appears sweet, inexperienced, honest, nice and sincere. Underneath the first impression and calm exterior, however, lies the tiger who will rip your heart out and eat it for dinner.

5. Tough Girls

Have you ever seen Holly Hunter in the popular television program *Saving Grace*? She plays Grace, a tough cop who was sexually abused as a child by a priest. She'll rough up a suspect, get a confession, drink straight from the bottle, have crazy, wild sex with her married police partner and go riding naked and bareback in the middle of the night. She's fascinating, appealing and very human. She's been hurt and she'll hurt you, but you are drawn to her.

6. Clean-Cut Warriors

Women are soldiers, police officers, FBI and CIA agents, politicians and sports figures, too. They fight for our country and represent us in the Olympics. They shoot guns, fly airplanes, drop bombs and break world records. They represent the positive attributes of the slang meaning of the word "bad." Men are attracted to their toughness, courage, eloquence and resolve. 2008 Vice Presidential candidate Sarah Palin seemed to come out of nowhere, riding in like Annie Oakley; men are discussing her beauty and great legs and women are rushing to copy her style of clothing and eyeglasses. Women warriors can intimidate, back men down and get what they want.

7. Successful Tycoons

Women can have money, power and a great deal of influence in business and personal relationships. They can run a company or agency, an institution or a government. Whether they are using finesse or force, many succeed. Highly ethical or questionably ruthless, tycoons will get their ways. Some men may enjoy the challenge of interacting or competing against these impressive women.

8. Players

Bad girls may go through a string of men by using their allure. Playing with men gets their sexual, financial, social and self-esteem needs met.

Another kind of player participates in a very different game: the Men's Ultimate Fantasy game. Bad girl players can be a man's personal dream whether it involves stripping, pole dancing, role playing (complete with costumes), kinky sex and even group sex. Television's *Swingtown* gives us a provocative look at couples mutually agreeing to switch partners. These players know how to be both nice and naughty, which most men find irresistible.

Just as with young boys, our young girls feel pressure to be provocative, sexual, bitchy and bad. Drama and chaos is intriguing.

They want to be noticed and accepted by the kids they consider cool.

QUESTIONS

- ◆ Have you ever fallen for a bad boy or girl?
- ◆ What attracted you to him or her?
- ◆ If you got burned or regret it, what happened? Did you keep going back to it?
- ◆ Would you do it again?

Chapter 13

Standing By Your Man

"And they lived happily ever after." As children, our fairytales tell us that love and romance have happy endings. As teenagers, we want boy/girlfriends, so we can feel all the excitement promised in the novels we read and the songs to which we listened. As young adults, we want to fall in love and get married. It is what we expect to happen and we feel left out if we aren't part of that experience. Careers, children, owning and furnishing a home and an active social life should follow.

So what happens when our relationship isn't going so well? The pictures in our head of what life is supposed to be are jeopardized. If we get married we say, "For better or worse, for richer or poorer, in sickness and in health." Nowhere in the marriage vows does it say anything about "happily ever after." We pledge to stay with our partner through adversity. While both men and women take these vows, historically women were expected to be in a subordinate role and many took the brunt of men's bad behavior.

The United States Constitution and its laws drew their foundation from British common law. Women were viewed as the property of first their fathers, then their husbands. Discipline of your property was viewed as desirable. The expression "rule of thumb" comes from British common law that gave men the right to use a stick or other instrument to discipline their wives, as long as it was no bigger around than the man's thumb. Each state has various laws relating to marriage and the archaic concepts have been slow to change. Women had to earn their rights, from voting to freedom from tyranny and abuse. Marriage was definitely less of a democracy and more of a dictatorship. Some couples still use marriage vows where only the women pledge to "love, honor and obey."

Modern culture is filled with both new and old examples that glorify men dominating women. Books, movies, plays and songs have shown women in submissive positions. In one old movie, "Stepford Wives" are supposed to be men's ultimate fantasy. They are robotically agreeable, gorgeous, soft-spoken and great mothers and homemakers. They never complain, are easy to control and love sex. How perfect.

Another example from the past illustrates accepted behavior of women and men seventy plus years ago. Columbia Pictures' *It Happened One Night* won five Academy Awards, including best picture, actor, actress and director. The comedy ends with the two main characters, played by Clark Gable and Claudette Colbert, falling in love. During the film, Colbert's character's father slaps her across the face and Gable's character calls her an "ungrateful brat," tells her to "shut up" and explains that she's on a budget. Her father approves when, at the end of the film, Gable's character says, "What she needs is a guy who will take a sock at her once a day, whether it's coming to her or not."

Many of the lyrics in rap music are particularly degrading to women. Some songs encourage macho men to use and abuse their women. From sexual dominance to physical control, the female is clearly to be conquered, then often discarded. In country music, Tammy Wynette sings about standing by your man, instructing women to understand their man's shortcomings and remain in his corner.

Standing by your man involves endurance when the going gets tough. Let's consider four reasons why women stay that were not previously mentioned:

1. You are proud of him
2. He has stood by you
3. Power, prestige and fame
4. Investment of time and energy

1. You are proud of him

From the quality of work he does to the way he conducts himself outside the home, you may be proud of your man. You might appreciate some of his characteristics and abilities or his interactions within your family. Comparing his best moments to his worst behavior can give you whiplash. Imagine the preacher's wife who sits with the congregation listening to her husband's inspirational sermon after he has yelled, berated and criticized her in the car all the way to church. Or the governor's wife who has watched him vigorously fight corruption, only to discover he has been generously paying prostitutes for years. How do they reconcile these two completely opposing behaviors? They may choose to focus on the qualities in him of which they are most proud.

2. He has stood by you

None of us is perfect. We have flaws. We have made mistakes. We may have our own abusive behavior to be ashamed of. If our man has accepted us as human, tolerated our bad deeds and remained in the relationship, it is possible that we will stand by him, too.

Some women have situations in their pasts that they deeply regret. Whether it is something that happened to you or something you did yourself, you may feel grateful to your partner for his acceptance and discretion. If your shortcomings or misdeeds have not discouraged his devotion, you may want to return the favor.

3. Power, prestige and fame

Though Hillary Clinton must have been hurt and embarrassed, she stood by bad boy Bill and then rose to the highest echelons of government and politics. Could she have done it if she had left him? Perhaps, but as a society we value standing by your man.

Being connected to a famous or powerful person has the often appealing effect of causing us to also be noticed, recognized, photographed and interviewed. It may be fifteen minutes of fame or lasting notoriety. Even if we become infamous, we have a small place in history. The attention may be from your local community to the nationwide glory of appearing on popular television news and talk shows. We are curious about the partners of famous men. Standing by them means you will also have a degree of power, prestige and fame.

4. Investment of time and energy

When a woman has remained in a psychologically abusive relationship for years, enduring the bad behavior of her partner, she may be hesitant to leave based on her investment of time and energy.

- ♦ I've spent ten years with him. I don't want to feel that it has been a waste of my time.
- ♦ After all the work I have put into this relationship, I'll feel like a failure if I go.
- ♦ I'm older now. I'm too tired and weary to start over. Besides, I'm afraid I'll just be dealing with some other man's lousy behavior.
- ♦ I helped make him a success. I'm certainly not going to leave and let some other woman enjoy all the rewards of my hard work.
- ♦ I've tried to leave before, but it's so hard and painful. I've been with him so long, I'm not sure how to make it without him.
- ♦ My children are precious to me and I certainly don't want some other woman who is his girlfriend or wife involved in their lives.
- ♦ I'm not willing to let his flaws and mistakes totally change the life I have developed over the years.

BERNIE'S STORY

We had been married almost ten years when a confluence of events in both our lives led to a total marriage breakdown. What followed were years of infidelity, broken trust, public embarrassment and the ultimate death of a marriage as we knew it. The emotional abuse inflicted on me by my husband and his mistress was so terrible that I quit eating for a while, I withdrew from most of my activities and I lived every day not sure I could continue. Our marriage now bears little similarity to the relationship we had in the best of times. It will never be the same. Trust cannot be restored once it has been broken so badly and so repeatedly. The idyllic, romantic view of marriage I held has changed and matured as every marriage must to survive. I am sure many people wonder why I stayed. The easier choice would have been to end it. Why should we stay together, especially in such a changed marriage? After much angst and therapy, it boiled down to these three things:

Firstly, at the time we had a history together of over fifteen years. This history encompassed our young single days, our early careers, births, deaths, family celebrations, friends—all those memories that cannot be recreated with another person or forgotten. If you believe in the Imago concept, I had, for better or worse, chosen on this first go-round the person who could best help me heal my childhood wounds. I began to ask myself why in the world another marriage or relationship would be any easier with another person who did not share this common history.

Secondly, we had a child together. This was perhaps the biggest driving force for me. My own mother had died when I was very young and I had a stepmother to whom I was not particularly close. I was determined that my child would not have the influence of another woman in her life, especially one of very questionable moral fiber. I wanted to be the only motherly influence in her life and did not and do not plan on sharing that with any other woman. I did not have confidence that my husband could be an effective single parent.

Finally, I came to understand that all this hurt and infidelity had little to do with me. All marriages have problems and rough patches. My husband immaturely chose to deal with those issues in our marriage by having a very hurtful and public affair. It was his choice, not mine. I did not drive him to do it and it had to be his choice to try a better way. Even though I did not legally divorce him, I did find a way to divorce myself from his actions and see them as very separate from the person I am. As a woman, I felt guilt for a long time because my husband chose to cheat on me. However, letting go of trying to fix it for both of us freed me to become more fully who I was intended to be—a process that I have not totally conquered.

I do not love my husband as much as I once did or at least not in the same way as before. There are things I still love about him and I care about his welfare but the "throw yourself under the truck for him" kind of love is gone. I know this happens to many couples who weather the storms of their marriages and stay together for a long time. I used to think some romantic love would return after time had passed, but I am not sure about that. When I think too much about it, I realize this is sad and that it would be untenable for many people. Habits that might once have been considered endearingly annoying are just plain annoying now. Faults that one could overlook, especially with the passage of time, are not so easily forgiven. Patience and forbearance are sometimes absent. Realizing day-by-day that there is nothing I can do to control his behavior is challenging. Always being vigilant in the relationship is exhausting and it makes it hard to reveal myself to him and share the things about me that are changing with age. It makes for an uneasy partnership at times. It is not the kind of partnership I dreamed of as a young woman, but it is what it is. Recently, I was looking through pictures of our daughter when she was a toddler and marveled at our smiling faces—my husband's and mine. We still smile in pictures, but my smiles are tempered with the knowledge that he could just as easily be missing from these photos, or me. I am grateful we have been able to cobble together a relationship that, while not perfect, works for us right now.

Chapter 14

Family Traditions

Traditions are beliefs and customs that are passed on through generations. No matter who raised you or where you lived, you were parented with accumulated traditions. Each family has value systems surrounding marriage and relationships, parenting and discipline, religion and worship, holidays and food, budgets and money, family and friends, power and control.

What were the values in your family? Were you allowed to:

♦ make mistakes or did you need to be perfect;

♦ express your emotions or did you have to hide your feelings;

♦ trust yourself and others or did you trust no one;

♦ make choices or were they made for you;

♦ be yourself or do you feel the need to meet someone else's expectations?

If you were never allowed to express emotions, make mistakes or have your own preferences, dreams and talents, you may have developed the feeling that you only really mattered in relation to another person. You may not recognize your core being and will seek to feel valuable and happy through other people and experiences. With no idea of how to feel complete, you search for meaning and purpose externally. Your need to connect with something outside yourself is fueled by your inner shame.

We live with voices in our minds that repeat all the negative messages given to us by people we loved or considered important. The messages are the foundation of our internal belief system. If you feel inferior, unappealing, unworthy or flawed, it generally stems from being verbally or psychologically abused. Criticism, ridicule, rage and physical or emotional abandonment leave us empty, sad, confused and in pain. When the abuse begins at a very young age, we don't judge our parents and find them inadequate or damaging. We believe that something must be terribly wrong with us to cause the people we love and depend on to treat us badly. We carry those feelings of shame with us, often for a lifetime.

A young child is not mature enough to question his parents' competency. The child does not ask, why do you not care enough about me to:

♦ listen and not judge or criticize;
♦ notice me;
♦ play with me;
♦ provide for me;
♦ include me;
♦ not hurt me;
♦ stay with me;
♦ let me be myself;
♦ allow me to separate from you;
♦ let me be a child and not have to take care of you;
♦ love me for me instead of what I achieve?

The pain of poor parenting creates holes in our souls. We seek to ease the pain with whatever we can find to fill the hurtful spaces. Solutions take many forms: relationships, sex, drugs, alcohol, shopping, gambling, eating, the internet or any behavior which initially comforts, but can become an addiction. In order to continue feeling comforted and filled, we must indulge our negative habit in increasing increments.

We need to consume more and more to feel better. The problem is the external solutions never really fill the empty space. We simply have no concept of how to do the necessary internal work.

What kind of partner do we choose to help us feel better? Harville Hendrix, Ph.D., calls the chosen one our "imago" partner. Imago is the Latin word for image. Essentially, your imago is a composite picture of the people who influenced you most strongly at an early age. In his groundbreaking book, *Getting the Love You Want*, he explains:

> We choose our partners for two basic reasons: 1) they have both the positive and negative qualities of the people who raised us and 2) they compensate for positive parts of our being that were cut off in childhood. We enter the relationship with the unconscious assumption that our partner will become a surrogate parent and make up for all the deprivation of our childhood. All we have to do to be healed is to form a close, lasting relationship.[21]

He goes on to explain that the most powerful attraction is to our caregiver's negative traits, so we seek to feel loved, appreciated and healed by a person who treats us in many of the negative ways that our parents did. It is what we feel we deserve, and it is familiar. However, we want to mend our wounds and resolve our feelings of pain or inadequacy, and we each put our faith in a person who helps recreate our childhood feelings. We usually won't see our partner as anything like our parents until the romantic love ends. At that point, the familiar dance begins. We still may not recognize the pattern repetition, but we are hooked into staying, hoping to get our needs met.

Some of the negative patterns that are traditionally played out within families:

1. Violations of Trust
2. Favored Child
3. Anger Issues
4. Fear and Worry
5. Perfection

6. Neediness
7. No Boundaries
8. Staying or Leaving

1. Violations of Trust

There are many ways to violate our family's trust. Lying is the common element present in all trust violations. Failure to disclose information or directly not telling the truth causes a large part of the damage.

Abuse in any form damages trust, because we begin with the assumption that someone we love should not hurt us. As we experience abuse or neglect, our parent or partner may foster our belief that we deserve or cause the abuse. We blame ourselves, feeling ashamed and unsafe. If you are abused by a person who cares, how can you trust anyone else? If Dad abused Mom, your family's tradition has taught you to inflict or accept abuse.

Frederick reveals the behaviors he learned from his psychologically abusive father:

> I hated seeing my dad berate my mother. He called her terrible names and made her cry. I felt so powerless. Now look at me: When I get angry, I yell at my wife, call her names and put her down. Sometimes when I am yelling, I see my mother's face and feel so ashamed.

We often learn how to express our anger by what we saw growing up. We also may find ourselves tolerating an abusive partner when we swore it would never happen to us. Attracted to the familiar, we recreate the dynamic of our family of origin.

Addictions in families also violate trust. "I counted on you not to be drunk, spend all of our money or become a drugged-out zombie." The multigenerational nature of addictions is rooted in genetics and acceptance. We can be predetermined through our chromosomes or environment to become or to live with an addict. No one welcomes this dilemma. Remember, we are all trying to feel better and we seek what we know as a remedy.

Cheating on your partner certainly is a trust violator. There are many ways one can cheat: sexually, emotionally, economically or psychologically. You can have sex outside of your relationship; you can become too close to a person other than your spouse, thus draining the intimacy out of your marriage; you could selfishly spend your family's financial assets; you can cheat your partner out of the peace of mind they naturally deserve.

Kevin reveals how his mother's behavior influenced him both early on and in his relationships:

> I loved both of my parents. My mom doted on me. I was her favorite son. She was also very controlling, watching and commenting on everything any of us did. Dad was more remote. I understand now that he needed to distance himself from her criticism. She cheated on him with another man. I found out about it and told my dad. He was devastated. At that time, I both loved and hated her. What did I learn? Women were to be loved and feared; you better cheat on them before they cheat on you; and you can never trust a woman.

2. Favored Child

Kevin's story also demonstrates some of the difficulties experienced by being a favored child, which can become an unwelcome pivotal role in the family dynamics. Depending on the extent of the favoritism, the child can be made into a "surrogate spouse," where a parent draws a child into intimacy which is mental, emotional and may be sexual. The child is never at fault. Of course, a child wants his or her parent's love, attention and approval, but does *not* want inappropriate adult intimacy. This kind of relationship robs children of their innocence and freedom as it binds them to their parents in an unnatural way.

A parent may "spoil" any or all of his or her children by giving them most of what they want and failing to discipline. This teaches children to expect everything without having to work for it and that they can get away with any behavior without negative consequences. The child internalizes "I can have what I want and do what I want."

Amy tells what it is like to be married to "a favored child":

My husband grew up with a mother who spoiled him. She gave him everything he wanted and to her he did no wrong. Occasionally she threatened to punish him, but she never followed through. He grew up so secure in her love that he thought he could get away with anything and nothing bad would happen. He never had to behave.

When I get upset with him now, he acts like a child. He expects to be able to still be a teenager, and he tries to turn me into his mom. He will be good for a while and then want credit for good behavior: "I've been so good. How can you get mad at me? I haven't gotten drunk and stayed out all night in two months! I think I deserve to have some fun."

A former favored child may unconsciously attempt to turn his or her spouse into a parent figure. If the parent gave the person what he or she wanted, as an adult the inner child wants to recreate getting all needs met through his or her partner. When the attempt is successful, the spouse who takes on the parent role may actually try to alternatively discipline and reward his or her mate. The unhealthy dynamic creates stress and tension for both.

3. Anger Issues

As discussed previously, anger is the least accepted and most poorly communicated emotion. We simply do not know how to handle it. Abusive, raging anger causes damage to everyone: the person expressing it, the person receiving it and anyone witnessing it, particularly children.

Never seeing the healthy expression of anger can also be difficult. We never get examples of what to do or say. We can make the assumption that anger is totally unacceptable if we never see it surface: My anger must be shameful, because I've never see my parents argue.

Gerry told of how his wife's perception of her parents' relationship pervades his marriage:

She grew up with parents who only argued quietly, behind closed doors. She never saw or heard even an angry discussion.

I grew up with loud, nasty, alcoholic fighting. I tried to hide, retreating from a world that was spinning out of control.

Very early in our marriage, she got angry, went into the bedroom and slammed the door. I came after her and said in an angry, fearful, controlled voice, "I need for you to never do that again." She understood how I had grown up and what I needed. She respected that request and she had no idea of how to argue.

Thus began our emotional "niceness." Over many years, we never fought, cheating ourselves out of increasing any intimacy and eventually distancing ourselves into oblivion.

4. Fear and Worry

There is an excellent chance that a person who is fearful, anxious or worried has a parent with the same characteristics. It is hard to operate in fear. There are so many things to worry about or be afraid of. We struggle with the concept that the vast majority of things we fear are totally out of our control. We think if we worry enough we will find solutions or at least prepare ourselves in case disaster strikes.

Anxieties cause us to feel insecure and inferior, as we realize we are not effectively navigating through life's predicaments. We create our own obstacles. We believe we are inadequate and deficient. We seek what we fear we lack. We search for peace, love, security, stability and a sense of belonging and family. We fear abandonment, rejection, pain, poverty, loneliness, emptiness and death.

Although we seek security and stability, we often choose a partner who uses our insecurities against us in the heat of an argument. If he or she knows we feel inferior, he or she will seek more control by pushing our inferiority buttons.

Karin discusses her feelings of inferiority as a child and now:

I grew up poor and I hated it. It was embarrassing to live off food stamps and free lunches, when lots of other kids at school had new clothes and shoes and had neat food in lunch boxes. I worked hard to have a different life. Now I have a nice home, a good car, new clothes and plenty to eat. My husband knows I still carry inferiority feelings with me all the time. When he gets angry with me he mocks how I now live, saying, "You know you don't belong in that restaurant, club or church. You are just trying to be a social climber, but you are nothing but trash."

5. Perfection

Feelings of inferiority can occur in those of all economic classes. Dana confides hers:

My mother wanted to live in the best neighborhood, drive the best car, belong to the country club and have the perfect children. In order to be perfect, we had to look perfect. She believed in the concept "the thinner the better." As I became a teenager, she got concerned about my weight. Looking back, I was a very normal size. She told me if I lost twenty pounds, she would buy me an outfit of clothing that was very "in" at the time and very expensive. She also assured me I would become more popular if I was thin. We had just moved to a new town and I was starting a new high school. I lost the weight, got the outfit and did make lots of new friends with the "popular kids." Is it any wonder that I developed an eating disorder, anorexia, and become dangerously thin? I ended up in the doctor's office, under 100 pounds, not having had my menstrual period for a year, losing my hair and freezing cold all the time. I was trying to be pleasingly perfect and just couldn't stop. No wonder I always have a voice in the back of my head that says you can't have successful relationships unless you are thin.

The concept of needing to be perfect is carried into our relationships, as we act out our beliefs with our spouses and our children. Being perfect allows no room for mistakes, messiness or rebellion, which are all normal life experiences. Perfection puts you in a box. A feeling of shame is conveyed if you try and move out of the box.

6. Neediness

The "he needs me" chapter explains why we stay in relationships where we feel needed. Our family of origin may have validated neediness.

Family members do need each other in healthy ways, but we often learn to be dependent on our family in ways that limit our growth and development. Unhealthy neediness encourages enmeshment, where family members are so entangled with one another that they do not know how to operate independently. A family's traditions may include:

♦ calling one another numerous times every day;
♦ not being able to make a decision independently;
♦ needing approval on a regular basis;
♦ sharing all secrets;
♦ talking about one another behind people's backs to form bonds;
♦ having vacations together;
♦ having every occasion and holiday together;
♦ having to attend the same church;
♦ having to live near each other;
♦ having keys to one another's houses and coming over without calling first;
♦ frequently eating meals together.

While many of these are nice traditions, it is the degree of neediness associated with the habits that can create conflict in relationships.

7. No Boundaries

In families where there are no boundaries, people experience having absolutely no privacy. Closed doors mean nothing; they walk in on each other. Drawers, purses, wallets, cell phones, computers and cars can be examined on a regular basis. They read one another's notes, messages, diaries and journals. They even have discussions while using the bathroom. There are no boundaries where I end and you begin. There is no private space around you that no one violates. If you did not grow up in this way and you marry someone who did, you end up feeling invaded.

Paul tells of his awakening to his wife's family:

> I fell in love with her and thought her family was great. They welcomed me enthusiastically and wanted to know everything about me. I found it so cool that they were so interested in me.

My family had been pretty distant and detached. Hers was warm and close. I just never realized how close, until I married her. They are always in our business. We have no privacy. Her parents have a key to our house and they walk in whenever they want. Sometimes they don't even tell us they are coming. It drives me crazy, but she thinks it's normal. I told her I can't live like this, but she just cries and says she doesn't want to hurt their feelings.

8. Staying or Leaving

Families have values about staying or leaving a relationship. Maybe no one in your family has ever gotten divorced or you have a parent who has been married three times. Either way, it impacts how you feel about trying to hang in there or your willingness to go. It is hard to leave a relationship you have committed yourself to, even when you are being psychologically abused. If your family's tradition is to stay no matter what, you feel internal and external pressure to keep the marriage together. If you saw a parent devastated by divorce, you may seek to avoid the same experience. If you experienced the effects of divorce as a child, you may be determined not to go through it as an adult. You may work harder at staying. Or you may have seen abuse as a child and your parents stayed together. The past need not negatively influence the present and future if you make the decision that you will not live in another abusive family.

What were your family's behaviors about these qualities: trust, having a favored child, anger, fear, worry, perfection, neediness, boundaries and whether to leave or stay in a relationship?

Though our families have a profound effect on us in numerous ways, we have a choice as to how we will live our own lives and can decide whether we want to honor all of our families' traditions or consider making changes and breaking the cycle of the damaging, unhealthy dynamics. Instituting new traditions in place of dysfunctional old ones can make vast improvements.

Chapter 15

But I Love My Partner

What is love anyway? It is all very confusing, but we seek the intensity of feeling that love brings. It can be euphoric, joyous, irrational and disastrous. Millions of books, poems, songs, plays and movies have been written on the subject. We seek to understand its complexities and experience its many dimensions. Perhaps love means different things to different people in varied situations. What do men and women in abusive relationships mean when they say, "But I love the other person so much"?

Let's consider these factors:
1. Opposite Sides of the Same Coin
2. Interlocking Puzzle Pieces
3. Desire
4. Healthy Love Connections

1. Opposite Sides of the Same Coin

"Your joy is your sorrow unmasked
And the selfsame well from which your laughter rises was often filled with your tears.

And how else can it be?
The deeper that sorrow carves into your being, the more
joy you can contain."[22]

The Prophet by Kahlil Gibran

The insightful quote from *The Prophet* by Kalhil Gibran explains that
the more deeply we experience one emotion, the more fully we can potentially feel the flip side. So out of sorrow can come joy. Our pain can become
our pleasure; hatred can become love; emptiness can be filled. The passion
of hate and love are closely aligned. We can fill our emptiness and gain
enormously through our losses. Negative experiences allow us to grow.

Perhaps the intense ugliness of psychological abuse causes us to feel
almost euphoric when it is replaced by kind, loving behavior. The
ending of a nasty incident signals relief. The calm after the storm feels
peaceful, even as you survey the damage. The storm can be dramatic,
intense, exciting and disastrous; we might also find it fascinating. The
true opposite of love may be indifference. When a person says "I'm not
'in love' anymore," he or she is expressing that the initial feelings of
intense chemistry and excited attraction are gone. It is the lucky few
who maintain the "in love" feeling, and generally they have worked at
keeping it alive. Mundane routines, stresses, pressures, lack of concern
about our appearances and critical negativity toward our partners erode
the "loving" feelings. Couples who put creative positive energy into
their relationships receive the payoff of loving feelings.

Psychological abuse does not always kill the "loving" feelings.
Despising what your partner says and does may mean you don't like him
or her much, but you can still love the person. You may be furious at
how the other person treats you, but passionately want to reconnect.
You can hate and love your partner; two sides, one coin.

2. Interlocking Puzzle Pieces

Some of the most powerful "in love" connections are formed from
involvement with a person who gives us what we feel we deserve, on a

conscious or unconscious level. The bond is formed from two people tapping into each other's belief systems. Intense feelings form over the perceived miracle that this person is exactly what you need, because they help play out your life patterns. They provide what you feel entitled to have. You initially believe this person is "just right" for you; "a match made in heaven"; a "dream come true." How did you get so lucky as to find someone who understands you so well?

The balancing of unhealthy connections has an endless array of possible combinations. Like interlocking puzzle pieces, we unite with our partners and begin the power struggles that ensue as we try to get our needs met. What seemed perfect initially begins to look flawed as we notice all of his or her traits that irritate and annoy us. In turn, the person is not so enchanted with us after seeing our imperfections. We feel discouraged and begin the often relationship-long process of coercing, pleading, pushing or trying to force our partners to make us feel "happy" again.

Ironically, the connection between two people can intensify from each person having the same negative belief system. Imagine watching a two person drama where both characters are given the same theme and are asked to improvise. Each individual acts out the theme, assimilating his or her own background, past experiences and knowledge. As the two try to intimately relate, their negative beliefs cause them to thrash against each other in hurtful, harmful ways. It is bewildering for each character to be attempting to play out his or her theme and find that, in the process, he or she has clobbered the other partner. It can be surprising and unintentional at first. Gradually, it becomes more calculating and resourceful.

Next, let's look more closely at four of these themes. Remember, few people are consciously aware that they have these beliefs:

a. No one really cares about me.
b. I deserve to be punished.
c. I am worthless.
d. Everyone leaves me.

Four Inner Insecurities

a. No one really cares about me.

If you believe that no one truly loves and cares for you, it is a very lonely, isolating feeling. Some people develop tough exteriors. They build figurative walls, which prevent others from getting too close, because they don't want to experience being disappointed. Some seek to desperately connect, not allowing their partners space to breathe. They may be clingy, fearful, needy or overly accommodating. Put the isolator together with the overly clingy, accommodating person and they will go around in circles, attempting to feel loved but believing no one really cares.

b. I deserve to be punished.

If you believe, for whatever reason, that you deserve to be punished, it is an open invitation for your partner to have a field day at your expense. When both people believe this, you can witness major psychological fireworks. Like the child made to offer up his or her behind to be spanked, you both, in a sense, offer up your rear ends to each other.

Stella grew up with a mother who put her to bed at night telling her how "pure" she was. A dutiful child, she was encouraged to confess any wrong-doings and accept her mother's displeasure, disapproval and eventual forgiveness. Once, she confessed to something she didn't even do, having no idea why. Later, she understood that the dynamic of confession and forgiveness was so entrenched in their relationship that she needed to have something to confess to play out their way of relating. As Stella became a teenager, her mother wanted Stella to be popular, bringing home lots of boys to introduce and entertain. Even though she received a lot of male attention, it remained important to Stella to be pure.

Steve grew up smart, athletic, popular and rebellious. He didn't mind standing up to authority and then facing the consequences. He had a gifted older brother who seemed to be the golden boy; everything turned out right for him. Steve struggled, studied and achieved. Each time he experienced success, he believed that some part of what he had accomplished would be damaged, tarnished or taken away from him. He didn't feel he deserved to keep anything good, so he unintentionally orchestrated losing what was important to him.

Stella and Steve met after each was divorced from long marriages. They both had experienced other relationships and were ready for a serious commitment. They fell deeply in love. They each thought the other was perfect and couldn't believe how lucky they were.

What went wrong?

In an effort to be honest and have Steve know and accept her, Stella confessed things about past relationships of which she was ashamed.

Steve punished her by being critical, highly emotional and verbally abusive. He had placed Stella on a pedestal and now felt she was forever tarnished. Steve tried to not see her differently but he was consumed by thoughts of her with other men. She tried to be perfect and pleaded with him for forgiveness for her transgressions (which had occurred before they ever met).

For years, they rode a roller coaster of high-intensity connections, mixed with psychological abuse and abandonment. He tried and failed to make her pure and perfect again; she tried and failed to get complete forgiveness and acceptance.

They eventually ended this unproductive dance. But during the time they spent together, which was filled with joy and sorrow, they mastered their theme of "I deserve to be punished."

c. I am worthless.

Feeling worthless may make you welcome any attention. Even negative attention seems better than none. In fact, the abusive behavior may be what you feel you deserve. Or feeling worthless may cause you to be ugly to your partner, because it doesn't matter how he or she reacts. His or her response simply confirms what you already know: you are not worthy.

You can easily see how this merry-go-round plays out. You can either give or receive abuse and it makes sense to you. It supports your belief system. Two people with the same thought process understand each other and can settle into a life of verbal and psychological torment, continually reinforcing the theme of worthlessness and shame.

d. Everyone leaves me.

Abandonment issues run rampant in modern society. A close family member may have died. A parent may have been absent due to divorce or desertion. A partner may have cheated or left.

Coming into a relationship believing you will be abandoned may cause you to:

- build "a wall" around yourself;
- treat your partner badly, causing the other person to pull away (the self-fulfilling prophecy);
- always have someone else "on the side" so that you have another person waiting;
- leave the relationship before he/she can;
- cling, plead, threaten suicide or give dire warnings of what will happen if he/she leaves;
- try guilting or manipulating your partner into staying.

Two people who connect, both believing they will ultimately be abandoned, may use a combination of all of the above behaviors. There will always be a psychological positioning in the see-saw relationship: I'll try and keep you; I'll leave you or make sure you leave me. I will seek to be loved, and then cause what I fear the most.

3. Desire

Susan explores the strong emotions that drew her to her partner:

When I was with him, the rest of the world slipped away. No matter where we were, I felt like I was home. Our senses were heightened and everything about life seemed more focused and intense. I was aware of my body and all of my feelings: alive and very excited. I wanted to be with him in every possible way with no barriers blocking our passion. We wanted to connect and become one for as long as that could last. Nothing else mattered. If he treated me badly, I still just wanted to get back to him. I didn't want it to end; but in time, it did.

Lust, passion, yearning, fire, hunger, craving and desire; these are all ways you can feel about another person. Is it love? Not really, but these emotions often get confused. The words we use to describe desire and passion have to do with intense emotions. We seek to experience these feelings at least one time, if not frequently.

What is it that we seem to desire the most? Many men and women want someone who is:

- hard to get;
- just out of reach;
- another person's love interest;
- popular;
- distant or detached;
- a challenge;
- ambivalent;
- physically attractive;
- sexually appealing;
- mysterious.

Often the guy who is a "jerk" or the girl who is a "bitch" embodies the characteristics just cited. We may not find ourselves attracted to someone who is simply nice, available, kind and enthusiastic, even though our minds tell us that person could be a good choice. Instead, our hearts flutter for the people who are mean, detached, arrogant and unimpressed with our interest toward them. Instead of choosing the security of a person who is devoted to you, you choose the experience of possibly unfulfilled desire.

Loving another person more than the person who appears to love you creates a powerful longing. The craving intensifies your desire. The object of your passion seems extremely important and valuable. We want the person who is hard to get and the struggle reinforces our conviction that this union would meet our deepest needs.

If you think your partner has more feeling for you than you do for him or her, you may feel secure. Have you ever taken someone for granted until the person got fed up and left, only to discover how much that person really meant to you? Your desire increased with their departure. What was plentiful became scarce and therefore more valuable.

4. Healthy Love Connections

There are some basic qualities and behaviors you need to have a healthy love connection. It is rare that each partner has mastered these things. Your self is always a work in progress.

♦ Know you are whole all by yourself.

Your partner cannot make you whole. It may feel like he or she does at first, but then you are angry, scared and frustrated when that sense of completion doesn't continue. You are a unique, fine, exquisite creation and you are complete as you are. You simply may not understand that yet. Life is a spiritual journey where you are forever changing and developing. Find your peace within the miracle that is you.

♦ Seek a partner you can respect, trust, admire and genuinely like.

Coping with and going through life with a person you feel this way about is a truly pleasurable experience. There is no room for fear, jealousy, suspicion and hatred when you choose a partner who has these qualities.

◆ Show love by word and deed.

Convey your love for your partner in the way you speak and behave. Allow yourself to give and receive. Demonstrate caring by doing the things that matter to the other person. Don't assume you know what matters to them; ask.

◆ Have a sense of humor.

Through the good and the bad, life's mysteries are best handled with a sense of humor. Laughter is medicine for the body and soul as well as the relationship's health. Don't turn the small stuff into big issues.

◆ Practice gratitude and appreciation.

Celebrate life each day by acknowledging what you are thankful for. Say it out loud or write it down. Appreciate that you and your partner are unique and the differences between you can enrich your relationship.

◆ Want what is best for the other person.

Do not try to control, take way from or diminish your partner. Allow your partner to be him or her self. Free yourself from jealously. Be your partner's cheerleader and promoter. If he or she truly loves you, his or her desires will not be harmful to you.

◆ Practice forgiveness every day.

Forgive yourself and your partner. This does *not* mean you tolerate abusive behavior! Healthy couples have many things to forgive and let go of. They clean the slate. They do not harbor resentments. It is a gift you give yourself and your loved ones to forgive, learn from your experiences and then move on.

If you feel you are "in love" with a person who psychologically abuses you, ask yourself:

◆ How do I feel about myself in this relationship?

◆ Do I feel I deserve the way he or she treats me?

◆ Do I believe that I am worthless or that no one really cares about me?

- Am I afraid he or she will leave me?
- Do I like and respect him or her?
- Can I imagine feeling whole and complete on my own?

Part III

Why We Leave

Chapter 16

The Last Straw

So why does a person finally leave a psychologically abusive relationship? The most common reason is that the receiver of psychological abuse simply cannot take it anymore. This thought may come as the result of a major disaster or a relatively minor occurrence that becomes the last straw. Most couples in psychologically abusive relationships layer the trauma, anger, sadness and frustration and never clean the slate by working through their issues. Even if apologies are made, there is rarely complete forgiveness and each incident is piled on top of the other occurrences. Over time, a huge pile of bad memories accumulates. The residual effect of the layered abuse is that positive, loving feelings gradually die and there is little strength or energy to hold that huge suitcase full of transgressions and keep going. One person loses hope, loses love, loses faith in the spouse and their union.

Larry and Linda's story shows how one partner finally reaches the final decision:

Larry and Linda entered their marriage, the second for both of them, passionately loving each other and united with the hope of compatibly blending their goals and families. Each had a sincere desire to enhance the partner's life. Although Larry loved Linda completely, he was hot tempered and jealous. Linda loved his positive, affectionate, supportive, humorous, intelligent, nurturing side. Unfortunately, this was offset by nasty name-calling, vicious mind games and a temper that erupted without any warning. She often thought of the line from the nursery rhyme, "When he was good, he was very good; but when he was bad, he was horrid."

As time went on, Linda just wanted to keep the good and get rid of the bad. She kept thinking things would change. They went to counseling. They renewed their vows. But the psychological abuse resurfaced and wore her down. Each time he moved out, she eventually took him back. This happened three different times! She couldn't imagine going through a second divorce. He had helped her with her kids, her career, her finances, her home and her parents. If she was honest, his bad boy side excited her and sexually he fulfilled lots of her un-met needs. But that same bad boy cursed her. He built her up only to tear her down.

A trip to the grocery store proved to be the last straw. By agreement, Linda bought the food for the household, since her teenage children were often at home. She had asked her kids what they wanted purchased for school lunches. As Linda and Larry entered the store, Linda and he headed for the delicatessen counter to order the requested sliced turkey. Larry began arguing with her that pre-packaged turkey was cheaper. Linda said she wanted to buy what the children liked. Enraged at her for not taking his suggestion, Larry yelled, "Fuck you," left the store and walked several miles home. Linda was stunned and humiliated as a woman, frying up sausages for customers to sample, sympathetically looked over at her.

Linda quickly exited the store and sat quietly in her car for a long time before returning home. A sense of peace came to her as she realized that as much as she still loved Larry, she simply could not take the abuse anymore. She actually felt relieved, and this time when he packed up to leave, her heart let him go.

In the scheme of other, even more hurtful psychological abusive behavior, a yelled "fuck you" in a grocery store appears relatively minor. However, one small event can be the last straw. Often partners wonder how they will recognize "the end." Some say that the time to go is the very first red flag, that there should be no second chances. However, when you love someone, that is difficult to do.

It does not matter how many people in your life have told you to leave your relationship and that you deserve a life free from abuse. Personal tolerance levels for your partner and his or her behavior determine when you leave. The encouragement of family and friends may give you the strength and confidence to make a change. Being able to relinquish or end the relationship hinges on your awareness of being finished. "I can't take it anymore" can be a desperate, frantic, urgent feeling; or it can be a peaceful, calm, tranquil knowing. Often, it is the calm feeling that allows a person to know he or she is truly done with the relationship. Each person, in his or her own time, recognizes when it is time to end the union. The negatives finally outweigh the positives. There aren't enough valid reasons left to stay. A partner's pleading, threats, promises or manipulations stop having meaning or resonating as believable. Exhaustion sets in. A person becomes too weary to care.

The exhaustion and weariness are often a result of the depletion of a person's core spiritual self. Continuous abuse drains our ability to feel any peace or find meaning in our lives. We feel fragmented. We can't seem to make simple choices or decisions without feeling confused or uncertain. Accomplishing anything productive seems overwhelming and unattainable. The relationship stops making sense. Fearing the loss of our essence, our inner self resonates within, guiding us to leave.

Jon's realization that he had to leave was gradual as his self-awareness grew:

Brittany constantly berated Jon. According to her, he never did anything right. He used to love to make her happy, but had given up trying, because it was impossible. Brittany was like a drill sergeant, handing out orders, calling him names and criticizing his performance. He could never do enough or measure up. It was hard to remember that they used to spend afternoons making love, then talking and laughing while cooking dinner together. Where had that woman gone? He hardly knew her. He'd become a slave to his unkind master. Deafness began to set in. Jon stopped hearing her demands and started listening to his inner voice that simply gave permission: *Run. You don't have to stay. There is another life for you. Go now.*

Loving someone should not require extreme endurance for bad behavior. Both partners can expect forgiveness for a fair amount of transgressions, but abusive behavior tests our limits. At some point, it is not worth the effort. A person should not be expected to have an endless capacity for being hurt.

Unfortunately, some people do not pay attention to the pleas of their partners:

- Please, let's work on our relationship.
- Can we go to counseling?
- I'm not sure how much longer I can keep doing this.
- I'm worn out.
- I need a break from you.
- Let's separate for a while.

If the psychological abuser is honest, that person could have seen the end coming. There were lots of warning signs and requests to fix the problems. He or she neglected to pay attention. The partner's detachment signaled gradual, then finally complete disengagement, not because he or she ever wanted to end the relationship, but because the receiver of the psychological abuse couldn't take it anymore.

Chapter 17

Final Temptation

In a letter to her spouse, Joelle describes their dysfunctional relationship of which she was, for so long, a part:

So many wasted days. We sit in silence, pass each other without acknowledgment, sleep in the same bed without touching. I'm being punished, or at least it feels that way. You are feeling sorry for yourself, sitting in a stupor, moping, pouting or simply needing to shut me out.

We can't resolve much of anything when we talk. I get frustrated and become critical. You refuse to talk, look at me or even be in the same room if you can help it. How long will it continue? A day, a week, maybe a month. So much wasted time.

I get busy. I take care of things that need to be done. I turn to my family and friends. I make plans without you. I don't know what else to do but to become as self-sufficient as possible. I try not to waste any days in my personal life, but this is a waste of a relationship. There is so much we could share that we miss.

The silence is deafening. When you are not in the house, the tension is gone and the silence is welcome and peaceful. How sad that being alone feels better than being together. You won't initiate a solution, an apology or a productive discussion. You will freeze me out until you are ready to resume compatibility. I am not allowed to be the one to decide when a thawing can begin. So I wait or I go to you, only to be shut out again. So many wasted days. I think I deserve more than this. I need someone to show he really cares about me.

When a person feels profoundly neglected or abused, he or she may be vulnerable to a new person who shows the hurt individual kind attention. The courage to walk out and stay gone is often as a result of meeting someone new. What we haven't been able to do for ourselves, we may accomplish when another person is waiting for us. While a new man or woman may not be a healthy reason to leave, the new person can be a powerful motivator.

There are many types of temptations:
1. The friend and soul mate
2. The lover you've never had
3. The helper/protector who empathizes about your psychologically abusive situation
4. The same person in a different package
5. The married man or woman
6. A same sex partner

1. The friend and soul mate
It seemed so innocent. He or she started out as a friend. Maybe you met the person at work, in your neighborhood, at the gymnasium, at church, on a committee, through a friend or in some other activity. You had common interests and began talking about simple things. The person seemed genuinely attentive and concerned about things that also mattered to you. He or she really listened. You looked forward to

opportunities to get to know the person better. Each time you were together, you were increasingly attracted. Over time, the friendship developed and you opened up about the problems in your personal life. You felt safe talking about the dysfunction. The person, in turn, shared information about his or her own life. You felt validated and connected. When you spent time with the new person, you simultaneously felt happy and peaceful. He or she seemed to be the soul mate you'd always wanted. You both felt understood, cherished and appreciated.

Friendships that develop into love can have a very strong foundation for change. If you get to know someone without any sexual involvement, you form the connection without all of the brain-altering chemistry clouding your judgment. As the bonding intensifies, you compare the new person to your current mate. The desire to be really known and loved is enormous. You feel you have found the perfect fit; you want the best for each other.

2. The lover you've never had

Since women reach the peak of sexual desire much later than men, women often aren't completely attentive to or knowledgeable about their sexual needs or abilities. There may be so many other priorities in women's thoughts that they don't worry about not having much desire, responsiveness or pleasure. Perhaps some women had little or no experiences before their current partners, so they accept the intimate connections they get. It's all they know. Maybe some women grew up hearing negative comments about having or wanting sex, which led them to suppress natural instincts. If they were told, "Men are like dogs, they just need to do it every once in a while" or "Nice girls don't really enjoy sex," they were probably confused by these messages. However, somewhere along the line, many sexually unsatisfied women figure out that some couples are experiencing fireworks. By just looking at a magazine rack, you will see that information about how to have a fantastic sex life is readily available.

What happens to a man or woman who ends up in an affair where the person has amazingly good sexual experiences? The person realizes what he or she has been missing. The body chemistry leaves the person feeling powerfully connected to the new lover. The partner in a dysfunctional relationship may wonder why he or she is settling for less.

Some scenarios are gripping:

The current partner is:	The new lover is:
uneducated or thoughtless	skillful and considerate
critical and judgmental	affirming and accepting
disrespectful or perverse	kind and caring
rushed and self-centered	lingering and giving
uninterested	very into the new relationship
obsessive	matched to your desire

Being in-sync with a partner where you relax and let go is a fulfilling feeling. If you find yourself having intense orgasms with someone else, when your old partner was never concerned about your experience, you naturally gravitate toward the new lover.

3. The helper/protector who empathizes about your psychologically abusive situation

The person who understands the partnership problems in your life, feels sympathetic and wants to help you seems to bring light and hope. If he or she wants to protect and defend you, you may choose to let him or her do so. If he or she takes the time and effort to truly understand all the other person's fears and concerns and shows a willingness to help, the psychologically abused partner feels grateful and appreciative.

The helper/protector can be a person who:

- ◆ listens;
- ◆ helps you sort through your concerns;
- ◆ gives or lends you money;
- ◆ provides help with moving or a place to stay;
- ◆ gives good suggestions and referrals;
- ◆ cares about your children;

- offers physical protection;
- confronts the psychologically abusive mate if necessary.

Some women who are frightened, for instance, seek out partners they feel can shield them from harm and assist them in leaving. If the new lover expresses outrage at what the abused person has lived through, it validates his or her decision to leave. If the new lover is incensed by how the abused partner has been treated, the lover appears safe to trust. The new lover's strength and concern help a psychologically abused person escape his or her abusive relationship and plan a new beginning.

4. The same person in a different package

This new person seemed so totally different from your ex, but darn it if you didn't fall for exactly the same type. If your initial chemistry was intense with your current partner and it feels remarkably similar with the new lover, take a long hard look at the new relationship. If you have never figured out why you were attracted to your abusive mate, you may not recognize repetition.

We can feel enormous attraction for
- what is familiar to us;
- what we feel we deserve;
- the struggle to meet our unmet needs;
- a challenge;
- anything that makes life easier or more pleasurable.

It is ironic to leave one man or woman for his or her fraternal twin. Nevertheless, it happens with amazing frequency. We don't do it intentionally and we are not amused when we discover our dilemma.

5. The married man

An affair with a married man or woman often begins with the premise that both people will have the same desire for caution and secrecy. It may feel safer, because you convince yourself that you don't expect him to leave his wife or her to leave her husband and feel he or she won't put any pressure on you. Believing you can prevent falling completely in love, you set out to just meet some of your needs for sympathy, companionship and/or sex "on the side."

Time goes by and women especially have a difficult time making love without feeling love. He or she begins to seem so perfect as compared to your psychologically abusive spouse. You think his wife or her husband just doesn't appreciate or adequately meet the person's needs. You fantasize trading places. He or she may be ready to leave the current mate or may say that it will happen someday but he or she can't just yet; besides you are married too. Wanting to be available for the new lover or fear of being charged with adultery can make some leave a psychologically abusive relationship. The new lover may never exit his or her own marriage, but he or she can be the final reason for the ending of your own dysfunctional union.

6. A same sex partner

In an increasing number of cases, a person may leave a current union for a same sex partner. Men and women can be in a marriage, because it was expected of them by their family, friends, culture, church, society and laws, but they are not really interested in, attracted to or in love with the person of the opposite sex. They can feel trapped and miserable. Their disinterest and/or disdain for their spouses cause great psychological pain, particularly when their partners have no idea of the other person's real sexual identity.

However, in other cases where the heterosexual partner is aware or suspects the other person's homosexuality, leaving for a same sex partner can be a relief to each person in the marriage. Many things from the past seem to fall into place and make sense. Each faces a struggle as he or she goes forward, dealing with the reactions of family and community. Prejudices and criticism can be strong. But for those facing the realities of their real sexual identities, the struggle can be worth the effort.

Affairs, by their very natures, have time constraints. The secret stolen moments seem precious and can be powerfully intense. The other person may seem so idyllic after being married to a psychologically abusive spouse. Finding someone new when you've endured psychological abuse can motivate one to do what is necessary to get away. We may not realize what we are doing, but we seek some sort of relief from the loneliness, neglect and fear of our abusive relationship.

Reasons for choosing a new relationship when you've been psychologically abused:

♦ The relationship gives you courage you didn't have before. You feel loved and validated. You know there is something better than your dysfunctional union out there, because you are experiencing it. If you leave now you won't have to be lonely.

♦ He or she gives you an ultimatum: leave the psychological abuser or I'm gone. The new lover may do this because he or she wants to be with you, feels guilty or afraid or because the new person is truly concerned about you and can't bear to watch the cruelty you are dealing with.

♦ You want the opportunity of a future with the new person. You believe he or she is the man or woman you want to spend the rest of your life with.

A note of caution: leaving for your love interest does not mean you will end up with that person. They may truly be your "transition person"—the one who helped you segue out of your dysfunctional marriage or relationship.

An affair does not provide the complete picture of what it is like to openly date or live with your new lover. It is impossible to view him or her accurately. Both people have bad habits and flaws they have minimized during the shared brief encounters. In addition, trust is usually a problem because you each have intimate knowledge of the lengths you both went to in order to see each other. If a new lover can cheat on his or her current partner, he or she could do it to you.

As your dysfunctional marriage or his marriage begins to unravel, nasty divorce issues may impact your new relationship, as may accusations and the battles of separation and settlements. Often you will hear your new lover or someone else explain what the ex says. You may think the other man or woman is crazy, unfair, just doesn't understand your lover or doesn't share the love for the person as you do. Be cautious.

If you and your new love remain together after your divorce, the real work of your new relationship begins after all the outside interference dies down. At that point, the two of you can begin to really see each other more clearly and decide if you want to continue your path together.

Chapter 18

Lost the Love

At some point when you're psychologically abused, you may totally lose loving feelings. This can be a reason to go. This is very different from not being "in love" anymore. It is not the same as the loss of the excited enthusiasm and chemistry you experienced during the early stages of a relationship. It is natural for the "in love" feelings to lessen or die. As the relationship goes on, you may lose the ability to love your partner, meaning because of the interrogations, punishment, power and other mind games, you have become indifferent to your partner, not as a person maybe, but as your mate.

Vickie looks back on her painful dysfunctional relationships:

When did I stop loving him? I am certain that I did love him intensely at first. By tiny millimeters over time, love died due to neglect, abuse, anger, sorrow, loneliness and, at times, even pity. I stopped respecting him as a person and I stopped caring about him as a man.

We killed it. He didn't act alone. I participated in the disaster we made of our relationship. We kept picking away at it, playing mind games until nothing was left. Along the way there were some good times, but they are almost non-existent now.

This happens over time, usually in small increments that are virtually immeasurable when they are happening. The causes are both large and small, major and minor, passive and aggressive, psychologically abusive and neglectful. You may not see the end coming or you may realize what is occurring. You may ignore the signs or beg your partner to pay attention and work on the relationship with you but get no response, anger or more games.

Once the love actually dies, it is usually not revivable. It is the one thing that therapy cannot fix. Some people may think their love has died, only to find it is buried under a mound of hurt, frustration, disappointment and pain. Clearing out those layered resentments may uncover positive feelings that still exist. You can't know for sure until you work on it.

Many women and men report experiencing defining moments at the end of their relationships that signaled the finality of their situations. Some examples of these defining moments are:

- Feeling indifferent to what he does, where he goes or who he is with.
- Not wanting to go anywhere with him or her.
- No desire to buy him or her a card or gift for an anniversary or other occasion.
- Avoidance of family events or being in family photographs.
- Lack of interest in anything involving the other person.
- Total detachment during sex or no sex at all.
- Fantasizing about him meeting someone else so he or she will want the separation.
- Realizing you are simply going through the motions of having a relationship with him or her.
- Complete lack of enthusiasm for working on the relationship.

Psychologically abusing or ignoring a person whom you love distances him or her from you. The abused partner protects his or her mind, emotions and spirit by withdrawing as much as possible from your behavior. The instinct is either to fight back or flee. One mental way to flee is to pretend it doesn't matter. Shutting down and toughening up are ways to believe you don't care. If you think and feel that you don't care often and long enough, it will begin to be true. Changing your thoughts about a person can change your feelings toward him or her. Self-defense can kill the love.

Rachel quietly conveys her inner emotions toward her husband:

At times, I absolutely hated Rob. We would be having a perfectly wonderful time together and then something changed. He became angry, nasty and abusive. At times, I could even figure out why. Everything had to be about him. He justified all of his actions and criticized me. I was the bitch. He was perfectly logical and reasonable. I was sick of his mood swings, sick of being called names, sick of never quite knowing with what I would be dealing. One minute he was kind and loving, the next he was a monster.

If I closely analyzed it, the kind and loving behavior was always on his terms. As long as he was getting what he wanted, things were fine. Otherwise he was spiteful and childish and self-centered. As long as he could feel like the good guy, Rob justified his selfish behavior. If he did something for me it was on his terms. If he bought me something, it was what he wanted me to have. If he ever asked me what I wanted, he ignored my responses if they were not what he wanted to do. I couldn't stand the pain of his breaking me down one more time. I hated responding to the passive-aggressive ways he pushed my buttons, then acted so innocent and self-righteous.

I really felt Rob was mentally ill. Thinking that didn't help much, because I lived with him and he refused to take medication. If I expressed not liking something he said or did, he would do it more often, because he knew it bothered me. It was a sick game. "Oh, you don't like being called a bitch? Then I'll call you a bitch anytime I want to. Oh, you want to keep the

kitchen tidy; I'll be sure and pile up my things to irritate you. I
see that you enjoy spending time with the children; I'll create a
distraction so that you have to pay attention to me. I know you
enjoy holidays, so I'll pick a fight to spoil the occasion."
Gradually, I gave up. I lost hope. I stopped caring. I
withdrew emotionally. I went through the motions of daily life.
I went to work, took care of the children, the dog, the house. I
saw my friends, read books and occasionally enjoyed an
entertaining television program or movie. The feelings of
hatred turned into indifference. It was a horrible way to live.
Just going through the motions of life, day after day.

As love slowly dies, many people will begin the grieving process. At
first you may deny or ignore the feelings of indifference, but you may live
this way for years gradually realizing what is happening. You didn't choose
for this to happen and it may be a very unwelcome experience. As time
goes on, you begin to accept the situation and feel a multitude of
emotions. You can feel sad at your loss, angry with the other partner for
his actions and not responding to your requests to work on it. You may
feel guilty and blame yourself for any of your own behavior that you are
ashamed of. You may also feel helpless, frightened and lonely. Many
people experience physical symptoms during grief and loss. The stress and
worry affect their bodies and resistance. Tension creates exhaustion,
feeling sick, lack of energy, inability to sleep well or wanting to sleep
all the time. You may lose or gain weight. You may feel exhausted and
have depression set in. You are unable to make good decisions and may
become confused, preoccupied and have a lack of interest in your normal
daily activities.

As you encounter any of these symptoms, you may see your medical
doctor for a checkup and be evaluated for medication. You may try
counseling. You seek solutions as you are trying to feel better. For some
people, the solution they choose is to leave their relationships. If this
becomes your choice, you may already have progressed through much of
the grieving process. If your partner did not see the end of the relationship

coming, he or she may be shocked at the calm conviction and strength you use in your decision making. The other person may never have noticed or cared about what you have been going through to get to this point. You may still care about your partner as a person. You may or may not value that person as the father or mother of your children. You may or may not wish him or her well going forward in his or her life. You may or may not be willing to go to separation counseling to help the other person understand what happened. It can be an opportunity for both of you to grow and learn. He or she may beg you to reconsider, not understanding that it is too late for you, because you have lost the love you once felt.

Harriet's story reveals the effects of one partner realizing he or she no longer has feelings for the other partner:

"I don't mean for this to hurt your feelings, but I don't think I ever really loved you," he said.

She had learned that statements beginning by someone saying they didn't want to hurt you generally meant they were going to. This did hurt. They had spent twenty years together. What did he mean by saying he didn't love her? She thought back to the beginning. They were just teenagers, enjoying high school successes, friends, dances and young love. Throughout college, they were anxious and excited to see each other on weekends and holidays. She wrote him long letters; he wrote her love poems. They talked and dreamed and planned a life together.

Picture-perfect wedding, career, home, kids and friends; they made all the dreams come true. He immersed myself in his career; she kept busy with family, friends, volunteering and eventually a job. Along the way they both stonewalled, isolated and tried to control each other and they drifted apart. She was the first to realize the mind games they were playing and begged him to pay attention to what they were destroying. He didn't and eventually they were left with only co-parenting.

Years later, he found a deep, meaningful adult love with his next wife. The intensity of that new connection left him feeling that he had never really loved anyone else.

We love people in our lives with the knowledge, experience and capacities we possess at that time. Our ability to connect is influenced by age, environment, insight, spiritual depth and maturity. We must ask ourselves, are we choosing a partner from a healthy peaceful center or a desperate, needy, clingy place? Have you ever decided on a spouse based on:

- seeing everyone else your age getting married;
- wanting to be a parent;
- harboring the fear of ending up alone;
- feeling pressure from your family;
- needing to legitimize a sexual relationship or pregnancy;
- desiring the other's assets, status or position;
- loving the other person's family;
- seeming to be an appropriate match?

A mate can come along at a time in our lives when we feel ready for the experience of love and marriage. Perhaps we have never fallen in love before, or we have and were deeply hurt by that person's actions. Safe or logical choices pop up and we convince ourselves that we can make it work. We may know we are settling, but the "bird in the hand" seems like an acceptable arrangement. Some couples make this work; others feel they have sold themselves short.

- I knew I was making a mistake when I was walking down the aisle, but I felt I had to go through with it.
- Even on the honeymoon, she criticized and irritated me.
- We were like impolite strangers trying to figure out how to live together.
- I couldn't bear the way he set traps for me and constantly watched me so I could never relax.
- She was such a nag. She picked on my table manners, my unfashionable clothes, my love making. I found myself taking every opportunity to get out of the house and spend time with my friends.

As you begin to come to grips with your psychologically abusive relationship and look back, it is hard to determine if your choices and decisions were made out of love. At the time you become involved in a relationship, you may believe it is love or know you are settling to get other things you want. Your gut may tell you more than your thoughts or emotions. The answer to whether you really truly love your partner can often be found in your "gut feeling." Stop analyzing or riding a wave of emotion. Settle into a quiet, peaceful place and your core self will give you the knowledge you are seeking. Simply be still and pay attention. What you need to know is there for you to see.

Losing the love for your psychologically abusive partner is a common reason to leave. As you grow, change and mature, you may choose not to remain with a person you can no longer love.

Chapter 19

Protecting Kids and Pets

I have heard some alarming accounts of psychologically abusive relationships which have become increasingly violent.

Nancy told a shocking story:
> My husband screamed at our pet and threatened to kill me. Somehow, I was able to get to the car and drive away. Hours later, when I came back home, my sweet golden retriever could not get up to greet me. Thousands of dollars in veterinary bills later, I took my dog and went to a friend's house. I never went back home. All those years of taking his abusive mind games and I finally left, because of the dog.

Sometimes threats against one's children or family pets may be the reason you finally leave a psychologically abusive relationship. What you had not previously been willing to do for yourself, you will do for them. Consider the same three topics as in chapter 8, this time in reverse order:

1. Well-being
2. Emotional Consequences
3. Practical Matters

1. Well-being

Physical safety is the first thing many people think of when they consider leaving. Perhaps you have seen your partner turn on your child in anger or you know your partner considers your pets dispensable, so he or she uses threats against them to demonstrate his or her capacity for torture and violence.

Psychological safety is equally important. Criticism, name-calling and mind games damage self-esteem. Threatening and terrorizing can become permanently implanted messages in children's minds. Seeing your child's head hung down in shame as your spouse berates him or her may motivate you to provide safety from the mental torture. Children are also deeply affected by seeing a beloved pet injured or killed. The trauma leaves deep psychological scars.

Keith discusses the animal abuse he saw as a child:

> I saw my father torture my dog that I dearly loved. He thought it was funny to tie her up and hang her so her feet couldn't touch the ground. Then he burned her with matches or prodded her with a stick. He punished me if I cried. I'll never get the images out of my head. I hate him to this day for what I saw him do. I was terrified of him and now I view him as a sick son-of-a-bitch who was never much of a man.

2. Emotional Consequences

Ann tells her fears:

> I overheard my teenage son talk to his girlfriend exactly the way his father talks to me. What kind of legacy are we leaving him?

It is not uncommon for children to identify with and emulate the dominant aggressive parent. They may hate what they see and hear, but still copy the abusive behavior. It is often less frightening to seek control of the relationship in order to feel powerful. The less abusive parent may be observed as the one getting hurt, so a child may choose what he or she views as the least vulnerable position. Children can also become verbally and physically aggressive as a result of the confusion and anger they feel over witnessing psychological abuse. At each developmental stage, abuse interferes with a child's ability to make normal progress.

If you leave your relationship, your children need age-appropriate information. Patience and tolerance are necessary. How you initially explain the separation and divorce influences children's emotional reactions. Tell your child:

This divorce is not your fault. You cannot control what is happening now. You did nothing to cause this and there is nothing you can do to get us back together. Your wishes will be taken into account wherever possible; however, adults are responsible for making unpleasant choices and decisions. You are not expected to take sides, and we want you to love us both. It's okay to feel angry, sad, guilty, hurt…

This conversation can also include any of the plans you have made that will involve them. Naturally, they will be confused and insecure and will want to know what your decisions mean for their lives. Allow them to ask questions. You won't have all the answers but assure the children you will provide information as you gain it.

Children should not be burdened with adult anger and confusion as you sort through your life changes. You may be emotionally depleted and physically exhausted, but your children should not be taking care of you or listening to your personal adult feelings. It is difficult not to talk badly about an abusive mate. Remember he or she is still your children's parent. Your children know a lot already about what has happened in the home and don't need more anger to deal with as they try to cope. They should be free to love both parents. Work toward increasing their sense of security.

It is vital to establish open, honest communication with your children. They should not be asked to lie about anything. They also should not be asked to pass messages or money from one parent to another. They do not need to be in the middle. Good communication requires attentive listening skills and appropriately handling upsetting information. Your children need to believe that you are a safe person to talk to and that you will help protect them. If they are being abused, you want them to be able to tell you, so that you can take the proper action. Seek professional help when you are unsure of what to do.

Blended families have challenges. The children have already gone through one divorce and if they are thrown into a new relationship with a stepparent and new stepsiblings, the adjustment is difficult. Any negative dynamics that develop in a blended family intensify the need to escape to protect yourself and your children.

Kelly reveals her own dysfunctional relationship:

> I thought we were going to be a perfect stepfamily. Boy was I wrong. We all seemed to have fun together when Clark and I were dating. However, once we were married and making a home with each other, things changed.
>
> Clark's ex-wife hated me, blaming me for their breakup. She constantly said nasty things about me to her kids. I couldn't really defend myself, because his kids always clammed up and didn't want to talk about it. It was his youngest child who repeated things without really understanding what he was saying. His older boy was sullen and critical of me and his daughter was haughty and sarcastic. His older two kids teased my two in ways that drove me crazy. His son called my daughter fat and told my son he was stupid, gay and uncoordinated.
>
> Clark seemed oblivious to what was happening. When I tried to talk to him about it, he defended his kids, saying they had gone through a hard time. He didn't want me correcting them. He felt they already had two parents and didn't need a third.
>
> He also gave his kids preferential treatment. He did fun things with them, excluding my kids. He thought it was normal

to have individual outings, but my two felt left out. We kept our money separate and he saw nothing wrong with giving his three kids extravagant gifts at Christmas and birthdays, while my two got the more meager presents I could afford. He said that my kids' dad would give them the things they wanted. I didn't think it felt good to them to see his kids opening gifts they would love to have gotten. Of course, Clark also didn't expect his kids to share, which they never did.

My son started wetting the bed. His grades suffered and his teachers said he was having trouble paying attention in class. He asked if he could quit his baseball team, saying he just wasn't interested in it anymore. He was losing all of his confidence.

My daughter became a bully at school, picking on both girls and boys. She was very aggressive, starting physical fights and getting suspended from school.

I again tried to talk with Clark. He said he was sorry, but felt it was clearly my problem with which to deal. He continued to see his three offspring as perfect angels. He refused to go to family or couples counseling. Even though I still loved him, I eventually left to take care of my hurting children.

3. Practical Matters

There are many practical matters to consider during a separation and divorce. If your partner is psychologically controlling and abusive, it is unlikely that he or she will suddenly be generous or cooperative. It is more likely that your partner will be destructive, threatening, unpredictable and protective of everything that person considers his or her own. He or she may fight with you about custody, visitation, child support, housing and possessions.

Remember, you can control only you and you probably need an attorney and counseling to help navigate these rough waters. If you feel that your children are likely to be abused or exposed to inappropriate people or activities when they are with your partner, talk to your attorney about your concerns. Supervised visitation is an option in these cases.

Your children are more likely to adjust and heal if you do your best to follow any of these suggestions:

- Do your own healing work so that you aren't holding on to your ex-spouse through your fear, anger and bitterness. Your children will notice it.
- Reduce the amount of conflict between you and your ex by refusing to participate in provocative arguments or situations.
- Find some new, healthy activities and friends for yourself and your children.
- Communicate with your children, their teachers and concerned counselors who can help.
- Give your children new age-appropriate, manageable tasks and responsibilities, which help them feel more accomplished and in control.
- Discipline in a healthy way. Do not stop expecting children to behave well because they are experiencing turmoil. It is vital to encourage them to express their feelings and thoughts, as their acting out behavior is often the result of unresolved feelings.
- Develop a support system. Do not expect your children to fill your needs. As you start to date again, realize that your children may be uncomfortable and anxious about what that means. Do not expect them to share your excitement about a new person and do not ask them to lie. Taking things very slowly helps everyone involved. Try to expose your children to good role models with healthy outlooks on life.
- Seek people and activities that will help your children develop confidence, have a spiritual foundation, establish good self-esteem and appreciate the blessings in their lives.

Chapter 20

Psychological Torture

You know if your partner is cruel by watching the way he or she interacts with the world around him or her. Does the person hurt others, just because he or she can? Does your partner seem vicious or inhuman to you, your children or your pets? Does your spouse seem pleased or amused by his or her own sick actions? The man or woman who randomly creates pain for any living thing is indeed a frightening person. At first, the behavior may be hidden from you. Then, you may see or experience things that seem unreal. You may attempt to convince yourself that surely you were wrong or misunderstood. Eventually, you can't deny what is happening and you know that staying with your partner appears to sanction the person's behavior. If he or she seems savage and inhuman, trust your gut that this is not a safe person.

Damaged and dangerous, such partners coldly calculate how to dismantle your sanity and control you completely. If you live with a person attempting to control your mind, you can eventually become a human robot or feel as if you are absolutely crazy. Some people are so damaged that they enjoy creating a torturous environment for their partners. It's like a game, played out for control or to watch the decomposition and destruction of another person. The game starts with small tactics and escalates into more serious threatening behavior. If this sounds scary and unsolvable, you are right.

It may start innocently enough, even seem fun at first. Alcohol, drugs, sex, gambling, shopping, food, internet games or thrill-seeking can initially be very pleasurable. No one intends to become addicted. If your partner is drawing you into his or her addiction, you eventually may need to escape to survive. It often takes some time to understand that you have entered a situation where you are losing control and are not making good choices. What appears harmless and enjoyable becomes destructive.

Jill reveals her frightening story:

I met him when I was newly divorced. I had tried to do everything right to be a good wife and keep my marriage together. Nothing had worked. After the marriage fell apart, I developed a "what the hell" attitude.

Randy came along with summer, sunny beaches and way too much alcohol. Life centered around feeling good. Sex had never been so exciting and dangerous. He introduced me to new adventures and I welcomed each new experience. I learned that my body could feel things I never thought possible. I was fascinated by a whole new world. There was always a party somewhere.

After about six months, I began to realize that Randy always needed to escalate the risk-taking. If there was nothing new to fascinate him, he got bored. I, too, was hooked on the adrenaline rush and the pleasure. I didn't want to lose him, so I went wherever he led me.

Looking back, I feel like I fell into a dark hole of seduction and perversity. He loved pornography. I was initially fascinated by viewing the naked girl with high heels and large breasts on the screen, who continuously made pleasurable sounds while a well-endowed male plowed into all the spaces on her body. It wasn't a turn-on for me; it was more of a curiosity. Later, I found those movies boring, tedious and sickening, while Randy loved watching them. He wanted me to duplicate the things we saw. I went through the motions with no feelings of intimacy.

There always seemed to be something new he wanted to try—the riskier the better. It wasn't about making love; it was about danger, excitement or the challenge of convincing me to try something different. I began to understand that trusting him was out of the question. Cheating on me would be its own thrill. If he never felt satisfied, then one woman would not be enough.

I grew to see Randy as having a constantly open mouth that could never consume enough to satisfy his ugly hunger. He was an addict. As I kept trying to feed his neediness, I was damaging my spirit. I felt empty. I was poisoning my soul while he continued to seek his own perverse sexual pleasure. I felt sucked into a rotting vortex and it scared me to death. I wanted out. I had to escape in order to not lose myself in the dysfunctional, damaging relationship I had chosen. My leaving was of little consequence to him, because there was always the next girl.

I left carrying with me the STD he never told me he had. It serves as a permanent reminder of a time when I lost hope and put aside my values and beliefs to walk on the dark side. When I came back into the light, I worked to regain my dignity and a whole new understanding of how I came to make bad decisions, where pain and pleasure were interwoven in an intricate puzzle. Eventually, I forgave myself. Now I find that I am more humble and don't judge other people the way I used to.

If you are wondering if your partner can change one of these scenarios, I believe there is realistic hope for addictions. Addictions can be managed through personal counseling and twelve-step programs. Whether your mate gets help is entirely up to him or her. Help is available, but it only works for people who seek it with the proper willingness to do the work needed to enter and maintain recovery.

If your spouse is extremely intimidating, cruel and inflicts psychological torture, it is, in my experience and research, exceedingly rare that this will change. Extensive, in-depth counseling with an experienced therapist may make a difference, but there is always the danger of the person regressing to old destructive behavior.

It is natural to be scared of losing the essence of who you are or losing your life. In fact, this is your gut telling you your partner poses real peril to you and those you love. This may give you the courage and motivation to leave. Escaping from a menacing person is a brave act. If you are ready to leave, it is important that you seek help and take every possible precaution to be safe. Men and women who fit into these psychologically abusive categories are dangerous, just as physically abusive individuals are. Do not underestimate what your partner can or will do. Be careful.

Chapter 21

Survival and Recovery

Surviving a psychologically abusive relationship and moving through recovery can take a great deal of time and effort. You will need to grieve the loss of your love, dreams, hopes and family. Your confidence is shattered as you try to start a new life on your own. You may not have the necessary funds and resources available. You may not know where you are going to live, how your children will adjust or how you will be treated by your family and friends. Everything seems uncertain and confusing. Where do you begin?

Michelle conveys her own difficult experience and the time-consuming process of leaving:

> My husband could not believe that I was asking for a divorce. I found it difficult to understand why he was surprised. I think he'd played nasty mind games with me for so long that he didn't even recognize that he was doing it. It is probably the only way he knows to act in a relationship. I couldn't take it anymore and my love for him had gradually died. I didn't want to argue; I just wanted out.

He started endlessly questioning me. That is the way he generally wore me down. I know he believed he could do it again. Then he got angry and badgered me about having someone else. That was when it all became so clear. He couldn't fathom that I could stand on my own two feet and take care of myself. He made all the major decisions and made most of the money, so he couldn't imagine how I would cope. I guess we both felt I had no identity outside of being his wife.

But I had come to the realization that if I didn't leave then, I would never find the self that had lost her way inside our tangled marital web. I looked directly into his eyes and calmly said, "No, I'm leaving you for me."

WHERE DO I BEGIN?

The first thing you may need to do is allow yourself to hit bottom. At times we spend an enormous amount of energy avoiding feeling pain and sadness. We are afraid of feeling lost, confused, alone or desperate. We may have difficulty imagining our life without our partners, but we may know we have to end the relationships. So we cling to staying busy, being around other people, working more hours or even holding our breaths to keep from experiencing the hurt. Imagine that you are dangling from a tree branch, you can't reach the tree trunk to climb down and if you let go you will fall. You are afraid you might die, but you realize you can't hold on to the branch forever. You don't know what will happen when you fall, but eventually you see that you have no other choices. Letting go of the branch and falling is very scary. The ground you hit may be hard, but you will not die. Yes, you may need help to patch yourself up, heal and go forward, but help is available. There are people to help nurture you, but first you may need to spend some time licking your wounds.

That is where healing often begins. When you comprehend your own ability to lick your wounds, you begin having the strength to grieve and recover. Of course, you don't have all the answers. At that moment, you may not have any answers. But you will find them one at a time, as each life question presents itself. You don't need to be in a hurry. This process of grieving and self-discovery takes time. It is not all painful. Some of it can be quite fun.

Continue your work of survival and recovery by finding out who you are and what you want. Discover your own likes and dislikes about everything. Start with your five senses. What do you enjoy tasting, touching, smelling, hearing or looking at? If you were offered a week to yourself to do anything you desired, money being no object, what would you enjoy doing? What is the most relaxing thing you do for yourself on a daily basis? How do you have fun? If you have trouble answering these questions, it may mean you have lost yourself somewhere along the way. If you go through your life on autopilot, just performing the next task that is required, there may be no time left in a day to meet your own needs. Maybe you can't even determine what those needs are. Many women and some men leave psychologically abusive relationships to find the selves they have lost or never discovered.

Psychologically abusive relationships prey on your insecurities, reinforce your shame and doubts, lower your resilience and damage your self-confidences and creativity. To restore our abilities and to regain the capacity to grow, we must nurture our wounded spirits. We need to slow down, read, meditate, pray and play. To stop our inner confusion and negative thoughts, we need to experience the simple gifts the world has to offer. Each person has preferences relating to joyful acts. Suggestions are boating, walking, jogging, exercising, gardening, reading, bubble baths, bird watching, sunbathing, beachcombing, painting, drawing, sewing, dancing, singing, kite flying, babysitting, animal play, blowing bubbles, listening to music, mountain hiking, river rafting, swimming, cooking, baking and laughing out loud.

The list is practically endless. Most activities are free or cost very little. They are a way to begin to add new dimensions to your life. It is not that any one thing is a solution. Putting joyful acts into your life on a daily basis creates the foundation for healing.

What about all your fears and insecurities? You must focus on the present. You have survived the past and you cannot live in the future. Be concerned with today. What can you do today to take care of yourself and to accomplish realistic expectations? Simply "do the next right thing." What a great and peaceful concept. Just do the next right thing.

Consider developing a positive comforting mantra. Create your own positive self-talk based on your own insecurities:

> I am okay. I can take care of myself. I can take care of my kids. It is normal for me to make mistakes. I will figure out how to solve them. There are solutions to each problem. I am smart. I can figure out what I need. I can find help when necessary. I will only focus on right now and not worry about the past or the future. I will take life as it comes and be fully aware of the present moment.

After some time of nurturing yourself, you may be ready to do your best work on accurately assessing the person you were before the relationship, the person you have become living through the destructive partnership and the person you most want to be. Begin by answering some tough questions:

- Did I like myself in my relationship?
- What would I want to change?
- Do I like who I'm becoming?
- What do I feel good about?
- What do I want to work on?
- Do I feel in control of myself?
- How can I be more focused and disciplined?
- What skills do I need to improve my life?
- Do I like my character and how I treat other people?
- Do I accept responsibility for my actions?
- Can I express my feelings in an appropriate way?
- Am I honest?
- Do I feel grateful for what I have?

Exploring the answers to these questions will take some time and energy. However, the rewards can be huge. If you want a healthy future relationship with yourself, your family and with an intimate partner, you increase the odds of these things happening by the work you do now. What about the complex subject of forgiveness? Do we need to forgive in order to move on? It is very difficult to forgive psychological and spiritual battering. Our bodies heal much faster than our spirits. Many people say they have forgiven, only to find many layers of anger and resentment of which they were unaware. Forgiveness is ultimately a gift you give yourself. Think of your anger, fear, resentment and memories as a huge boulder you carry on your back. Forgiveness is the means of chipping away at that heavy burden. It can happen in stages, over time. It can be done partially or with a total release. It is not that you forget what happened. It is that you let go of that huge layered boulder. You dump it down a hill, roll it over a cliff or simply set it down. Use the image that works for you.

Equally important is forgiveness of yourself. Look at your total self and your words, deeds, thoughts and feelings. Own all of who you are, even when it makes you uncomfortable. The emotions, thoughts and behavior that you are the most ashamed of or uncomfortable with generally exist in your dark shadowy side that you have attempted to hide or disown. This requires a lot of unproductive energy. Take a look at what you find most distasteful in other people. You may find you possess the same qualities and characteristics that you hate in someone else. Consider the comments and criticisms your partner and others have made about you and decide if any of those remarks could possibly be true. As we acknowledge and embrace our total selves, warts and all, we begin to awaken and release our energetic spirits. Only then are we free to experience life and relationships more fully.

In the process of acceptance, love and forgiveness, we are provided with our own guides for moving forward. Self-knowledge allows you to see the work you want to do. Eckhart Tolle, in his insightful book *The Power of Now*, states, "Life will give you whatever experience is most helpful for the evolution of your consciousness."[23] We are provided with everything we need to solve our problems, answer our questions and have peace of mind. Use everything that has happened to you to have greater insight, become less judgmental, more compassionate and live more fully.

DON'T DWELL IN NEGATIVITY

The contributing scholars and teachers in Rhonda Byrne's valuable book *The Secret* discuss how we attract our own life's circumstances. If we dwell in negativity, we will attract negativity. If we concentrate on sending positive energy out into the world, we will attract positive energy back to us.

The work you do on yourself should be designed to bring your best self more completely into the present moment. The intention is not to have you continue focusing on your shortcomings, regrets or sorrow. We must fully own who we are and where we have come from, then bring our whole selves into this moment to live a life of endless positive possibilities. It does not mean that no other bad thing will happen to us. Pain and pleasure are woven into all living. As we live in peace with ourselves, we make better choices and believe in our competency to create, love, worship and enjoy. We all can move forward and transcend our transgressions. We do not need to remain stuck. Each day is a gift. In order to fully appreciate that gift, we must be peacefully present and aware of all the intricate nuances of each moment. The ability to stay centered and aware requires effort. We need to frequently stop and refocus so that we are not too caught up in all our daily activities and anxious concerns.

Laughter is healing and relaxing. Much of what we find humorous is what resonates as true. When we identify with a person or situation, we can share a common amusement of where life may find us. Gwen's story reveals her own journey to self-awareness:

It was March 17, and Gwen had only been separated from her husband of seventeen years for a few months. She had known him since she was sixteen, married him at twenty, and they had two children together. When they separated, she bought a townhouse and began to learn how to live on her own for the first time in her life.

On that St. Patrick's Day evening, she left home to give a short speech at a political meeting, endorsing a friend who was running for a district court judgeship. She was finding that the stress from all her life changes was causing her to be compulsively neat, so on the way out the door she gathered all her trash into a plastic bag to throw away in the parking lot dumpster. As she dropped her trash into the large, just emptied dumpster, her key ring holding all her keys snagged on the plastic bag and went into the dumpster with her trash. She heard the metal thud of the keys hitting the bottom. *Darn, I'll have to go in and get them*, she thought.

She climbed up into the opening, and as she jumped down and hit the dumpster floor, the heavy metal door slammed shut and latched closed. After a stunned moment she realized: *Oh my God! I do not believe this! I am locked inside a dumpster in a green skirt, black wool coat, heels and black suede gloves.*

The ordinarily busy parking lot was extremely quiet. She repeatedly yelled for help and then thought: *Who's going to open this door, not knowing what they will find?*

Yelling for help and hearing no sound, she decided to climb back up on the door ledge and push the heavy top open with her head. It hurt and she became aware that she was stuck doing an Oscar the Grouch impersonation, because she couldn't lower the top without smashing her fingers. She had to continue clutching the ledge where the top lowered. If she let go, she would fall backward and hit the bottom.

After a while she saw an elderly lady drive up and get out of her car. "Excuse me," Gwen said politely. "I am locked inside here. Could you open the door and let me out?"

The very startled lady asked, "How did you get in there?"

"I promise I'll tell you if you let me out," Gwen said.

The lady was quite shaken as she opened the dumpster door. Gwen climbed out and spent some moments calming the woman down and explaining what had happened. She actually made it to the political meeting in time to speak. She did not describe her adventure, thinking that would not gather any new supporters for the friend whose candidacy she was supporting.

Much to her co-workers' delight, she told her story the next day at work. The story got retold many times to family and friends. Gwen figured she may as well laugh at herself as she ventured into independent living.

If you venture into single living and make the inevitable mistakes, be patient and tolerant with yourself. It is very normal to be scared, confused, lonely and sad. You won't immediately have all the answers. You will not do everything perfectly. Keep a sense of humor and at your low points think: *At least I have yet to lock myself in a dumpster!*

Part IV

How Do I Decide?

Chapter 22

You've Been Hurt

Perhaps you have never identified yourself as a person in a psychologically abusive relationship. If you haven't experienced any physical abuse, you may have thought, *I'm not one of "those women or men."* Historically, it was necessary to concentrate efforts on *battered* women in order to bring attention to an enormous problem that was conveniently ignored or overlooked by law makers, law enforcers and service providers. It was necessary to be militant, be vocal and form coalitions in order to be heard. Feminist, anti-feminist, professionals, victims and many volunteers came together with a common purpose: change laws, educate the community, help train law enforcement and provide shelter, counseling and other needed services for battered women and their children. We lobbied for legislation, wrote grants for funding and appealed to national, state and local entities for donations and meaningful changes that would make a difference in the lives of women and families dealing with domestic violence. The grassroots movement involved people in all races, religions and socio-economic positions. The problem was known to be in all neighborhoods and all professions. No one was immune and women experiencing physical abuse began to understand that they were not alone or unusual. Victims became survivors as they came forward, told their stories and asked for help. Susan Schechter, in her book entitled *Women and Male Violence: The Visions and Struggles of the Battered Women's Movement*, describes in interesting detail the evolution of changes in laws, attitudes, services, families and individual women.

In the decades since the movement began, experience and research has helped to broaden our knowledge of other abusive relationships. We now understand that there are many types of abuse occurring in varying degrees in millions of relationships. We can also now acknowledge, without fear of decreasing or damaging services for victims, that women inflict abuse as well as receive it. In order to assist relationships and families, we must understand all the dynamics of what is occurring, without gender prejudice. In some relationships, one person is clearly abusive, while his or her partner is the victim. At times, these labels are unproductive, as both people can engage in abusive behavior and it is more productive to concentrate on changing the relationship dynamics. We must focus on changing the complex spectrum of all types of abusive behavior and move toward healthier individuals and families. While physical abuse can kill, maim and disfigure, other types of abuse leave permanent emotional, mental and psychological scars. So far in this book we have focused on one of the less recognized forms of abuse and looked at how psychological abuse manifests and why we stay or leave.

You have the right to live a life free from intentionally or unintentionally inflicted pain. Whether the abuse is physical, verbal or psychological, you are entitled to have a fulfilling, satisfying relationship. When you have accepted your partner's behavior for a long time, it is often hard to step back and, in a more objective manner, determine if you find his or her behavior unacceptable. Would you want anyone you care about to be treated the way you are? If the answer to that question is no, then what are your options?

1. You can leave.
2. You can stay and do nothing.
3. You can stay and work on yourself and perhaps the relationship.

1. You can leave.

If you have determined that you do not want to continue in your relationship, you may choose to leave. There are many excellent resources to help you prepare and maximize your safety precautions. If your partner is dangerous and threatening, plan carefully for your departure, taking with you all the items you will need in your immediate future. If possible, prepare to leave when things are calm and you are not in jeopardy of being physically harmed. Contact individuals, organizations and agencies ahead of time that may provide assistance. You need to feel that you are not isolated. There are people who will help you, but you do need to search them out and contact them.

If your mate is psychologically and not physically abusive, you still will need a support system to help you with information, emergency funds, shelter and emotional support. Perhaps you have no idea how one will react. Be cautious. Think through all your options and the potential consequences of your decisions. The "better to be safe than sorry" rule applies here.

Some women and men leave as a temporary separation, in hopes that their partners will seriously want to devote time and energy to changing the relationship dynamics. If your mate still loves you, leaving may be a real wake-up call. He or she may not want to lose you, and your departure will be a signal that you can't tolerate their psychologically abusive behavior. Some who thought their mates would never leave are shocked to find that the other people have made final decisions.

A note of caution about leaving: It should not be used as a manipulative game. The results are always uncertain. Your spouse may be unwilling, unable or uninterested in working on the relationship and making changes. The person may not feel he or she needs to do anything differently. They may actually welcome the separation. Some partners admit to orchestrating departures through their abuse or neglect. This kind of partner knows if he or she continues the stonewalling, threats, criticism and psychological torture long enough, the other person will go and then the abusive partner doesn't have to look bad for leaving.

Some mates may say and do whatever it takes to get you back home, only to revert to their old selves when they feel you have settled back into the relationship. You want to believe he or she's changed, because really you don't want it to be over. You thought leaving would make the other person change. You could discover that the good behavior and promises were just to get what the other person wanted. They may even have believed that they would change, but then were unwilling to keep working on it once things returned to normal.

If you both determine that you are willing, counseling may be extremely helpful at this critical time, when one person is saying he or she will not put up with any more abuse and the more psychologically abusive mate is motivated not to lose the marriage. Begin by seeking group therapy or enlist individual counseling if possible. Let your therapist help you determine when and if couples counseling is appropriate. Use all available resources to learn and grow. If the other person still loves you and you still love your partner, powerful changes can take place. You both need to make a commitment to continue counseling, especially after the honeymoon phase during reuniting is over. The problems don't change or get solved overnight, and stopping one type of abusive behavior can bring on different issues and problems. Be aware of the important fact that one type of abusive behavior can morph into another. Real sustained changes can take place with effort, good will and determination.

Gina reveals:

> I didn't want my marriage to end, but I knew I couldn't continue to live with his verbal and psychological abuse. I was exhausted, mentally and emotionally. I was willing for it to be over if things couldn't change, so I left. I can't believe I waited so long. During this period it was like he was finally hearing me and paying attention. He said he didn't want to lose me and that he realized he'd hurt me. I was already in counseling, so I asked him to go for himself, and eventually we went as a couple. I had to get over my anger about the fact that it took me leaving for him to want to change. I guess my willingness to put up with it was a way of giving him permission to continue. I wish I had stood up for myself years ago, but I couldn't find the strength until now.

2. You can stay and do nothing.

You don't have to do anything differently. You are not in a race. You do not have to make any changes. No one else should judge your life and your decisions, unless you are abusing someone else or putting your children in danger. That becomes a different matter and you must find help in order to address these issues. As long as you are the only one directly impacted by your relationship, you may decide it is manageable.

If after reading this book you still don't know what you want to do about your psychologically abusive relationship, there are many factors to consider. If you choose not to confront your partner's psychologically abusive behavior, but wish to improve your outlook, here are some coping tips, strategies and suggestions:

    a. Your life is no fairy tale.

    b. Stop self-pity.

    c. Get by with help from friends.

    d. See yourself clearly.

    e. Sometimes fuzzy is fine.

    a. **Your life is no fairy tale.**

Become more realistic about your relationship and what it is composed of. Choose to look more closely at its components and your partner. Give up the magical thinking about your mate. What you see now is what you get. You can benefit by having clearer, down-to-earth expectations of your mate. Can you imagine the person saying or thinking any of the following things?

    ♦ I'm the king or queen of my castle. I'm in charge. You do what I say. I hold all the power, money and control. I can tell you what to do, and you should obey.

    ♦ Everything is about me. I love myself, and whatever happens will be evaluated for how it impacts me. I'm important. The world should revolve around me.

    ♦ I'm angry as hell. I'm angry and resentful and I have every right to be. You'd better watch out. I need to blow off some steam.

- I've got a problem. It's not my fault. I can't help it. It's beyond my control. You need to understand and make allowances for my behavior.
- You scare me. Why do you always want to be so close? I don't want to be tied down. Intimacy and commitment are not my things. Don't try and tell me what to do. It doesn't really matter what you need, back off.
- Oh, poor me. I've had a tough life. Bad things always happen to me. I am unlucky. I need to be taken care of. You should feel bad for me.
- Please fix it. I count on you to make things right. You always know what to do. I can't be expected to repair anything. It's your job to keep the peace and make everything run smoothly.
- You have a problem. I don't know what is wrong with you. I'm fine but you're not. You are the one who causes all the trouble. You need help. It's not my fault.
- I won't grow up. I'm Peter Pan or Sleeping Beauty, and don't expect me to mature. It's fun being a kid. Grown-ups are too serious and you are a drag.
- I'm scared. I won't really say so, but you know that deep down, I'm frightened and insecure. Please protect me and understand if I lose my temper, it's because I don't want anyone to see that I feel weak.

You may recognize your mate in one or several of these examples. Feel free to come up with your own statement that characterizes what he or she says and does. It helps to understand what you are coping with and what to expect in the future. Don't waste energy trying to change the other person. It helps to understand the mind-set your partner approaches you with. Don't buy into the idea that you caused the behavior or that you need to help your mate fix things you are not responsible for.

b. **Stop self-pity.**

The only time that feeling sorry for yourself is productive is when you get so sick of your own pity that you get angry at yourself and are ready to do things differently. Otherwise, self-pity may have you stuck in a victim mode.

If you perpetually feel like a victim and identify yourself accordingly, you may prevent your own healing and recovery. There is hardly a person alive who has not had some trauma in his or her life from which he or she needs to recover. No matter how bad your situation is now or has been in the past, you do not want to let helplessness, devastation and confusion paralyze you. Self-pity can lead to powerlessness. When you feel there is nothing you can do to feel better, then your situation will not improve. Some people have significant trauma stored away like computer files in their minds. If this applies to you, you may not even be able to access the information in these files, as parts of your mind may have shut down or walled off the files to protect you from seeing or re-experiencing hideous information and feelings. You may be exhausted from carrying around too many heavy mental files.

Give yourself permission to rest and recuperate. When you are ready to open and examine the files, you can, although it may require professional help to safely navigate your way through past horrors. Whatever is stored in your memory you have already lived through. If you are an adult who is capable of making decisions, you can make your present vastly different from your past. If you find that you are dwelling in self-pity, ask yourself what you can do to feel better. It can be as simple as exercise, meditation, laughter, rest, reading or self-pampering. Ask, pay attention and follow through. Don't hesitate. Try different things until one thing or the cumulative effect of all the things you try makes a difference.

Some people who are stuck in victim mode repeatedly tell their stories to family, friends, acquaintances, co-workers, physicians and therapists. They may even tell strangers who will listen. Of course, it is validating to have another person take the time to listen to us, but continuously talking about your dysfunctional relationship becomes tiresome, exhaustive and unproductive. People may avoid you if they feel you repeat the same complaints over and over again without taking any action. Acute trauma victims often need to tell their stories many times in an accepting therapeutic environment in order to heal, but the average person cannot assist with the necessary help. Some victims of psychological abuse stay stuck in the drama or the consistent addictive pattern of telling what has happened to them and experiencing no relief or healing. Counseling and self-exploration can help you determine your motives and reasons for repeating your stories. Ask yourself what you are looking for. There may be other answers and ways to meet your real needs and desires. If we know what we are seeking, we are more likely to find it.

Another way to avoid the pitfalls of self-pity is to volunteer some of your time and energy. Do something you would enjoy to help another person in need. Step out of your life and into someone else's world who can benefit by knowing you and sharing your gifts. Use your creativity or let someone train you to help a certain individual, family or group of people. There are a wide range of things you can do to share your talents, your blessings and your spirit. You can schedule your time with an existing organization or you can spontaneously have giving days filled with your own random acts of kindness.

c. **Get by with help from friends.**

Whatever our life situations, friends can be vital parts of our well-beings. Some are new, some old. Some friends are there for certain parts of our lives. They are our work friends, church friends, volunteer friends, school friends, neighbor friends, club friends or our child's friend's parents who also become our friends. Some friends are great for certain activities, events, occasions or celebrations.

These relationships can be particularly important when you are enduring psychological abuse. Close friends cannot only help you see more clearly, give you a chance to vent, help you in deciding how to move forward and give you an outlet but also bring satisfaction that you are not enjoying in your primary relationship. I feel especially blessed by nine friends of mine. We have supported one another through volunteering, work and friendship for many years.

On one evening we discussed why we all think friendship can be so important to well-being, especially in stressful times and when one is enmeshed in a psychologically abusive relationship:

True close friends put no pressure on each other to be anything other than who we are. We totally accept each other's choices, decisions, changes and the right to be different, opinionated and even wrong. We know we make mistakes, and we sincerely apologize and make amends if we have hurt or injured one another in any way. We communicate and can say what we feel. We don't pretend that we have all the answers or that we can fix a major problem like a psychologically abusive relationship for each other. We have faith and confidence that each of us will find our own paths as we make our way in the world. We are not there to judge, but to listen and discuss. We have a history together where we have stood by each other through marriages, divorces, childbirth, illnesses, family deaths, painful problems, job stresses and life changes. We care deeply about each other's children and grandchildren. We help each other age gracefully, with a sense of humor and great camaraderie. We share our hopes, dreams, fears and concerns. We tell each other about great books we've read, movies or plays we've seen and places we have traveled to. We can go weeks or months without talking (although that is rare) and pick up conversations right where we left off, without missing a beat. We are not jealous of each other. We enjoy that we have other friends and experiences that enrich our lives. We buy small thoughtful gifts for one another just because we care. We are comforted by each other's presence and if we need a hug, we know where the best ones are. It is totally safe to be vulnerable and to fall apart. We will be consoled by each other's love and ability to endure our pain, because we understand or empathize with what the other woman is feeling. We know how to keep a secret and we don't betray each other. There have been devastating events we weathered together, and we know that sometimes being silent but present is the most powerful healer. Mostly, there are happy times: Many shared years of lunches and dinners, glasses of tea and bottles of wine, laughter and tears, parties and celebrations, gossip and funny stories. We are each other's extended family, there through the triumphs and tragedies, a phone call or email away, making life rich and pleasurable. We count each other as our true blessings.

If you have not been fortunate enough until now to find close friends or if your psychologically abusive partner has forbidden or discouraged you from having friends, it is never too late to start. Develop the habit of spending more time chatting with people you know or new people you meet. Listen to them and share some small things. Trust is built over time. These friendships grow and develop. Search for women or men who listen to you, care about your concerns and will not violate your confidence by telling a secret or talking about you behind your back. The best way to find a good friend is to be one. Be the kind of friend you would like to have. If someone hurts your feelings, don't give up. You may want to tell him or her how you feel or if you think it's a lost cause, move on. There is a world full of people who can benefit from your friendship as you will benefit from theirs.

d. **See yourself clearly.**
      It is always important to understand who you are and what you are doing. If you have decided that at this point in time you

will stay in your marriage or relationship with a psychologically abusive partner and not change, improve or end it, think about how you can know and like yourself better. Ask:

+ Am I a fixer, helper, caregiver, victim or avoider?
+ Am I more dominant or more submissive?
+ Do I believe I deserve what I want or deserve what I am getting?
+ Do I accept blame for things I didn't cause?
+ Do I do things in my relationship that I'd like to change?
+ Do I see myself as strong or weak?
+ Do I love myself?
+ Am I taking care of my body, mind and spirit?

It is often difficult to realistically evaluate ourselves. We all have some negative messages from childhood that we have unconsciously accepted. Our outward appearances are sometimes given more attention than our personalities, abilities, qualities, values and characters. Since birth we have lived in a pop culture that bombards us with images that show us we aren't measuring up. From Barbie dolls to scantily clad airbrushed models, pop music divas and television and movie stars, we can't possibly attain or maintain such perfection, which is, after all, only an illusion. No wonder too many twelve-year-old girls are worried about being fat and ugly, and by the time they graduate from high school they might be asking for breast implants, liposuction or plastic surgery. Too many boys think they must be sports stars, incredibly muscled and cool. The quest for perfection can last a lifetime and aging scares us, so we lift our faces, inject botox, seal off parts of our stomachs and become exercise addicts. We devote an enormous amount of time and money to being less of something we are or more of something we aren't. What God, our parents and nature gave us isn't acceptable.

Psychologically abusive partners may have heavily damaged your self-esteem, too:

♦ Are you going to wear that? Don't you think it's too tight? It makes you look bigger.

♦ Aren't you going to the gym today? You'll never look like a real man if you don't work out.

♦ Are you really going to eat that? Do you know how many calories it has?

♦ Maybe you should try a different hair color. I've always thought redheads are hot.

♦ Why not try a Brazilian waxing? I think taking off all the hair would be sexy.

♦ How about a hair transplant so you won't look so old.

The list is endless and I'm sure you can add to it. The message is that your natural self is just not okay. We do live in a world where there are many options available to us. If you decide to change your appearance because you want to, that's fine. However, if you change to meet someone else's standards, it probably won't satisfy your partner, who'll just pick on something else, and you most likely will not feel more attractive.

Try making a positive appraisal of yourself, inside and out. Notice your strengths and natural beauty. Praise yourself out loud. Concentrate on what you like and ignore your exterior flaws. We all have them. Be your own cheerleader. Changing your attitude to one of self-appreciation will bring you the very peace which shines outward as true beauty.

e. **Sometimes fuzzy is fine.**

Have you ever gotten new prescription eyeglasses and then began noticing all the dust on your furniture or dog hair on your floor to which you hadn't been paying attention? Or looked into a magnifying mirror that shows every line and wrinkle that you had been ignoring? What did it hurt to ignore those flaws? How did it help you to pay attention to them?

Sometimes, we simply must acknowledge that life is full of imperfections and focusing on them is not going to change them. Some situations and behaviors are worth ignoring while concentrating on what you can change or what you won't tolerate. So, for all the acceptable flaws, sometimes fuzzy vision is just fine. Use energy toward growing, changing and improving while accepting that life is mysteriously, fascinatingly imperfect.

3. You can stay and work on yourself and perhaps the relationship.

"I've broken my own heart so many times, trying to make my psychologically abusive partner into what he or she isn't."

Well said. Whether you stay in your psychologically abusive relationship or go, remember, you cannot change another person; you can only change yourself. You can only truly control you. What does that mean? It means that right now, this moment, you can make the decision to start taking care of yourself. You have answers inside of you. Search for all the ways to nurture your body and spirit, and you will eventually find solutions. Here are some ways to get started:

    a. Move in the right direction.
    b. Develop an invisible shield.
    c. Be your own best friend.
    d. Be still and wonder.
    e. Be active and take charge.

a. Move in the right direction.

Madeline shares her self changes, written in an exercise directed to her husband:

I used to be sweet. I was nice and friendly and lovable. I didn't snap, yell or bark at anyone. If I had an issue with something or someone, I could talk it out in a calm, appropriate manner. I was fun to be around and I enjoyed other people.

What happened, you ask? Where is the sweet girl you used to know? Well, let's see: I've been yelled at, called names, lied to, abused and abandoned. I work hard from early morning until late at night. I have a job that shows me the worst things that people can ever do to each other. I'm tired, cranky and hormonal. I miss being with the people I love. I often feel I don't do enough or measure up. I feel angry, resentful and disappointed way too often.

Sometimes I wish I could crawl onto your lap and have you comfort me, but I wouldn't dare. You would think I was crazy and would have no idea what to say. Besides, if I show any weakness, it doesn't work for you. You need for me to be strong and competent. You need for me to always do my part to take care of things. I am not allowed to fall apart.

So can the sweet girl become a bitch? The answer is yes. The sweet girl was innocent, optimistic and hopeful. The bitch is more of a realist and sometimes a pessimist. The bitch has an attitude. Who do I want to be? Somewhere in between the sweet girl and the bitch, I think. I'd like to take what life has taught me and use it to do something special. I'd like to do more playing, resting, reading, laughing and loving. I want to work less and spend more time with the people I love. I need alone time and the space to think and be creative. I could care less if I'm sweet or bitchy, as long as I'm moving in the right direction.

If you keep doing the same things and don't like the results, it's time to try something different. You have no guarantees about how anything you do will work out, but think of using positive energy. Do something positive for yourself and maybe for your partner too. The positive energy you send out is not wasted on you. Feeling good about one thing leads you to think of another creative way to interact in your world.

b. **Develop an invisible shield.**
There are some hurtful words and actions that seem impossible to ignore, but at times it is helpful to ignore temper tantrums of your mate. If you choose to remain living with your

partner despite the partner's psychological abuse, you want to take away his or her ability to push your buttons and cause you to do or say things you will regret.

Imagine that you carry an invisible shield that you have with you at all times. If hurtful words and non-physical negative actions are directed at you, you can use the shield to deflect them. I know this sounds kind of crazy, but you want to make his or her psychologically abusive behavior clearly about the other person and less damaging to you.

If you are ready to address the partner's destructive behavior, you want it to be from a position of strength, instead of responding to the abuse while you are hurt and angry. It is very difficult not to allow the bad words and actions of someone you love to hurt you. If you can minimize the damage, you will decrease the other person's power and focus the problem back where it belongs. Please be aware that he or she may choose to escalate the psychologically abusive behavior if your partner doesn't feel he or she is adequately getting to you. You may need to leave the room or the house to protect yourself. At all times be aware of your physical, mental and emotional safety.

c.   **Be your own best friend.**

Recently, I was shopping for a gift for someone else, and I found something I really wanted, as well as finding the gift for my friend. I was trying to decide if I could really afford to splurge on myself when the saleswoman said, "If you really want something, sometimes you have to be the one to make it happen." I thought, *what a good saleswoman with a great message.* We often cannot expect that someone else will meet our needs and wants. We have to be willing to take things into our own hands and nurture our own selves. Direct some of the kind, nice things you would do for a good friend toward yourself. Affirm your own goodness and treat yourself often to positive attention.

d. Be still and wonder.

Slow down, be still. Rest, mediate and pray. Get comfortable with the image of yourself floating around in space, unattached, unconnected, undefined and unpredictable. Let your mind wander down new roads that lead to knowing yourself more fully. What do you need? What do you want? What matters to you? What do you want to do that you haven't yet done?

We hear the messages about slowing down and being fully present, but it is very difficult to do. Pay attention to your surroundings. What do you see, hear, smell, taste and feel? Enjoy the sensations that are pleasing to you. Fill your life with more of those things. Minimize the irritants. Turn off the technology. We've become addicted to devices and it often conflicts with searching for yourself. Turn off the man-made noises. Notice what you now can hear, inside and outside. Perhaps you want to change the way your surroundings look by bringing new colors or designs into your home or office. Rearrange the furniture or get some new pillows or inexpensive art. Try some new foods. If you don't enjoy cooking, there are so many new, creative carryouts. Try some new scented candles or potpourri. Comfort yourself with a new blanket, stuffed animal, soft nightgown or robe.

Recently, I stayed at a wonderful bed and breakfast inn. I had a leisurely breakfast, walked, took a bath in a wonderful tub, read a great book, shopped at fun stores, had afternoon tea and a relaxing dinner. I realized that I could easily do every one of those things at home, but I hardly ever do and I certainly don't do them all in one weekend unless I'm on vacation. Why don't I? I'm always driven to try and get everything done before the workweek starts. I could treat myself to a free vacation at home and I would not have to buy gas for my car to travel! Plan your own at-home mini-vacations.

Spend a little time each morning and each evening recognizing your blessings. I heard my grandson say my name for the first time recently. I am thrilled! It is the little things that can make a difference in our lives.

e. **Be active and take charge.**
   Some old advice is essential: eat right, sleep well and exercise. Watch your intake of drugs and alcohol. Get help for any addictions. Eliminate destructive behaviors.
   If you are depressed or anxious, see a physician for a medication evaluation and a counselor for therapy. It is normal for your moods to be altered when you are in a psychologically abusive relationship and are trying to make changes in yourself.
   Organize your living and working spaces. Clear out the clutter and clean. Having your space in order helps you feel more in control.
   Plan things you can look forward to doing. Do not let an abusive spouse spoil your fun.

Working on your relationship is easier if both people are willing to participate. If your partner is uninterested in marriage or individual counseling or in trying anything new, you still can strive to be your best self in the partnership. Here are some final suggestions.

 ♦ Notice and praise the actions you appreciate. Let him or her know what matters to you.
 ♦ Do something for your partner that the other person would enjoy.
 ♦ Talk and act in ways that you would to a new love interest. Eliminate criticism and sarcasm. It is unproductive.
 ♦ Encourage positive progress.

If you are raising children, you are a living daily example to them. What you do is much more powerful than what you say. Be conscious that they are watching you and give them the gifts of honesty, dependability, trust, kindness, spiritual exploration and forgiveness. You control your words and actions. Strive to be a person they can admire.

If you are raising a daughter, you are showing her how to be a woman or how men treat women:

 ♦ Take care of yourself so she sees what healthy living is about.
 ♦ Behave in a relationship the way you would like her to behave. You are showing her what a woman should expect from a man

and what a man expects from a woman.

- Teach her that men and women are wonderful and fascinating people who have the capacity to be kind and respectful.
- Be truthful and consistent so that she can trust you.
- During her childhood, don't make her your confidante or best friend. She deserves a childhood free from adult responsibilities.
- Teach her that both men and women should be nurturing and responsible.
- Tell her that she deserves to be treated in a non-abusive way and that she should not settle for less. She should also learn not to be abusive with her words and actions.
- Show respect and expect respect from your partner.

If you are raising a son, teach him:

- Women and men are special, wonderful, complicated and unpredictable.
- You will love women and be confused by them, but you do not need to control them.
- If a woman is nasty and abuses you, move on. Someone else will appreciate and respect you.
- Forgive and forget your partner's crazy, nonsensical, irregular, non-abusive behavior.
- Let her be herself. You be yourself.
- Don't compromise yourself or your values.
- Show respect for yourself and for her.
- Be willing to equally share chores and responsibilities.
- Do no harm with your words or actions.

Chapter 23

Hurting the One You Love

Until this point in our journey together we have been focusing on those of you who have been victims of psychological abuse. Now we want to turn, in this chapter, to speaking directly to the perpetrators. Both genders can be psychologically abusive. No person should play mind games and hurt the people he or she loves. If you are the abuser, how can you stop? Here are some simple, straightforward answers to commonly asked questions:

1. Why do I hurt the people I love?
2. What can I control?
3. How can I be successful in sustaining changes?
4. What else do I need to know?

1. Why do I hurt the people I love?

Understanding how psychologically abusive behavior develops is not intended to provide you with an excuse. It is wrong if someone abused you and it is wrong if you injure someone else. The knowledge of what formed the way you think, feel, talk and act can be the first step in making changes.

Many factors contribute to the adults we become. It begins at conception. Our genetics are like the pre-wiring for our temperament. Hence, some babies are easygoing and happy while others are tense and fussy. The way your brain and nervous system interact can be a setup for having a quick explosive temper. Scientists have now provided us with a myriad of medications that can help with predetermined moods and reactions by changing the neurotransmitter serotonin levels in our brains.

The next big impact is the environment we experience from birth to adulthood. If you grew up with parents who inappropriately expressed their anger, you were being taught a negative way to deal with your own angry feelings. Hating what was happening in your home, you were powerless to stop it. As an adult, you may find yourself speaking or acting in the same abusive manner, because that is what you learned from your role models. Not having heard healthy ways to communicate, you may have no clue where to begin.

An abusive home does not foster good self-esteem. Even if you had some positive loving attention, any abuse or neglect can cause feelings of unworthiness and shame. You may feel incapable of attracting and keeping a good, healthy relationship. Anger and hurt over past experiences are carried into adulthood, and you may punish someone you love for your abuser's past behavior.

Perhaps you never experienced any abuse or neglect in your home. Did your parents separate and you felt abandoned or confused? Did you have a single parent who never exposed you to a healthy relationship? Or maybe you feel that you did see good relationships, but you had a parent who was fearful, anxious, controlling or emotionally detached. It is possible that you had a parent who was too close to you in ways that felt unhealthy or uncomfortable and that did not allow you to feel secure about maturing into an independent adult. Everyone's situation is different, but your upbringing impacts who you become and how you relate to your mate.

In your teenage years and in early adulthood, what kind of men or women did you find yourself attracted to? Do these people have any of the characteristics of either of your parents? Do you experience the same dynamics in your close relationships that are similar to what you observed in your family home? You may seek out men or women who seem different from your family, only to find you have fallen in love with someone who acts like one or both of your parents. If you had a critical, judgmental parent, you may, without intending to, have chosen a critical, judgmental partner. If Mom yelled threats and criticism and Dad stonewalled, you may find yourself with a screaming wife whom you now ignore, repeating a pattern you never dreamed of copying.

Genetics and environment also contribute to two other important factors: your mental and physical health and addictions. Handling anger and frustration are more difficult while in poor health or under the influence of addictive substances or behavior. Not feeling well, experiencing guilt or shame or using mind and mood altering substances often leads to poor impulse control. Feeling depressed or anxious can leave little tolerance for another person.

Fear is another reason we hurt someone we love. Some commonly expressed fears:

♦ I am afraid of loving her too much. I feel so vulnerable.

♦ What will I do if he leaves me?

♦ Suppose she finds someone else more appealing.

♦ I don't want to be alone.

♦ What if I lose my job, can't support or contribute?

♦ Do I satisfy her sexually?

♦ I'm afraid of being judged, criticized or abandoned.

Past relationships can also influence how you treat your current partner. If your former girlfriend, wife, boyfriend or husband cheated, it is difficult to trust and have faith that your present mate will not also cheat. Maybe you were unfaithful and never caught, so you are suspicious of what your partner is doing that you don't know about. Carrying guilt and shame for your past unforgiven behavior can cause you to project anger toward others. The shame can be for your own actions or something bad that was done to you that you internalized and felt you must have deserved.

You may fear the power you feel that your partner has over you. You may be deeply in love with him or her and feel that you need him or her in a way that scares you. You may think about the other person's strengths, good looks and kindness and worry that if you find this person wonderful, so will others. You may become tormented by jealous reactions over his or her friendliness or even professional interactions with others. You are scared of losing the person and do not enjoy realizing how vulnerable you are, knowing you would be devastated if the other person hurt or left you.

Ben opens up about his obsessive love and his psychological abuse of his partner:

> I worshipped and adored her. She was a walking dream to me. I felt lucky to be with her, and I would always tell her how much I loved her, and I knew she loved me too. At times, I felt she was perfect.
>
> It consumed me that she had ever been with other men. No one else should have ever touched her. I obsessed about her other relationships. I knew they were before we ever met but I would imagine in great detail the intimate interactions she must have shared. I was creating visions in my mind, but I knew how she was with me, so I would think of her being that way with other men. It nearly drove me mad.
>
> I've always had a hot temper, but I never wanted to hurt her. I wanted her to love and be proud of me. I wanted her individual attention. I understood that there were other people and things that she needed to focus on, but inside I hated losing any of her time or attention. She was the best part of my world.
>
> So what did I do? I let my fears and anger build inside of me until I exploded and punished her for my weaknesses and insecurities. I raged and yelled and called her terrible names. I put her down, thinking it would relieve the pressure and make me feel better. Instead, I felt like shit. During those angry outbursts, I looked in her eyes and saw my reflection. I saw how I

looked to her, and I felt her disappointment and hurt. It made me even more furious to realize what a jerk I was to be so mean. She was my angel, and I became her devil. When I couldn't stand myself any longer, I left and stayed gone awhile. I hated being away from her, but I had to collect myself and build my confidence back up. I felt stupid and ashamed of what I had done and went back with my devil tail between my legs. I always expected her to take me back. In time, she always forgave me and we had a great time being happily back together…until the same terrible thoughts and feelings started building up again. I couldn't stop them. I often wished I had a giant eraser that could make those tormenting fears disappear.

I hoped the relationship would never end, but if I am honest with myself, I knew I was killing it. I was so afraid of losing her that I actually caused it to happen, by never fully getting control of myself. I think back to the time I'd walked out the door with her on her knees begging me not to go, and I feel like a fool. She had enough love and faith in me that I could be a better man. I guess I didn't have enough faith or strength or love for myself to make it happen. We broke up. Years have passed and I still think of her every day. I hope that she remembers our good times and the love we shared. I hope she is happy and knows that I still love, worship and adore her.

A man or woman with inner strength, compassion, competency and assertiveness can be a very exciting, enjoyable partner. Do not fear the other person; celebrate him or her. If admired, praised and appreciated, that person can become your dream mate. Partners with the right kind of centered confidence can speak their minds appropriately; have fulfilling jobs; plan, organize and accomplish tasks; have fun doing almost anything; may enjoy sex with a reckless abandon; and can love you completely. You'd be a fool to shut that down. Don't mess that up. Encourage your partner and count yourself lucky.

2. What can I control?

A great deal of abusive behavior is an attempt to punish or control another person. It is a great illusion. Thinking you have established power over your partner means you have neglected to see his or her true thoughts and feelings. If you love your partner, do you want him or her to despise your words and actions? We all have parts of our minds and souls that we don't give anyone else access to. He or she has places you can't reach. Your partner may follow your orders to keep the peace and resent you each step of the way. Coercing or manipulating your partner's behavior does not mean you have created a safe relationship for yourself. In fact, the more the abuse occurs, the more likely it is that he or she will eventually leave.

The only person you truly have any control over is yourself. We are a blend of feelings, thoughts and actions. You cannot control your feelings. There is no little switch inside us that can be flipped to stop unwanted feelings or to create emotions that are not there. We must accept our feelings and learn to express them in productive ways. Our thoughts are somewhat more malleable. As we read, listen to others, study, participate in a group or worship, we can shape and change our thoughts. Unwanted or negative thoughts can be changed into healthier, more productive ways of thinking. Our behavior is where we have the most control. You can decide what you want to do between now and when you go to bed tonight, and in most cases, your plan can be followed. Changing your thoughts and behavior will eventually impact your feelings. If you are practicing positive thinking and liking your decisions and actions, you will feel better. You will begin an upward spiral of well-being where consistently affirmative thoughts, behavior and feelings are working together in harmony.

What does this mean? It means you have the ability to stop being psychologically abusive. You can make up your mind to change how you act and what you say. With some hard work, new ways of communicating and behaving can be implemented. The opportunity is available to do things differently. Just deciding you want to change is a start, but this doesn't make it happen. You have to break old habits and learn new ones. You won't do it perfectly. There may be five steps forward and two back. Build on the three positive steps and keep going. How do I get started?

a. Learn to recognize your triggers and understand your anger.
b. Examine your need to control.
c. Own up to your abusive behavior.
d. Genuinely apologize and make amends.
e. Don't expect a quick fix.

a. Learn to recognize your triggers and understand your anger.

One of the first steps to breaking old habits is learning to recognize what triggers your abusive behavior. Think of what your partner says or does that increases your fear, hurts your feelings or triggers your anger. We all have figurative buttons inside us that when pushed, create strong emotional reactions. Our partners know where our buttons are and they push them when they are lashing out and want to cause us pain. You may by pushing his or her buttons. No matter who is button pushing, this is underhanded fighting.

Intentionally or unintentionally, some men or women push their partners' buttons. Why? It may be because it's all he or she ever learned in the past. It may be because it is the established system in which you both operate to act out your feelings toward each other. He or she pushes your buttons, you abuse; the abusive person becomes the bad one, and the other person becomes the victim. Sometimes, when one partner tries to change his or her abusive behavior, the other doesn't know how to handle the changes and increases that person's button pushing to test the partner's limits.

Ethan and Eliza were mutual psychological abusers.

Ethan had a problem temper. He loved his wife Eliza completely and he was proud of their home and family. When they fought, he often threatened Eliza: he slammed doors, threw things, punched walls and stood over her menacingly. Later he was filled with remorse and pain.

Eliza had grown up in an abusive home. She couldn't believe that the knight who had rescued her was now hurting her too. She found herself fighting back and at times they had terrible battles. Since he was physically stronger, she thought of other ways to get under his skin, calling him names and putting him down. She told him he was exactly like her father, whom they both hated. She scratched him, leaving marks she knew other people would notice.

Ethan knew he had to do something to save the marriage. He sought professional help and made great changes in his behavior. Eliza, while grateful for his efforts, found herself confused by the changes. One night, Ethan did not respond to her usual button pushing during a fight. In an act of supreme frustration, she reached inside her panties, pulled out her bloody sanitary pad and tried to smear it in his face. She realized she needed to seek her own professional help.

Take away the power of someone else pushing your buttons by recognizing what he or she is doing and then learning not to respond. Pretend you are an outside observer to your arguments with your spouse. Watch what he or she does and how you react. Remove the power of your partner hurting you by refusing to allow the person's words to irritate or anger you:

Oh, I see that she is pushing my buttons now and I refuse to let myself lose control. I will not give her the satisfaction of using her words or actions to anger me to the extent that I'll do or say something I'll regret.

Remember, you can only control yourself. You can't control someone else. You can only do your part to change your behavior. It is up to your partner to look at his or her part in the system you both have created. Do not use *any* of your partner's behavior as an excuse to be abusive. If you justify your actions based on what he or she does, you will never be able to stop what you are doing. The example given is an extreme, but people are not perfect. Your spouse may do things you don't like or that make you unhappy or angry. Nothing he or she does is an acceptable excuse for you abusing your partner. You have other options. You can talk with him or her about the things that bother you. In return, you need to listen to your partner about his or her concerns. You can seek couples counseling. If all else fails, you can leave the relationship. Abusing your partner should not be one of your choices.

Anger is a normal, natural feeling. It is what you do with your anger that often becomes the problem. If you refer back to chapter 3, you can read the description of the effects of anger on your brain, as well as the rest of your body. Anger and stress cause your brain to signal chemicals, such as adrenaline, to be sent out into your body, preparing you for action. Unless you have been programmed or trained to be a ruthless, calculating assassin or brutal abuser, your system revs up to fight or flee. If your instinct or experience makes you flee and your partner follows you wherever you go, trying to talk, resolve things or continue arguing or complaining, a fight will generally ensue. By that time, your brain and body are ready for a fight. Imagine that your body chemicals and nerve endings are like thousands of little soldiers, well prepared for battle. Additionally, you very well may have a reservoir of shame from past angry thoughts, feelings or actions that were directed toward you or that you directed toward someone else. The shame intensifies the strength of your soldiers. Your negative memories are stored in a memory bank, ready to be withdrawn during a fight. This often happens without your conscious intention to make a withdrawal from that negative memory bank.

Examples of common negative thoughts:
- You always put me down.
- Stop complaining. You don't appreciate anything.
- You make me so mad. It's all your fault. You always do this to me. You cause me to act this way.
- You are embarrassing me in front of my friends.

◆ You never listen or pay attention to me.
◆ I'm sick of you spending so much money. No matter how many times I say something, you still do it.
◆ I'm tired of you criticizing me. Nothing I do pleases you.

Negative thoughts in your mind join forces with the present problem and feed your fire. The anger builds and eventually erupts into a nasty crescendo. If the intense angry outburst becomes abusive, then your actions, thoughts and feelings make additional deposits in your negative memory bank. You haven't solved anything and have probably just made things worse for you and your partner. What are some inappropriate ways to use your anger?

◆ Controlling – getting him or her to do what you want. Getting your way through verbal or physical force.
◆ Punishing – making him or her feel bad through degradation, put-downs or hurting feelings in any way.
◆ Attacking your own shame – punishing yourself, feeling you are bad so you deserve to be self-abusive.
◆ Avoiding other uncomfortable feelings – feeling anger instead of fear, jealousy, sadness or even love.
◆ Enjoying the power of anger and the adrenaline rush – creating anger for the rush can lead to becoming addicted to anger.

One rule to follow: If you are scary, then stop! It does not matter if you don't think you are out of line. If you are scaring him or her, then your behavior is a problem for the other person. It may have to do with your partner's past experiences, nervous system and chemical constitution. Whatever the situation, if your anger scares or hurts your partner, you need to find a different way to express it.

There are positive, healthy purposes for your anger. It may alert you that something is wrong or that you may be in danger. It can help you escape from an unpleasant, uncomfortable or dangerous situation. Anger can help bring you out of despair and depression or move you along through the grieving process. It is a wonderful motivator to do something positive and productive that you have been needing to do. What are some ways to deal with your anger which will avoid filling up your negative memory bank?

♦ Self-awareness – Sit alone, still and quiet. Be aware of your body's sensations. Breathe deeply, slowly and fully. Examine what is bothering you. Decide why you are upset or concerned and if your thoughts or feelings remind you of any situations or experiences from your past. Become fully aware of what you are thinking and feeling.

♦ Switch gears – If your thoughts are negative and irrational, do not continue brooding or obsessing, as you are fueling a damaging fire. Distract your negative thoughts with positive thoughts. Intentionally think of things you appreciate and are grateful for. Watch a funny or heartwarming movie or television show. Read something interesting and enjoyable, not dark and violent. Talk to someone who is positive and affirming.

♦ Move your body – Exercise, swim, work out, run, do active chores. Do something positive to elevate your heart rate and pump that serotonin into your brain.

♦ Fill your positive memory bank – Concentrate on intentionally creating positive experiences and memories, for yourself and for your partner. There are thousands of ways to be helpful, kind or romantic. Do things that make you feel good and that you enjoy doing. Then do things you know will make the other person feel good and that your partner will enjoy receiving. It doesn't matter what you get in return. The benefit to you is the increasing deposits in your good memory bank. A high balance in this account may be the measure of your true wealth.

b. Examine your need to control.

Perhaps you are seeking some kind of security or guarantee about your life when you attempt to control your partner. You may think if you keep him or her "under your thumb" your partner will never leave or betray you. Perhaps you feel that it's acceptable to use dreadful conduct with your partner, because he or she is supposed to put up with you. Sometimes we show the people we love the most our worst behavior, rather than our best.

Maybe other things in your life seem out of control, so you try to rule your home environment. Are you experiencing any of these feelings?

- Feelings of powerlessness or worthlessness.
- Irrational thoughts.
- Frequent anger.
- Jealousies and suspicions.
- Worries over job or money.
- Ignored or not cared for.
- Frustration and resentment.
- Concerns about your children or family.
- Fears over a variety of issues.
- Disappointed over many losses.

If any of these apply, you may seek to feel better by dominating or bullying your spouse. This does not work to solve any of your concerns and it pushes him or her away. The anger and resentment your partner will feel towards you keeps him or her from being your ally. How can he or she want to be supportive to someone who is hurting him or her?

Make a list of all the ways you have been trying to control your spouse. What specific behaviors did you use? I'm sure your partner will be able to add to your list if you ask the other person to explain what that person feels is controlling. Think about how your actions are working for you. How are they impacting your partner? What is the end result of your controlling behaviors?

c. **Own up to your abusive behavior.**
This is a hard task. Most people minimize, deny or don't seem to be able to accurately recall their negative actions. Start another list. What have you specifically said or done that could possibly be construed as abusive? Try to objectively recall your words, tone of voice, body language and conduct. What have you said that your spouse found hurtful? Did you intend to distress him or her, or were you simply thoughtless? Have you ever played mind games with your partner? If you were physically violent, what did you do? Think about how you feel during and after your harmful behavior. If you felt justified in any of your abusive actions, you are unlikely to change. Remember, taking responsibility for your behavior, regardless of what has been done to you, is crucial to improving any relationships you have now or in the future.

While painful to examine, acknowledging your behavior is an essential step in this process. If you do not comprehend what you have done wrong, you cannot feel the remorse that is necessary to be able to move to the next step. It is important to not only understand what you have done, but also the total impact on your spouse and your family. Your actions are like the stone that is thrown into the lake. The rock goes down hard and the ripples spread out in increasingly wider circles. You must work at comprehending exactly how you have hurt the people you care about. Nobody enjoys this careful scrutiny. The purpose for this examination is not to shame you. It is to help you realize and acknowledge the consequences of your actions. *If you don't get it, you can't stop it!*

It is important not to make assumptions about how your family feels. You may know how you have felt in the past when someone hurt you, but hurt is not necessarily experienced the same way by someone else. Each person has the right to his or her own reactive feelings. The only way you can empathize is to begin by asking and having the patience, tolerance and endurance to hear your partner's pain, sorrow and anger. Often this is most easily accomplished in a therapeutic environment with an impartial counselor who also facilitates feelings being safely and accurately expressed.

Consider the impact of the abuse of your wife or husband on your children. What are you teaching them by your example?

- ◆ Fear and insecurity – Children can't help but be frightened and insecure after hearing and seeing abuse. Trust me, it doesn't matter if they are in another room with the television set on or playing computer games. They hear you.

- ◆ Learned ways to express anger – You are teaching them how to express anger, fear and frustration by watching you act out.

- ◆ Gender roles – Your sons are learning how to assert themselves and how to treat women. Your daughters are learning how to treat men. Both sexes are learning how their gender should be treated. Do you want some person treating your child the way that you treat his or her mother or father?

- ◆ Shame – Every child who grows up in an abusive environment grows up to feel shame. Do you want to leave a legacy of shame?

- ◆ Difficulty trusting and low expectations of what they can experience in a relationship – Children know what went on in their families. They may want more for themselves, but not believe they deserve it. Most people end up marrying what is familiar to them.

Once you have fully considered the numerous ripple effects of your negative actions, you may be ready to move on to something positive that does not gloss over the past. This process is intended to move you into a healthier present. When you rush through this comprehension, you miss important issues that factor into the healing of yourself and your family. The intention is not to browbeat or punish you. It is understood that you have many wonderful qualities.

d. **Genuinely apologize and make amends.**
You may never have apologized or you may have said "I'm sorry" a million times. This apology is different. This is the kind of apology that comes from a deep and thorough understanding of your actions and the pain they have inflicted on someone you love. This is an apology with a sincere desire for forgiveness and a sustained commitment to not repeat your abusive behavior.

He or she may not forgive you. That is not the part that is in your control. Your sincerity should not be impacted by what you hope to get in return. Through your own soul searching, studying and owning your dark side and genuinely apologizing, you make vows to yourself to change. That is your job. The other partner's forgiveness is his or hers to give, not yours to demand. In time, the other person may be willing to find partial or complete forgiveness. Your work comes first and should not be conditional on what you receive.

Another way to ensure good progress is to make amends. You may want to ask the partner what he or she would like. Even if the partner is unwilling to discuss this, simply being thoughtful and kind is a start. Again, this behavior can't be a bargaining chip to get something you want. Make amends that would be significant. Learn what matters to him or her, what makes your partner feel understood and loved.

e. **Don't expect a quick fix.**
This process is a way of life, not a quick fix. It's like deciding you want to weigh less, then going on and off a diet. It doesn't work. Changing eating habits for life means you

maintain a weight loss.

One of the common problems that people have is expecting fast results and then being able to get "back to normal." "How long is this going to take?" and "When will we be done with this?" are questions that demonstrate that you don't yet get it. Be patient. Changing attitudes and behaviors requires hard work that is well worth the effort.

Only your partner can decide if he or she wants to work on your relationship. It is their choice. It could be too late. Your partner may not have enough loving feelings left to want to work on it. The person may be too hurt to really know how he or she feels. You must do your work for you. Your partner will make up his or her own mind. Do not try to push or coerce your partner into doing anything he or she is not ready to do. Healthy relationships require two willing partners.

While some men and women are not highly motivated or interested in sex, many find their intimate sexual connection with their partners to be the most meaningful, affirming part of their relationships and while some men and women's sex drives are unaffected or undeterred by abusive behavior, most have very little interest in sex after they have been hurt, angered, frustrated or demoralized. At this point, why would he or she want to be vulnerable and expose him or her self to you? Don't expect sex after you have resorted to abusive mind games. Depending on what has happened, you may have a long way to go before your partner is ready to jump into bed with you. While it may make you feel better, it is generally not any solution for the other partner until that person can recover and preferably feel that some understanding and some positive progress has occurred. In addition, don't assume that everything is fine if he or she does desire sex. Having sex and having forgiveness are not the same thing. Maybe you both can agree to have "make-up sex", but sex can also occur out of a simple interest in being sexual and the issues at hand are far from being resolved. There is a difference between communicating mentally and emotionally to resolve difficulties and communicating sexually for a release or for pleasure. The greatest pleasure comes from creating peace of mind before sharing your bodies.

3. How can I be successful in sustaining changes?

♦ <u>Learn to communicate more effectively.</u>

Everyone who comes in to counseling with relationship problems needs to learn to communicate in more productive, healthy ways. The most common challenge is how to express angry feelings in a non-abusive manner. Most people do a fairly good job conveying happy, loving thoughts and feelings. We usually haven't learned acceptable ways to resolve our hateful angry issues. Learning how to have a fair fight is important, because all viable relationships will experience disagreements. Learn to listen; take turns talking; do not resort to button pushing; use non-abusive words; have respectful body language.

Do not take offense and get angry at every little thing. You are not at war. You don't need to attack. You are supposed to be a team. Let a lot of small stuff go. Ignore some of the negativity. He or she may be in a bad mood or have a bad habit of using sarcasm and negativity when expressing him or her self. It is okay to tell the other person what bothers you without overreacting to it. Deflect and dismiss minor irritants. It is truly not worth arguing over the hundreds of things people argue about. It is normal to be annoyed by many of your partner's habits, but we all have them. Allow your partner to be who he or she is and focus on what you like about the person. Avoid unnecessary visits to hot spots. When you know an issue between you is sensitive and perhaps irresolvable, try not to have avoidable discussions or arguments about it. Deal with the present without piling on issues and feelings from the past. Simply discuss what is currently going on and don't make it a bigger problem than it really is. Remember, there is no such thing as winning if people you love get hurt. Avoid competing with your partner. Do not throw nasty hurtful darts thinking you will win. Your goal should be to be heard and understood and that will not happen if your partner has to defend him or her self.

♦ <u>Practice a healthy lifestyle.</u>

You cannot make successful changes without taking care of yourself. Be nice to yourself and develop a sound mind and body.

> ▶ Eat and sleep well.
> ▶ Get help for any mental or physical health problems.
> ▶ Address any addiction issues.
> ▶ Exercise regularly.
> ▶ Have good, supportive friendships.
> ▶ Develop healthy outlets and interests.
> ▶ Take time to nurture your spirit.

♦ <u>Seek professional help.</u>

Often abusive behavior cannot be changed without some outside insight, teaching, modeling or support. Help can come through many professionals. Seek assistance from a person who is a good match for you. Most communities have experienced ministers, competent agencies, good treatment programs and a variety of mental health professionals. Psychiatrists are medical doctors and they are the appropriate people to assess if medication is needed. Psychologists provide testing and therapy. Counselors, social workers and marriage and family therapists are available to help you with this issue. Whoever you contact, make sure they are licensed professionals with training and experience in dealing with the problems surrounding abuse. Seek someone you feel comfortable working with. It won't be as bad as you may think. The right person for you can end up being extremely helpful.

4. What else do I need to know?

♦ If you continue the abusive behavior, he or she can certainly leave. This is sad on many levels. It breaks apart a family, impacts children, is expensive and is very painful.

♦ The grass is not greener. All relationships have some problems. You carry yourself and your behavioral problems into any new relationship. Thus the new one may be just as unhealthy or more so.

♦ Work you do on yourself now is beneficial in the future. Being your best self and liking what you say and do help you to be successful and nondestructive in both your personal and professional lives.

♦ What does she want? Here is a list of things women commonly express wanting from their partners.

  ▸ Don't control or abuse me.

  ▸ Listen and really understand what I am saying.

  ▸ Talk to me about important things and express your feelings.

  ▸ Help! I can't do it all. I need you to do your share of the work around the house and with the kids.

  ▸ Notice and appreciate me. Compliment and thank me sometimes.

  ▸ I like verbal and physical affection that is not always about having sex.

  ▸ I need some time out to take care of me. Everybody needs a little pampering.

  ▸ Let's have fun together again. I miss the way it was in the beginning. Plan something enjoyable for us to do.

Ask your partner to read this list and add anything that is important to her.

♦ What does he want?

  ▸ Don't control or abuse me.

  ▸ Listen and really understand what I'm saying.

  ▸ Sex is important to me. Communicate that you want me. Tell me what you want.

  ▸ Don't lecture me about working long hours, understand I do it for us and our family.

▸ Appreciate my efforts to help with the housework and kids. Don't make fun of my efforts.

▸ Don't criticize and make fun of my friends.

▸ Let me enjoy some leisure time activity with my guy friends. Don't lecture or threaten me.

▸ I'd like to see you being happy with me.

Ask your partner to read this list and add anything that is important to him.

Chapter 24

It Takes Two

We have taken a journey together. Let's look back at some of the issues upon which we have focused as we made our way along our path. This will help guide you and your partner forward into a healthier more satisfying future whether you separate or remain in the relationship. You have gotten to the place you are now together. You have individual and couple issues. We have seen that your goal as an individual should be to learn and grow. This can be accomplished by the insight and understanding achieved through careful attention to your own feelings, thoughts and actions in your relationship dynamics. As a couple, your goal should be to change the unhealthy destructive interactions and replace them with positive affirming behaviors. Whether you stay together or split apart, what you learn personally will be useful in this or a future relationship.

SEPARATION AND DIVORCE

The person who wants out gets his or her way. That is a hard concept for some people to understand but it is true. If your partner no longer wants to be married to you, for whatever reason, you cannot force the other person to stay unless you are terribly abusive and manipulative. You cannot make a person have feelings that he or she no longer has. It may be against your wishes, your values or run contrary to your own feelings, but your mate may not have any desire to continue working on your relationship. It may be frightening to think of being abandoned. You may feel lost and confused. You may be extremely angry at your partner and perhaps at yourself.

Separation and divorce does not have to be a nasty, gut-wrenching process. Regardless of how you may feel at this moment, if you have decided to leave the relationship or you partner has, there is a future for you beyond this marriage. The more collaborative and cooperative the separation and settlement, the greater the chances of operating peacefully and productively within your new circumstances. You actually have the opportunity to have a better relationship in your divorce than in your marriage. If you have children together, the quality of your separated interactions is vital to their health and well-beings. Even if the divorce is not your choice, seek a better relationship as an ex than as a husband or wife. Be a better, more involved, more appropriately loving parent. Seek your own healing to come to terms with yourself and your life's experiences.

Here are some suggestions:

- ◆ Do not attack your partner with your words, actions or deeds. Do not try to provoke, coerce, manipulate or control. Do not attempt to punish your ex, because you are angry and unhappy. Meanness or cruelty only prolongs your suffering and accomplishes nothing.
- ◆ If there are children, work out reasonable arrangements. Do not bad-mouth your ex. The kids have a right to love both of you. Do not share your adult feelings and problems with children. Do not interrogate them about what is happening at your ex-partner's, unless you have a reason to believe they are being abused or neglected. Do not put them in the middle or ask them to relay messages or money. Pay attention to their needs.

Listen to their feelings. Seek any needed assistance to help them cope.

♦ Minimize conflict requiring legal intervention. The more issues and financial arrangements you work out on your own or with a mediator, the less money spent on an attorney or investigator. Be honest about assets. Do not try and hurt the other person out of anger and spite. Seek reasonable resolutions pertaining to dividing assets, custody arrangements and support payments.

♦ Remember that you once loved this person and perhaps you still do. Do not let hatred contaminate your life going forward. The kinder you are to your ex, the freer your spirit. Further trauma you create or experience poisons your well-being.

♦ Take care of your own needs. Explore a meaningful life independent of your mate. Create a living environment that feels warm and welcoming. Spend time with positive people. Avoid spending time with anyone who is negative, judgmental or critical. Combat the negative messages that you carry in your mind. This is a time for new beginnings.

♦ Seek out helpful resources. Counselors, ministers, support groups and healthy insightful friends can provide needed assistance. Many churches now have divorce recovery programs that you usually may sign up for, even if you are not a member of that church. There are endless ways to grow. Learn to fully embrace your pain and fully enjoy your pleasure.

♦ Many people experience symptoms of depression and anxiety during this period. Evaluate yourself with the following criteria from the DSM-IV.

  ▶ Depression – experiencing five or more of these feelings or issues:

  Sad, empty, tearful or irritable most of the day.
  Little interest or pleasure in daily activities.
  Noticeable weight loss or gain.
  Can't sleep well or sleep all the time.
  Move slowly or are very agitated.

Tired and no energy.
Feel worthless or guilty.
Can't concentrate well or make good decisions.
Contemplate dying or consider suicide.

▸ Generalized Anxiety – experiencing three or more of these problems:

Feel edgy or restless.
Tired often.
Can't concentrate or blank out.
Irritable.
Tense muscles.
Trouble falling or staying asleep, restless sleep.

You may be clinically depressed or anxious, especially if you have a family history. However, chances are you simply have an adjustment disorder that includes these symptoms. A psychiatrist can evaluate whether you need short-term medication, and a therapist can help you make the needed adjustments and recover from your trauma. Try to evaluate your mental health checkup as impartially as you consider any other necessary treatment. There is no shame in seeking this help. You are not going crazy, even though sometimes it may feel that way. The majority of people in a therapist's office are seeking assistance in adjusting to difficult life circumstances.

STAYING TOGETHER

If you choose to stay in your relationship and your partner is unwilling to work together on changes and improvements, the previous two chapters focus on what you can do for yourself. If, as a couple, you want to work toward a healthier marriage, you must both agree to commit to the therapeutic process. I very strongly recommend joint counseling with an experienced, empathetic therapist.

What does commitment mean?

♦ It won't ever work if one or both of you keeps leaving as a contingency plan in his or her mind. This often happens when counseling is the last ditch effort to save the marriage, but no love remains to energize the necessary work. Or the leaving contingency is a defense mechanism which involves detaching in order not to get hurt: You can't really get to me if I'm almost out of here.

♦ You cannot be involved with anyone else. If you are having an emotional or physical relationship with a person outside your marriage, you drain off a part of yourself. You can't really work on your marriage if you are involved with two relationships.

♦ You must be willing to lower your defenses, look at your own behavior and concentrate on making *your* changes. If you come to counseling only hoping to get your partner to change, you'll miss the opportunity to have a significantly better relationship.

♦ Risk being vulnerable. This is extremely difficult when you've already been hurt by your mate. If you tear down your self-created protective wall, you can be open to sharing and receiving. You may not like what you hear, but it is your therapist's job to help the process feel safe and to teach non-abusive ways to share thoughts and feelings. The more work you put into the process, the greater the personal benefits. If both of you openly invest in learning and growing, the results can be fun, exciting and enormously useful. Positive experiences tend to multiply. When we have success, we are motivated to do our part in the team building.

I would like to be optimistic and tell you that every relationship can be repaired and become healthy. The truth is that is not the case. Sometimes, one or both people are unwilling or unable to grasp the negative impact of their psychologically abusive words and actions or if they understand what they are doing, they are unwilling or unable to change. Perhaps they are so emotionally or psychologically damaged that they cannot appropriately interact with their partners or respond to the opportunity for new behavior. They may firmly believe they are "right" or justified in their actions. They may be comfortable with the existing power and control dynamics.

Even if only one person changes through counseling, the relationship system is altered. The partner has choices about how to react to his or her spouse's new behaviors. He or she may escalate the abuse to try and get the other person back under control; he or she may want out of the relationship or be willing to examine and change his or her own behavior.

The good news is there is hope and help for most relationships. You have loved and lived with your mate for some time. If you both choose to not give up on the relationship and have a willingness to work on it, here are some suggestions:

1. Stop the abuse.
2. Listen to your partner.
3. Communicate and compromise.
4. Praise the positives.
5. Be patient.
6. Develop a shared vision for your future.
7. Have some fun.

1. Stop the abuse.

Make a commitment to yourselves and to each other to stop the abuse by controlling what you say and do. In addition to stopping the obvious abusive behaviors discussed in this book, there are other negative actions which commonly build up after years of living with abuse. Dr. John Gottman, in his book *Why Marriages Succeed or Fail*, calls them the "Four Horsemen of the Apocalypse." They are criticism, contempt, defensiveness and stonewalling.[24]

> You are a stupid, lazy, bitch who can't even keep a clean house. I am sick of your constant complaining. The reason I am never here is because you won't leave me alone. It's your fault that I get so angry. I don't intend to talk to you the rest of the weekend.

This example statement clearly hits all of the four horsemen. The husband has succeeded in putting his wife down, acting disgusted, blaming her for his actions, getting her angry and then refusing to talk. Obviously, this stonewalling will get you nowhere but separated—if not physically, then emotionally.

If you have been psychologically abusive in your relationship it is important to work on self-awareness. Ask yourself:

♦ What makes me angry?

♦ What hurts my feelings?

♦ What actions or situations push my buttons?

♦ What negative things do I have in my mind about myself and about my partner?

♦ What causes me to feel inadequate, powerless or like a failure?

♦ What body sensations do I experience when I get angry?

♦ Do I feel that when experiencing intense rage my brain floods and my ability to reason shuts down?

♦ After I have calmed down, have I ever not remembered what I have said or done?

♦ Do I blame other people, alcohol or my past for my abusive behavior?

♦ Do I feel entitled to act the way I do?

♦ How do I feel after I have been abusive: proud and powerful, angry and tense, sad and remorseful, confused and disoriented or just numb?

♦ What techniques have I used in the past to keep myself from being abusive?

♦ Am I willing to explore new methods for de-escalating my anger and approaching my partner more appropriately?

Focus on doing no harm. Give the best you have to offer. Be a team of two and work *with* your partner. Cherish your loved ones. Treat your spouse as kindly as you would treat your best friend. If you choose to navigate through life together, do your part to make it a positive, memorable journey.

2. Listen to your partner.

Listening is often the hardest part of good communication, because most of us do not try to really understand what is being said and the feeling behind it. Women often feel more understood and validated by their girlfriends than their mates. Research into the way men's brains process male and female voices was done at the University of Sheffield in England. According to the findings, men use different parts of their brains when listening to women's and men's voices, and according to a funny editorial by Bill Ferguson of the *Macon Telegraph* "the hapless male, through no fault of his own, is forced to engage in a difficult sound-processing activity just to try to keep up with what women are saying."[25] Many women are repetitive in hopes of being heard.

We often assume we know what our partner is saying and our minds jump ahead to formulate our own responses. We may interrupt or close down and never fully hear the content or meaning of what is expressed. Also, we listen through our own filters, so that many messages are received differently than the senders intended. A person who is fearful of criticism or reprimand may feel he or she is being yelled at, even if the partner never raised his or her voice. Anger is a normal, natural feeling, but even if it is appropriately expressed, many people feel attacked when they hear anger from their mates.

It is said that the sentence men hate the most is "We need to talk." Many women seem to have a higher tolerance for discussing problem issues, while many men look for quick solutions, avoid the conflict or simply do not want to deal with anything that could possibly mean they might need to change. Endless discussions of problems are generally unproductive. A few minutes of really listening is easier than hours of repetitive dialogue.

3. Communicate and compromise.

It is important for couples to argue effectively. Bumping up against each other verbally is often the way we work through a problem or difference of opinion. Couples may argue over anything and everything from loading the dishwasher, folding the towels, cleaning the house, disciplining the children, interacting with the in-laws, spending money, whether to have sex, honesty, fidelity and religion. There are thousands of other issues that come up.

Some couples argue over every little thing and seem to have an endless tolerance for disagreement. They may remain married and argue about the same issues well into their eighties. In other couples, one or both people cannot tolerate too much or any conflict. The biggest problems seem to come when one person is quick to argue while the other abhors arguing or when abuse becomes part of the picture and turns arguing into unhealthy fighting.

Refusal to ever argue can also damage the relationship, as both people gradually drift apart through the unwillingness to confront, connect, disagree, then hopefully compromise and resolve some issues. Not arguing means you stuff or deflect important feelings. You cheat the other person out of hearing and knowing you more completely. The partnership dies a slow death from neglect and emotional abandonment.

You can have positive communication about difficult issues. Practice showing respect for your partner even if you don't agree with what he or she is saying. Learn to express your own feelings, wants and needs. Be willing to share your dreams and deepest wishes. Don't assume you know what your mate is thinking or feeling; ask the other person. Limit your discussions to the current issue rather than bringing up all your past grievances. Don't push your partner's buttons with remarks you know will really hurt the person. Don't exaggerate or over-dramatize an issue. Too many tears or feeling martyred doesn't solve anything. Avoid making judgments about your partner's character or person, and do not generalize with "you always," "you never" or "you should." If you are too angry to speak, ask for a time-out, but suggest a time in the near future that you are willing to revisit the discussion. Do not totally shut down. Argue in private, not in front of family, friends or even strangers.

Compromise is necessary when an issue requires an answer. Ideally, both people should be willing to give a little to help the situation. In some cases, one person clearly gets his or her way. If one wants a child and the other doesn't, there is no such thing as half a child. Couples often argue over money, housework, child rearing, family issues and sex. Compromise is abundantly possible in each of these areas. Or you may be paired with your opposite in the realms of introvert/extrovert, neat/messy, spender/saver, late/on time and wanting sex once a day/wanting sex once a month. Again, there are lots of opportunities to compromise.

One couple, Henry and Helena, who came to me for counseling, were both concerned that they couldn't take much more of their relationship. They still loved each other, but that feeling had significantly diminished. They were also finding it hard to continue to be attracted to each other, as they were both filled with anger and resentment. They did not want their marriage to end, although they had both considered it. They had a lot to be thankful for: good jobs, a beautiful home, two children that they both adored, supportive family and friends and a partnership with many strengths but their dysfunctional relationship was jeopardizing their future together.

Helena's Side

I get so frustrated with Henry. I can't seem to get through to him in a way that brings about any changes. He'll agree to do something, but after a day or maybe a week he is back to the same behavior. I know I get bitchy and complain a lot, but I don't know what else to do.

Among my issues is that he wants more sex, but I don't feel any emotional connection with him. I need more positive attention. He often gets angry and either yells and calls me names, even in front of our kids, or won't speak at all. I feel we are angry at each other way too much. When we try to have some fun, he only wants to do things with his friends or family. If we are with my friends or family, he looks and acts miserable or just ignores them.

Another reason I don't want sex is his smoking. It's smelly and I hate tasting the cigarettes on his breath so I don't want to kiss him. Yes, I knew he smoked when I married him, but he promised he would stop when we had kids. He uses the nicotine patch, but soon he's back smoking again. Even though he promises not to smoke in the house, I come home and find that he has and he leaves his cigarette butts lying around. I worry about the danger to the kids and me from second-hand smoke, plus I hate the example he's setting for them.

Then there is his negative behavior. He lies. He doesn't tell me the truth so often that I don't know when to believe him. It can be about anything, big or small. He usually won't carry his cell phone or if he has it, he won't answer and then he makes up an excuse about why he couldn't. It is very hard to trust him after so many lies. There are times he stays out all night and won't explain where he's been.

I realize I'm not much fun, but I am exhausted. The baby still wakes up some at night and often just wants me. I work hard at my job and I like a clean house. I never feel like there is any time to relax. After work, both kids need our time and attention and there is so much to do around the house and to get ready for the next day. I could really use more help. I know he is tired too, and he's fine with the house being messy, but it drives me crazy. It could get done so much quicker if he would help me.

In addition, I am resentful about the way we deal with money. I get paid well for what I do and I make more than he does, but he controls our finances. He complains if I go shopping for myself or the kids, but we seem to always have the money for big items that he wants to buy.

We used to have so much fun together. I felt like he was totally in to me and he would plan things for us to do. We used to talk about everything and I was so happy and excited to be with him but all that has changed.

Henry's Side

She *always* reminds me of how hard she works and that she makes more money than I do. I handle the finances, because she would suck at it, which she readily admits. She shops to entertain herself and to feel better, but I only comment on her purchases when I feel they are really frivolous. We have been able to do a lot of things because of my money management. She also conveniently forgets that I brought more assets into the marriage.

I'm not a bad guy. I do a lot around the house. I think I'm a hands-on involved father, and I handle all of the cooking or I run out and pick up our meal. I'm never doing enough to please her. She's critical and judges everything I do. I don't ever fully please her.

Yes, I do lie and at times I don't answer my phone. I lie to tell her what I think she wants to hear or to get her off my back. I avoid talking to her sometimes to get a break from her complaints and demands.

I hate it that she never really relaxes. She's unhappy, negative and uptight. I enjoy just flopping on the sofa and watching TV or playing video games, which drives her mad. It's hard to plan anything fun, because if any little thing changes or goes wrong, she freaks out and can't handle it. Often, it means we don't do something we were looking forward to.

I know I lose it and yell. I hate that I do that, especially in front of the kids. The pressure of her complaints, criticism and demands build up until I explode. I'm quiet afterwards, because I am angry and ashamed.

I want more positive attention too. We go months without sex, and she never initiates it. Most of the time when I approach her, she comes up with a reason not to and turns me down. How does she expect me to feel about that? I know I shouldn't be smoking, but it is the one thing I really enjoy. It calms me down and relaxes me.

She used to be excited when she saw me and that made me feel great. Life didn't seem so hectic and we really enjoyed each other. I had so much energy to plan things, because it was easy to please her. There isn't much pleasure left in our relationship.

Turning It Around

Life became more complicated and stressful as Henry and Helena had more responsibilities and two children to take care of. They had less time for themselves and for each other. The more pressures they experienced,

the less positive energy they directed toward the relationship.
Their behavior toward each other became negative and at times, psychologically abusive.

They were willing to change their behaviors and attitudes. Both of
them accepted the concept that they would each have to focus on what
they could change in themselves and stop trying to control the other person. They needed to concentrate on being their best selves in the marriage.
They also agreed to set aside more time for quality couple interactions.

Henry agreed to:

♦ Work on lessening his smoking habit. If he did smoke, he
  agreed to only do it outside the house and to immediately
  dispose of his cigarette butts. He also agreed to brush and use
  mouthwash afterward.

♦ Stop lying. He knew this was a bad habit, and he pledged to
  correct any lies, if he slipped up. He also agreed to carry his cell
  phone and answer it as well as communicate with Helena if he
  was going to be out late.

♦ Help more around the house if Helena would make *short* lists
  of things she would like him to do.

♦ No longer use abusive language and to tone down the yelling.
  Notice and compliment her on her many positive qualities.

♦ Do something special for Helena or give her a gift that she said
  she would like to receive.

Helena agreed to:

♦ Work on decreasing criticisms and demands.

♦ Learn ways to de-stress and relax. Find personal fulfillment in
  something that interested her.

♦ Express appreciation for things that Henry did. Make lists as
  he requested. Praise his positives.

♦ Be willing to initiate sex with an interest in them both
  enjoying it.

♦ Do something special for Henry or give him a gift that he said
  he would like to receive.

Henry and Helena began planning more pleasurable couple time. They each took responsibility for putting more positive energy toward the relationship. They began to have more fun, to correct and apologize for their mistakes. Their vision for the future included keeping the other person as a friend and partner.

4. Praise the positives.

What was it about your partner that made you fall in love? What attracted you to him or her? Somewhere inside, those good qualities remain; unfortunately they have just been joined by some negative abuse. In all probability, you were drawn to the very person who can help you learn your most challenging life lessons. Keep an open mind and discover what is right in front of you to see. Discover the need to come out from under your relationship's oppression into the light of freedom.

Be your best self. Each person struggles with annoying insecurities, self-doubts, fears, failures and traumas. The reaction could be to punish the people who will put up with your bad behavior. Instead, be a person you can respect and enjoy. If you really like yourself, have made necessary changes and the relationship still isn't working, then you have an answer about the potential of the union to be different.

What can you do to be your best self as you relate to your mate?

- Notice things you like and comment on them. Praise positive qualities and actions.
- Let go of petty arguments and practice forgiveness every day, for yourself and each other. Do not layer transgressions so that you always carry anger and resentment.
- Build on what is good in your relationship. Maximize your union's strengths and minimize the weaknesses.
- Express gratitude. Everyone enjoys the positivity of hearing that they are appreciated.

5. Be patient.

It takes time to re-establish trust and rebuild the foundation of a relationship. Psychological abuse makes it difficult to trust that our partners have our best interests in mind and that we can count on them to care for us. Begin by asking your partner for small manageable changes that are not too difficult. Experiencing the pleasure of successful transitions is infectious.

Realize that a person is not going to alter his or her essence. We are all flawed. Hopefully, you like the core spirit of your mate. Practice empathy. Try to walk in your partner's symbolic shoes. See the world from his or her perspective. Offer friendship, even when you are the most challenged. Get to know each other better and find more common ground to enjoy, while still honoring each other's uniqueness.

Taking the steps to create a healthier union will not have smooth forward progress. Expect some regression into old familiar behavior. Each person is responsible for owning and correcting his or her mistakes. Sincerely apologize, acknowledge what you have done wrong and listen to your partner's reactions. Learn from the consequences of your behaviors and let that guide your future actions. We are most likely to make a sustained change if we fully feel the impact of our hurtful conduct.

6. Develop a shared vision for your future.

Sharing dreams and goals can set your marital stage for more teamwork and less dissention. You may have different approaches to life, different values and desires, but it is important to listen to each other and develop a vision that accommodates both partners' wants and needs. Brainstorm and plan together:

Each of you take two pieces of paper. At the top of one write "Wishes For Me" and at the top of the other write "Wishes For Us". Then on each paper list a column of topic areas. Write all of your plans and dreams for yourself as an individual and as a couple for each topic. Let your imagination soar. Don't hold back. Write down any and everything you would like to have. Include big and small wishes in each category. Even if your wishes seem impossible, include them.

Some topics and potential themes to consider:

♦ Physical – caring for your health, dieting, exercising, cooking, working out, hiring a personal trainer, watching your weight, going to doctor checkups, sharing physical activities. These can include walking, running, tennis, golfing, biking, swimming, sports, gym, gardening, baking, home improvements, etc.

◆ Emotional – resolving difficult feelings and hurts, getting appropriate medication or therapy, making apologies and amends, nurturing self and each other, developing healthier relationships, laughing more, slowing down, meditating quietly, reducing stress, helping each other, etc.

◆ Mental – developing your mind; going back to school; reading more interesting books; learning a new skill, craft or language; studying another country or culture; learning the history of your family, geographic area, nation or government; listening to interesting speeches or lectures; visiting art galleries, museums and local festivals, etc.

◆ Spiritual – taking a spiritual journey or retreat, visiting different churches in various denominations, studying many religions, praying, reading books with different viewpoints, meditating, taking a yoga class, worshiping in whatever way you are comfortable, immersing yourself in nature, contemplating our universe, etc.

◆ Financial – setting goals for what you have now – income, assets and debts, dreams for the future, what kind of savings you want, where you want to live, do you need another job, what do you want to have in the bank and what do you want to buy, wish lists of big and small items, etc.

◆ Friendship – considering types of friendships you want to develop, things you want your friendships to include in individual and couple friends, what you want and need from each other in order to be better friends, how your bond can grow to take you through life and into old age – i.e. listen to me and don't try to fix it, go shopping together, go to movies or plays that I like, go to a football game with me, learn about a sport I like, watch a movie I like with me, etc.

◆ Adventure – deciding how you can have more fun and excitement at home and away. It can be anything you can imagine: camping out under the stars in the backyard, picnicking in the park, candlelit bubble bath, movie marathon with popcorn and pizza, white-water rafting, hiking, zip-lining, mountain climbing, world traveling, beach combing, skinny dipping, crazy and spontaneous sex, afternoon siestas, midnight drives, learning a new dance, seeing your favorite performer in concert, visiting all the national parks, taking a cruise, etc.

Plan a time to get together and share your lists with your partner. Applaud and promote each other's dreams and ideas. Do not put down or criticize any hopes or thoughts. This is an opportunity to develop a shared vision. If you care about your mate you will support his or her wishes and encourage his or her endeavors. As a couple, you can use these wishes and suggestions to enrich your present. Many of your ideas you will be able to be put into practice right now. They can be realized today. Each of you must be responsible for doing what you can do to make your individual and couple wishes come true. Enjoy!

7. Have some fun.

Couples counseling and relationship growth can be hard and stressful. Devoting time to enjoyable experiences reminds you of why you got together in the first place.

Each of you make a list of at least five things you really enjoy having your partner do for you and at least five things you would enjoy doing for your partner (not what you think they want to receive, but what you would truly enjoy giving). These can be things you used to do, still do or have never done but would enjoy. There are no wrong answers. Exchange lists. Notice if the things your partner most wants to receive match up with what you enjoy giving. As an act of love, practice giving your partner the things that are most important to him or her.

Take turns planning a date. Set mutually agreeable times for each date. When it is your turn to plan the date, plan something you would enjoy doing. If it is your turn to go along on the date, your responsibility is to have a positive attitude and a sense of humor. So, if he plans to go bowling and you hate bowling, approach it with a good attitude and simply enjoy. Back when you were dating, you each knew how to look good and be cheerful, so that the other person would want to see you again. Use that same energy to plan and prepare for your dates. The idea is to have fun. It is not necessary to spend money. It is vital to have a good disposition and an open mind.

Use small moments in your day to build on your intimacy. A quick call, text message, email or note can be a bright spot in the day. A hug, pat, kiss or compliment is appreciated. A small thoughtful gesture or gift is nice to receive.

Plan vacations that your time and money will allow. Consider the interests of each person. If he wants to hike in the mountains and she enjoys the beach, alternate choices of vacation spots and take turns exploring the other's joy.

Laughter is a critical component of fun. It is healing and bonding. Even if you find different things funny, laughter is contagious. Seek out humorous books, movies, comedians, programs and stories. Share humorous life experiences.

When you and your partner share all these positive activities, hopefully your sexual desire is awakened or intensified. An exciting, mutually satisfying sex life can increase intimacy, relieve stress and stimulate passionate relationship energy.

Every relationship has its own unique character and complexity. I hope that reading this book has helped you feel less alone in your journey toward stopping, changing or ending psychological abuse. Choosing your future path can be challenging and confusing. Regardless of the decision you make about whether your relationship should end or continue, I hope you've realized that you have the right to take care of your needs and be the person you most want to be. My wish for you is that you make your privileged time in this world meaningful and filled with the joy of a peace created from within.

Acknowledgments

My most sincere appreciation goes to:

♦ My daughter, Rebecca Kitchen, who unselfishly gave me her time to type this manuscript and provided me with support and encouragement when I was frustrated and uninspired. I do not think I could have completed this book without her.

♦ My husband, Ron, for understanding that writing a book while continuing to work meant that he did not get much of my time and attention and for doing a lion's share of the work at home.

♦ My agent, Mary Sue Seymour, and my editor, Dr. Joan S. Dunphy, along with the entire staff at New Horizon Press for their help, patience, insight, knowledge and willingness to take a chance on a new author.

♦ The nine women I am fortunate enough to call my closest friends: My business partners, Nancy Ball, Karen Elliott and Kathy Glenn. They have my respect and admiration as we journey through our professional lives. The other members of the Tammy Wynette Fan Club: Jane Cauthen, Linda Hiatt and Julia Nile. They are my original mentors and co-workers in the quest to understand the impact of domestic abuse and the finest dinner companions and inspirational women. A special thanks to Julia for her hours of typing and enthusiasm for this project. And finally to Robin Sullivan, Pat Vreeland and Barbara Wales. They are my extended family and hold places in my heart where dreams feel safe and loved.

I also offer my thanks to the people who were willing to share their stories about their lives and relationships. I greatly appreciate your generosity and courage.

End Notes

1. National Resource Center on Domestic Violence (May 2007), 1-800-537-2238.
2. Anthony Storr, *The Essential Jung* (Princeton University Press, 1983), 97-117.
3. Doug and Naomi Moseley, *Making Your Second Marriage a First Class Success* (California: Prima Publishing, 1998), 86.
4. Margaret Mitchell, *Gone With the Wind* (New York: The MacMillian Co., 1936), 716. Note: The word *frankly* was only said in the movie version.
5. Donald Patterson, "Fury's Fatal Toll," *Greensboro News and Record*, 22 September 1995, D1.
6. Neil Jacobson and John Gottman, *When Men Batter Women* (New York: Simon and Schuster, 1998).
7. Caroline Myss, Ph.D., *Anatomy of the Spirit: The Seven Stages of Power and Healing* (New York: Harmony Books, 1996), 25-26.
8. Tim Yeadon, "Vernon cops plea in slaying," *Greensboro News and Record*, 18 July 2002, B5.
9. Phyllis Trible and Hershel Shanks, "Wrestling with Scripture," *Biblical Archaeology Review* (March/April 2006): 46.
10. Ibid., 51.
11. Janis Abrahams Spring, Ph.D., *After the Affair: Healing the Pain and Rebuilding Trust When a Partner Has Been Unfaithful* (New York: HarperCollins, 1996), 242.
12. Winifred Gallagher, "I Confess: Six Ways to Right a Wrong," *O, The Oprah Magazine*, June 2002, 198.

13. Robert A. Johnson, *Owning Your Own Shadow: Understanding the Dark Side of the Psyche* (San Francisco: HarperCollins, 1993), 17.

14. Ibid., 18.

15. Ibid., 89.

16. Richard Rohr, *The Enneagram: A Christian Perspective* (New York: The Crossroad Publishing Co., 2001), 32.

17. John Bradshaw, *Healing the Shame that Binds You* (Florida: Health Communications, 1988), 119.

18. "Sexiest Men Alive: Sexiest Cabinet Member," *People*, 2 December 2002, 92.

19. "Army's counseling scrutinized," *Greensboro News and Record*, 27 July 2002, B9.

20. Alex Tresinowski and Nicole Weisensee Egan, "Under Suspicion," *People*, 3 December 2007, 102.

21. Harville Hendrix, Ph.D., *Getting the Love You Want: A Guide for Couples* (New York: Harper & Row, 1988), 82.

22. Kahlil Gibran, *The Prophet* (New York: Alfred A. Knoff, 1926), 28.

23. Eckhart Tolle, *The Power of Now* (California: New World Library, 1999).

24. John Gottman, Ph.D. *Why Marriages Succeed or Fail...And How You Can Make Yours Last* (New York: Fireside/Simon & Schuster, 1994), 68-102.

25. Bill Ferguson, "Huh? Why men don't listen to women," *Greensboro News and Record*, 16 August 2005, A9.

Bibliography

Alcoholics Anonymous. 3rd ed. New York: Alcoholics Anonymous World Services, Inc., 1976.

Allen, P. *Getting to "I Do".* New York: Avon Books, 1994.

Argrove, S. *Why Men Marry Bitches: A Woman's Guide to Winning Her Man's Heart.* New York: Simon & Schuster, 2006.

"Army's counseling scrutinized." *Greensboro News and Record* (2002).

Arterburn, S. and M.J. Rinck. *Avoiding Mr. Wrong: And What to Do If You Didn't.* Nashville: Thomas Nelson Publishers, 2001.

Barnett, O.W. and A.D. LaViolette. *It Could Happen to Anyone: Why Battered Women Stay.* California: Sage Publications, 1993.

Beattie, M. *Beyond Codependency and Getting Better All the Time.* New York: Harper/Hazelden, 1989.

Berne, E. *Games People Play: The Psychology of Human Relationships.* New York: Ballantine Books, 1964.

Bradshaw, J. *Family Secrets: The Path to Self-Acceptance and Reunion.* New York: Bantam Books, 1995.

———. *Homecoming: Reclaiming and Championing Your Inner Child.* New York: Bantam Books, 1990.

———. *The Family: A New Way of Creating a Solid Self-Esteem.* Florida: Health Communications, Inc., 1988.

———. *Healing the Shame that Binds You.* Florida: Health Communications, Inc., 1988.

Brown, J.E. *Why Do We Stay: In Abusive and Unhealthy Relationships.* Baltimore: America House Book Publishers, 2001.

Brown, S.L. *Counseling Victims of Violence.* Virginia: American Association for Counseling and Development, 1991.

Byrne, R. *The Secret*. New York: Atria Books, 2006.

Carlson, R. *Don't Sweat the Small Stuff…and It's All Small Stuff: Simple Ways to Keep the Little Things From Taking Over Your Life*. New York: Hyperion, 1997.

———. *You Can Feel Good Again: Common-Sense Therapy for Releasing Depression and Changing Your Life*. New York: Plume/Penguin, 1993.

Chapman, G. *The Five Love Languages: How to Express Heartfelt Commitment to Your Mate*. Nashville: LifeWay Press, 2007.

———. *Loving Solutions: Overcoming Barriers in Your Marriage*. Chicago: Northfield Publishing, 1998.

———. *Hope for the Separated*. Chicago: Moody Press, 1982.

Chodron, P. *When Things Fall Apart: Heart Advice for Difficult Times*. Boston: Shambhala Publications, Inc., 2000.

Corey, G. *Theory and Practice of Counseling and Psychotherapy*. California: Brooks/Cole Publishing Company, 1991.

Cory, J. and K. McAndless-Davis. *When Love Hurts: A Woman's Guide to Understanding Abuse in Relationships*. New Westminster: Womankind Press, 2003.

Cowan, C. and M. Kinder. *Smart Women, Foolish Choices: Finding the Right Men, Avoiding the Wrong Ones*. New York: Clarkson N. Potter, Inc./Publishers, 1985.

Diagnostic and Statistical Manual of Mental Disorders. 4th ed. Washington, D.C.: American Psychiatric Associates, 1994.

Eckhart, T. *The Power of Now*. California: New World Library, 1999.

Engel, B. *The Emotionally Abused Woman: Overcoming Destructive Patterns and Reclaiming Yourself*. New York: Fawcett Columbine, 1990.

Evans, P. *The Verbally Abusive Relationship: How to Recognize It and How to Respond*. Massachusetts: Adams Media Corporation, 1992.

Ferguson, B. "Huh? Why men don't listen to women." *Greensboro News and Record* (2005).

Ferguson, D. and T. Ferguson. *One Year Book of Devotions for Couples*. Illinois: Tyndale House Publishers, Inc., 2001.

Fisher, B. *Rebuilding: When Your Relationship Ends.* California: Impact Publishers, 1981.

Freeman, J. *Women: A Feminist Perspective.* California: Mayfield Publishing Company, 1989.

Gallagher, W. "I Confess: Six Ways to Right a Wrong." *O, The Oprah Magazine* (2002).

Gertler, S. and A. Lopez. *To Love, Honor, and Betray: The Secret Life of Suburban Wives.* New York: Hyperion, 2005.

Gibran, K. *The Prophet.* New York: Alfred A. Knoff, Inc., 1923.

Goldberg, H. *What Men Really Want.* New York: Penguin Group, 1991.

Gottman, J.M. *The Seven Principles for Making Marriage Work.* New York: Three Rivers Press, 1999.

———. *Why Marriages Succeed or Fail…And How You Can Make Yours Last.* New York: Simon & Schuster, 1994.

Gray, J. *Mars and Venus on a Date: A Guide for Navigating the 5 Stages of Dating to Create a Loving and Lasting Relationship.* New York: HarperCollins Publishers, 1997.

———. *Men Are From Mars, Women Are From Venus: A Practical Guide for Improving Communication and Getting What You Want in Your Relationships.* New York: HarperCollins Publishers, 1992.

Harley, W.F. *His Needs, Her Needs: Building an Affair-Proof Marriage.* Michigan: Fleming H. Revell, 1986.

Hendrix, H. *Getting the Love You Want: A Guide for Couples.* New York: Harper & Row Publishers, 1988.

Hershenson, D.B. and P.W. Power. *Mental Health Counseling: Theory and Practice.* New York: Pergamon Press, 1987.

The Holy Bible. Revised standard ed. New York: The World Publishing Company, 1962.

Jacobson, N. and J. Gottman. *When Men Batter Women.* New York: Simon & Schuster, 1998.

Jeffers, S. *Feel the Fear and Do It Anyway.* New York: Fawcett Columbine, 1987.

Johnson, R.A. *Owning Your Own Shadow: Understanding the Dark Side of the Psyche.* New York: Harper San Francisco, 1991.

Johnson, R.A. *He: Understanding Masculine Psychology*. New York: Harper & Row Publishers, 1974.

Kirschman, E. *I Love a Cop: What Police Families Need to Know*. New York: The Guilford Press, 2007.

Latus, J. *If I am Missing or Dead*. New York: Simon & Schuster, 2007.

Lerner, H.G. *The Dance of Intimacy: A Woman's Guide to Courageous Acts of Change in Key Relationships*. New York: Harper & Row Publishers, 1989.

——. *The Dance of Anger: A Woman's Guide to Changing the Patterns of Intimate Relationships*. New York: Harper & Row Publishers, 1985.

Madaness, C. *Sex, Love, and Violence: Strategies for Transformation*. New York: W.W. Norton & Company, 1990.

Martin, D. *Battered Wives*. New York: Pocket Books, 1976.

McGee, R.S. *Excerpts from the Search for Significance*. Texas: Rapha, 1994.

McGraw, P.C. *Relationship Rescue: A Seven-Step Strategy for Reconnecting with Your Partner*. New York: Hyperion, 2000.

——. *Life Strategies: Doing What Works, Doing What Matters*. New York: Hyperion, 1999.

Meske, D. *Our Six Emotional Needs*. Wisconsin: IAS Marketing, 1988.

Miller, M.S. *No Visible Wounds: Identifying Nonphysical Abuse of Women by Their Men*. New York: Fawcett Columbine, 1995.

Mitchell, M. *Gone with the Wind*. New York: The MacMillan Co., 1936.

Moseley, D. and N. Moseley. *Making Your Second Marriage a First-Class Success*. California: Prima Publishing, 1998.

Moss, L. *Why Doesn't She Just Leave?* San Jose: Writers Club Press, 2000.

Myss, C. *Anatomy of the Spirit: The Seven Stages of Power and Healing*. New York: Harmony Books, 1996.

National Resource Center on Domestic Violence, 2007. 1-800-537-2238 ext. 139.

Nicarthy, G. *Getting Free: You Can End Abuse and Take Back Your Life*. California: Seal Press, 1982.

Patterson, C.H. *Theories of Counseling and Psychotherapy*. New York: Harper & Row Publishers, 1986.

Patterson, D. "Fury's Fatal Toll." *Greensboro News and Record* (1995).

Peabody, S. *Addiction to Love: Overcoming Obsession and Dependency in Relationships*. California: Celestial Arts, 1994.

Peale, N.V. *The Power of Positive Thinking*. New York: Simon & Schuster, 1980.

Peck, M.S. *The Road Less Traveled: A New Psychology of Love, Traditional Values and Spiritual Growth*. New York: Simon & Schuster, 1978.

Pizzey, E. *The Watershed*. New York: Harper Paperbacks, 1983.

Portez, M. and B. Sinrod. *The First Really Important Survey of American Habits*. California: Price Stern Sloan, Inc., 1989.

Norwood, R. *Women Who Love Too Much: When You Keep Wishing and Hoping He'll Change*. New York: Pocket Books, 1985.

Rice, E.K. *Finding Your Soul Mate Handbook: The Journey of Attracting and Creating Loving and Successful Relationships*. North Carolina: Rice & Associates, Inc., 2001.

Rohr, R. and A. Ebert. *The Enneagram: A Christian Perspective*. New York: The Crossroad Publishing Company, 2001.

Rosemond, J. *A Family of Value*. Kansas City: A Universal Press Syndicate Company, 1995.

Ruiz, D.M. *The Four Agreements*. California: Amber-Allen Publishing, 1997.

Santrock, J.W. *Life-Span Development*. Iowa: Wm. C. Brown Publishers, 1983.

Schechter, S. *Women and Male Violence: The Visions and Struggles of the Battered Women's Movement*. Boston: South End Press, 1982.

"Sexiest Men Alive: Sexiest Cabinet Member." *People*, December 2002.

Shoshanna, B. *Why Men Leave*. New York: The Berkley Publishing Group, 1999.

Spring, J.A. *After the Affair: Healing the Pain and Rebuilding Trust When a Partner Has Been Unfaithful*. New York: Harper Perennial, 1996.

Stern, E.S. *Loving an Imperfect Man: Stop Waiting for Him to Make You Happy and Start Getting What You Want Out of Life*. New York: Pocket Books, 1997.

Storr, A. *The Essential Jung*. New York: MJF Books, 1983.

Tolle, E. *The Power of Now: A Guide to Spiritual Enlightenment*. California: New World Library, 1999.

Tresniowski, A. and N.W. Egan. "Under Suspicion." *People*, December 2007.

Trible, P. and H. Shanks. "Wrestling with Scripture." *Biblical Archaeology Review*, March/April 2006.

Viscott, D. *I Love You, Let's Work It Out*. New York: Pocket Books, 1987.

Weiss, E. *Family and Friends' Guide to Domestic Violence: How to Listen, Talk and Take Action When Someone You Care About is Being Abused*. California: Volcano Press, Inc., 2003.

Wexler, D.B. *When Good Men Behave Badly: Change Your Behavior, Change Your Relationship*. California: New Harbinger Publications, Inc., 2004.

Whitfield, C.L. *Healing the Child Within: Discovery and Recovery for Adult Children of Dysfunctional Families*. Florida: Health Communications Inc., 1987.

Wiesel, E. *Night*. New York: Bantam Books, 1960.

Williamson, M. *A Woman's Worth*. New York: Random House, 1993.

Yeadon, T. "Vernon cops plea in slaying." *Greensboro News and Record* (2002).

Zukav, G. *The Seat of the Soul*. New York: Simon & Schuster, 1989.